# the ketogenic cookbook

## NUTRITIOUS LOW-CARB, HIGH-FAT PALEO MEALS TO HEAL YOUR BODY

Jimmy Moore
and Maria Emmerich

Victory Belt Publishing Inc.

Las Vegas

First Published in 2015 by Victory Belt Publishing Inc.

Copyright © 2015 Jimmy Moore and Maria Emmerich

ISBN-13: 978-1-628600-78-0

The authors are not licensed practitioners, physicians, or medical professionals and offer no medical treatments, diagnoses, suggestions, or counseling. The information presented herein has not been evaluated by the U.S. Food and Drug Administration, and it is not intended to diagnose, treat, cure, or prevent any disease. Full medical clearance from a licensed physician should be obtained before beginning or modifying any diet, exercise, or lifestyle program, and physicians should be informed of all nutritional changes.

The authors/owners claim no responsibility to any person or entity for any liability, loss, or damage caused or alleged to be caused directly or indirectly as a result of the use, application, or interpretation of the information presented herein.

Front and Back Cover Photography by Hayley and Bill Staley

Interior Design by Yordan Terziev and Boryana Yordanova

Meal Plans by Craig Emmerich

Printed in the U.S.A.

LSC 0516

# contents

## recipes

# Introduction

*One cannot
think well, love well, sleep well,
if one has not dined well.*

—Virginia Woolf

A ketogenic diet—one that calls for a low-carb, moderate-protein, and high-fat nutritional intake—has become more and more popular in the past few years as more and more people are looking for a nutritional approach to optimizing their health that is based on a real foods–based diet and can be tailored to meet their individual needs. In fact, the term *ketogenic* was the fifth-most Googled diet search term in 2013. And although you may have heard that getting into a state of nutritional ketosis is an ideal way to lose weight, it is so much more than that. We'll share why within the pages of this book.

Before we dive too deeply into the subject of ketogenic diets and share some delicious recipes that fit within this lifestyle, we'd like to introduce ourselves to you and explain why we decided to write this book, which is sure to become a resource you will turn to again and again as you begin your own low-carb, high-fat journey to better health. The two of us came to this way of eating by very different paths, but we now stand united in our passion to empower people with the same life-changing message.

# Jimmy's story

Growing up, I was always the fat kid in class. I was routinely picked last on the playground for any athletic endeavor, ruthlessly made fun of because of my weight, and generally thought of as a nerd and a freak. Because I was such a social pariah, I had to come up with ways to deal with the rejection I was feeling. Ironically, that meant eating more and more food to cover up the pain. And because my mom was a single parent for most of my childhood, she did the best she could to find the cheapest food possible to feed her two growing boys and little girl. That translated into meals based mostly on processed carbohydrates.

Hamburger Helper, Fruit Loops, Coca-Cola, Little Debbie snack cakes, macaroni and cheese, ramen noodles, cheeseburgers with french fries, and other crappy carbage comprised nearly everything my brother, sister, and I ate growing up. It was the Standard American Diet that most people have consumed since the 1970s. What's ironic about all of this is that at the same time, my mom was trying to lose weight by eating a low-fat diet. So that meant that, while we kids were eating all of that junk food, she was consuming rice cakes, fat-free ice cream, salad with fat-free dressing, and other so-called healthy foods. I would have loved to have taken video of this with an iPhone back in the 1980s because I'm sure it was a peculiar sight!

It shouldn't be surprising to anyone that as I grew into an adult and began making my own nutritional choices, I continued to eat the way I had been taught growing up. Some people have this idea that when you become an adult and move out on your own, you suddenly know what proper nutrition is. If only! No, that's ludicrous. You eat the way you grew up eating, and for me, that meant more and more junk food, fast food, and carbage. Needless to say, through college and into my late twenties, I was gradually getting bigger and bigger while my metabolism was getting worse and worse.

Every few years I attempted to lose weight and get healthy. But what that generally meant in my mind was eating a low-calorie, low-fat diet and getting lots of cardiovascular exercise. The problem with this model for tackling my obesity and propensity for health problems was that it could never satisfy my deep cravings and hunger, and I was always left wanting more. I went through phases of trying everything that made sense to me on some cognitive level, including drinking Slimfast (eww!), taking Dexatrim diet pills, and, of course, eating a low-fat diet. In fact, in 1999 I tried a very low-fat diet after my brother, Kevin, at the age of thirty-two, had a series of heart attacks in the span of one week that nearly killed him. Since I was only four years younger than he was, I knew I had to do something drastic to avoid the same fate.

So here I was at the age of twenty-seven eating virtually zero fat and consuming such foods as "naturally fat-free" marshmallows. Or the "always a low-fat food," Twizzlers. It says it right there on the packaging, so it must be true, right? And the sugary version of Coca-Cola was totally devoid of fat, so I had that from time to time as well. Because of my mom's low-fat diet days back in the 1980s, I was just accustomed to fearing fat as the grand enemy of my weight and health. And while I did indeed lose weight eating that way, one thing kept dooming me to fail time and time again—H-U-N-G-E-R!

My wife, Christine, will tell you that I was not a pleasant man to be around when my stomach was growling and I needed to eat. And when you cut the fat out of your diet, hunger is inevitable. I felt like I was going crazy. I now know that my brain was screaming at me to feed it the fat it needed to operate as it was supposed to. Instead, I suppressed those urges and willed myself to succeed—which I defined almost solely as losing weight. While I did indeed lose a good amount of weight doing this, the other intangibles required for lasting success—hunger control, steady mood, mental acuity, energy—were steadily crumbling beneath me. The beginning of the end came one day with a fateful request from Christine.

When I'd been on my low-fat diet for nine months, Christine asked me if I would go to McDonald's and order her something. I asked her if I could have a Big Mac meal "just this one time," since I was quite literally starving after months upon months of eating low-fat. I think you can guess the rest of this sad story. That "one time" became time and time again over the next four months as I rebelled against that low-fat diet, eating everything I could get my hands on regardless of nutritional content. Predictably, I gained back all of the weight I had lost and then some. All of that work was down the drain, and I was right back where I had started.

In the fall of 2003, I was the biggest I'd been in my entire life and about to turn thirty-two (the same age my brother was when he had his heart attacks). At the time, I thought I weighed around 330 pounds. Since I am six-foot-three-inches tall, I carried my weight well. But there were signs that my health was starting to go downhill, with my doctor putting me on prescription medications for high cholesterol, high blood pressure, and breathing problems. I was a mess, and Christine was always trying to convince me to try again to lose weight. But because of my past experiences with dieting, I came to one sobering conclusion—if losing weight and getting healthy meant hunger, pain, and frustration, then I'd rather be fat and happy eating whatever I wanted. This was a very dangerous mentality that I allowed to creep into my head, but it is pretty indicative of the attitude that most people have toward healthy living.

A series of events that took place in 2003 began to awaken me to the idea of giving a pursuit of health another go. At the time, I was a substitute teacher in a middle-school English class. One day, while writing the day's lesson on the chalkboard, I heard a boy say loudly from the back of the room, "Man, Mr. Moore is really fffffffaat!"

As you can imagine, the entire class of preteens burst into laughter, and I turned around and started laughing to keep from crying. But as blunt as that comment was, the kid was right—I was very fat and, even worse, on my way to becoming seriously ill with a heart attack like my brother, and quite possibly headed toward an early grave if I didn't change something about the way I was living my life.

Another event that helped me realize how bad I had gotten occurred at my church's annual fall festival, where kids and adults alike were climbing up and down a rock wall. I remember looking at the wall and thinking how easy it would be for me to do it. When it was my turn, they suited me up with the climbing gear and away I went to climb to the top and back down. But my moment of glory on the rock wall was short-lived, as I couldn't make it more than two steps before slipping and twisting my ankle. With so many people watching my defeat, it was one of the most embarrassing moments of my life. I remember thinking to myself, "What in the world is wrong with me that I can't even climb a silly rock wall?!"

As other quality of life issues began to manifest—ripping my pants, needing assistance getting up out of a chair, hating to go on an airplane or to the movies because my rump didn't fit in the seats, and receiving obvious looks of disgust from complete strangers—my wheels started turning about what I could do this time to lose weight. There was no way I was going to go on yet another low-fat diet after my previous experiences. What could I do that would be different, leave me satisfied and happy with the foods I was eating, and produce a lasting impact not just on my weight but also on my overall health? Surely such a diet had to exist.

As it happens, my dear mother-in-law, Libby, gave me a copy of a diet book for Christmas in 2003, right as I was thinking about all of this perhaps more seriously than I ever had before. What's interesting is that she had given me diet books for Christmas every year for most of my marriage to Christine, but that year, she got me a book that was unlike any other nutritional health book I had read before, and it changed my life forever. That book was *Dr. Atkins' New Diet Revolution* by the late, great Dr. Robert C. Atkins.

Curiously, when I lost weight on that nearly no-fat diet in 1999, many people thought I had done it on Atkins. But I remember telling anyone who said this to me, "That's one of the most unhealthy ways you could possibly lose weight. I would never do a low-carb diet like Atkins." Well, here I was just five years later, reading the book for myself to finally see what it was all about. And honestly, as I began looking at this diet, I thought Dr. Atkins was completely nuts, based on everything I'd ever heard about a healthy diet. *What does he mean, eat fewer carbohydrates? Doesn't he know that's where you get your energy from? Then he says to eat more fat? This author is a cardiologist and he's telling people to eat butter, full-fat meats and cheese, cream, and other fat-rich foods? Does he want people to raise their cholesterol, clog their arteries, and have a heart attack?* But as I continued to read and began to understand the purpose of cutting carbs and increasing fat and protein, I decided to give it a go. After all, it was perhaps the one thing I had never tried in all my years of going on diets.

As so many people do every year, I decided to make it my New Year's resolution to lose weight beginning on January 1, 2004. But before I could start on this new diet plan, I had to determine my starting weight. Remember, I thought I weighed around 330 pounds, because the bathroom scale in my house only measured up to 320 pounds. I remember driving around to various gyms to find a scale that would give me an accurate starting weight, but all of them gave me an error message. What in the world was going on? Finally I went to a Gold's Gym and asked if I could use their scale. They said I could and told me that it would measure up to 500 pounds. I remember thinking that I wasn't anywhere near that big.

When I stepped on that scale in Gold's Gym and saw a "4" at the beginning of my weight, my heart immediately sank. *Do I seriously weigh over 400 pounds?* Yep, 410 pounds, to be exact. And it was at that very moment that the true severity of my morbid obesity stared me in the face. I needed to do something that would not be temporary, but permanent. And while the idea of eating low-carb and high-fat seemed crazy based on everything I had ever seen or heard, the time had come to give it a try. It was time to trade sugary soda, Little Debbie snack cakes, fast food, and junk food for bacon, eggs, cheese, butter, green leafy vegetables, steak, cream, and more. This was a do-or-die moment for me, and I was ready to rise to the challenge.

After a few days of discomfort, my body began to adjust to the new diet, and just two weeks after removing sugar, grains, and starch and replacing them with real, whole fats and proteins that actually nourished my body, I felt normal, for perhaps the first time in my entire life.

I had a huge burst of energy once I had removed all the carbage from my diet and replaced it with the quality fresh food that my body was truly craving, and in the first month, I lost thirty pounds. WOO HOO! Then in the second month, I was so energized that I had to let it out on the treadmill at the gym, walking at a speed of three miles per hour for ten to fifteen minutes. Keep in mind that I still weighed 380 pounds. I tell people I was weight lifting—all that weight I was carrying around was plenty of weight to lift! By the end of February 2004, I had lost another forty pounds.

After one hundred days, I had lost a total of one hundred pounds, and I knew I was on to something bigger and more special than anything I'd ever tried before. I was getting healthier, without deprivation, cravings, hunger, or any of the other stuff that had ruined every single weight-loss attempt I'd ever made. I had finally discovered a way of eating that was delicious, nutritious, and completely effective at giving me back my health. I ditched my breathing medication after a few weeks. Where I'd once gotten dizzy standing up from the couch, within a couple of months I no longer needed my blood pressure medication. And nine months into my low-carb, high-fat lifestyle, I let go of my final prescription medication, for high cholesterol, because my body was transforming from one addicted to sugar and carbohydrates to one that was finally operating the way it was intended to.

At the end of 2004, I had lost a total of 180 pounds, and my life was about to shift in ways I couldn't ever have imagined. The Atkins Nutritionals company contacted me about featuring my success story on their website, and I began receiving e-mails from people all around the world asking me how I did it, where they could connect with me, when I was going to write a book about my experience, and more. My initial reaction to this attention was, "Will you people leave me alone?!" But then I got to thinking that it would be fun to share the journey I'd just gone through to help educate, encourage, and inspire others in their own paths to a healthier life.

In early 2005, a buddy of mine who had a political blog suggested that I start blogging about a low-carb diet. My first question to him was, "What the heck is a blog?" But once he explained, a blog sounded like the perfect tool for getting the word out and sharing all the information I had learned about nutrition and health. Plus, I'd loved to write as an English major in college, and now I would have an outlet to use that for a good purpose. Thus was born *Livin' La Vida Low-Carb,* which is now one of the most popular nutritional health blogs in the world.

In early 2006, I made a fortuitous connection when Kevin Kennedy-Spaien sent me an e-mail telling me how much he loved my blog and that if I spoke half as well as I wrote, I'd be a great podcaster. I became a contributor on his now defunct *Health Hacks* podcast, and soon we launched *The Livin' La Vida Low-Carb Show with Jimmy Moore* podcast, which has been a perennial top-twenty nutrition and fitness health podcast on iTunes for nearly a decade. It's the longest-running health podcast on the Internet and hit episode 1,000 in 2015! Additionally, I now do a podcast on Fridays called *Low-Carb Conversations with Jimmy Moore, Dietitian Cassie & Friends,* where we look at the latest health headlines and offer up thoughts and opinions about them from the perspective of low-carb living.

Since 2013 I've released two books with my coauthor, Dr. Eric C. Westman, an internist and researcher at Duke University: *Cholesterol Clarity: What the HDL Is Wrong with My Numbers?* (2013) and *Keto Clarity: Your Definitive Guide to the Benefits of a Low-Carb, High-Fat Diet* (2014). After the overwhelming success of *Keto Clarity,* my publisher asked me to write a cookbook of ketogenic recipes. My fans have been begging me to share recipes in a book for a long time, but the idea of sitting down and meticulously measuring out a quarter cup of this and a teaspoon of that makes me want to pull my hair out. Don't get me wrong, I love to cook, but my way of cooking involves a lot of eyeballing the ingredients and making tasty food without the stress of being precise about measurements and cooking times. But a cookbook done right most certainly needs precision. So I asked my publisher if I could collaborate with someone who knows a thing or two about recipe development and a real foods–based, ketogenic way of eating.

Although I love my *Cholesterol Clarity* and *Keto Clarity* coauthor Dr. Eric Westman (and can't wait to start collaborating with him on the next in our *Clarity* series), he's certainly no wunderkind in the kitchen (you know, I think he'd burn water if he tried to cook!). When I started thinking about who would be the perfect fit for my philosophy on ketogenic diets, one name immediately rose to the top of the list: Maria Emmerich, the talented and extremely knowledgeable expert in ketogenic nutritional health. She's already self-published a whopping seven books chock-full of amazing low-carb recipes, including a book dedicated solely to ketogenic diets called *Keto-Adapted: Your Guide to Accelerated Weight Loss and Healthy Healing.*

Those of you who have read *Keto Clarity* may recognize Maria as one of the experts featured in that book, and she's got quite a following of people who appreciate her extraordinary ability to make delicious foods that fit within a healthy low-carb, high-fat template. When I called her to suggest joining forces on a cookbook, the only way I could describe her response would be to compare it to the reaction of an eleven-year-old girl being told that she was going to meet One Direction backstage after seeing them in concert. Oh yes, she was head-over-heels giddy about the opportunity to collaborate with me on a book, and my publisher immediately fell in love with Maria's infectious enthusiasm and passion for making mouthwatering ketogenic dishes.

Thus was born the idea for the cookbook you are holding in your hands, and we are thrilled to provide this much-needed resource for a nutritional approach that has been gaining major steam in recent years. The recipes in this book all fit within the low-carb, moderate-protein, high-fat template and are composed of real foods. Maria and I both believe that this way of eating is an important aspect of a healthy lifestyle and is essential to completely heal your body from damage caused by the modern-day food culture, which has led to the epidemic of chronic diseases such as obesity, diabetes, heart disease, and worse. *The Ketogenic Cookbook* is designed to provide you with information about incorporating a low-carb, high-fat approach into your life and arm you with plenty of recipes that fit within that nutritional framework.

# Maria's story

I never really thought about my weight and health very much as I was growing up because I always saw myself as a perfectly normal kid. But all of that changed one day when I was a sophomore in high school. I asked my friend if I could try on her cute jacket, thinking that we were about the same size, but it quickly became obvious that the jacket was tighter on my body than I realized when one of my classmates started loudly singing "Fat Girl in a Little Coat" to the tune of "Fat Guy in a Little Coat" from the movie *Tommy Boy.*

As you can imagine, I was mortified, and everyone started laughing at me and mocking me for being overweight. That moment was the beginning of a great awakening inside me and prompted me to make a change in my health. In fact, it was the catalyst for my interest in nutrition and exercise, which eventually resulted in my becoming a nutritionist. I often think about that embarrassing experience whenever I need to remember why I do what I do. (I saw the guy who sang that song about me at a wedding a few years back, and he was shocked that I looked better than I did in high school. Sweet revenge!)

I worked hard in high school to get enough exercise and eat what I thought were healthy foods, following the food pyramid and government guidelines, which meant lots of carbohydrates and whole grains. I went on to study exercise and nutrition in college, and right after college, I developed severe irritable bowel syndrome and acid reflux. I couldn't even drink water without getting reflux. I was searching for a true solution, not just medication to help the symptoms, when I remembered taking my dog, Teva, to the veterinarian when I was in high school. She'd been losing her hair in patches, and the first question the vet asked me was, "What are you feeding her?"

It was a question I had never been asked even once by doctors I had seen over the years, and I started pondering why. Why do drugs, not nutrition, seem to be physicians' first choice of therapy? I decided to dig deeper into this subject, and that led me to look closer at a low-carb, no-grain diet, based on what I'd learned in school. I decided to cut out most carbs and all grains, and my symptoms immediately began to improve. It was the first step on my path to a ketogenic diet, but I wouldn't take the next step for many years, and it took some difficult times to get there.

In 2007, my husband, Craig, and I had some really tough curveballs thrown our way. I was a rock-climbing guide and totally loved it, but when the economy took a nosedive that year, Craig lost his job and our primary source of income vanished. We were utterly devastated and had to temporarily put off our dream of adopting children. There we were with no money, no insurance, and a heavy burden on our shoulders that challenged our marriage in ways we couldn't have imagined. It all took a toll on us, both physically and mentally, but we didn't throw in the towel.

One of the things I love most about Craig is his perseverance—a trait we have in common—and we pushed back. I quit that rock-climbing job and decided to become a nutritionist. I didn't have a lot of clients at first, so I started self-publishing books in my free time to help supplement our income. We also started tightening our budget, having "date night" at home and renting movies from the local library. These prudent measures and our willingness to tighten our belts saved our finances and our marriage from devastation.

That year, we really struggled to put on a smiling face for our family and the people in our lives. I remember for Thanksgiving, Craig made a "Thanksgiving box." We asked everyone to write what they were most thankful for on strips of paper and place them in the box. The strips of paper were anonymous and were read out loud for everyone to hear. The fun part was guessing who wrote each one; the most meaningful words usually came from someone we would have never guessed. My mom kept the strips of paper to remind us all where we came from to get where we are today. That gave me hope for a better tomorrow.

And things did get better. Craig got another job as a product manager at a company that made software for hospitals. I took on more clients as a nutritionist, and I loved helping them find better health through improved diet—something that I still found doctors never considered. But in my work with clients who had severe metabolic syndrome and diabetes, I found that their blood sugar levels weren't improving enough despite limiting carbs and sugars. I remembered learning in college that since the body can't store protein, it turns excess protein into sugar, and I decided it was time to limit not just carbs but also protein. In other words, I stumbled onto a low-carb, moderate-protein, high-fat diet—a ketogenic diet—and it made all the difference for my clients, and for me.

Now that I am keto-adapted—my body burns fat, not sugar, for fuel—my life and my body are running better than they have in many years. My fitness and energy levels are through the roof, and I'm truly happy. Although I was never athletic growing up, now I am more active than the vast majority of the population. At the age of thirty-four, I run every single morning not because I have to but because I love it. I'm not training for a race or trying to lose weight. I just love it! I know, I'm weird, but it is who I am.

We adopted two beautiful toddler boys in November 2011. As luck would have it, Craig lost his job just a few months later, in April 2012, and we had to reassess where we were and what we would do. That's when he decided to leave the corporate world for good and stay at home with the boys full-time, homeschool them, and help me in my nutrition consulting business. No longer were we trying to have lots of stuff to keep us happy. We found joy in downsizing our lives and enjoying the precious

moments we share as a family. There is a great quote by Marcus Aurelius: "Remember this, that very little is needed to make a happy life." We still fight the mentality that we need more, but we've prioritized our family, our health, and our time together making memories.

Eating a ketogenic diet hasn't changed my love of food—I've always loved to eat and I always will. Even as a young teenager I often cooked and baked for my family. My signature dish was lasagna. And now, because I understand how to balance macronutrients to keep a meal ketogenic, I love creating keto-friendly versions of classic dishes. My family still enjoys all the foods I remember from growing up, just modified to be healthier. Now my son Micah's favorite food is my Lasagna Roll-Ups (page 206)!

I'm thrilled to be collaborating with my friend Jimmy Moore on this cookbook. We both want you to enjoy tasty foods that fit within a real foods–based, low-carb, high-fat, ketogenic way of eating. It will enhance your health in ways you could never imagine.

**Are you ready to step up your game in improving your nutrition? In these next few chapters, we'll dive deeply into what *ketogenic* means and why it is so important in your pursuit of health.**

# What Is the Ketogenic Diet?

*The difficulty lies not so much in developing new ideas as in escaping from old ones.*

—John Maynard Keynes

If you want to know what people are interested in these days, look no further than what they're Googling. The world's most popular online search engine keeps tabs on the most common search terms, and when it comes to searches related to diet, it's not surprising to see that the latest gimmicks—including juicing, detoxifying, cleansing, and even an all-fruit diet—are attracting the most attention. But amidst these dubious ideas for getting healthy are actually some incredibly effective ones. Take a look at the fifth-most popular diet-related search term on Google in 2013—a word that started popping up on the diet scene in recent years, *ketogenic.*

You may have already heard of some form of this word before, perhaps *keto, ketosis, ketones, ketogenesis*, or *keto-adapted.* It's been becoming increasingly mainstream in recent years as scientific studies have strongly supported the idea that a ketogenic diet improves several aspects of health. This has obviously piqued the curiosity of the general public, particularly the many people who are desperately looking for an answer to health woes that have been getting worse and worse on the standard calorie-counting, fat-cutting, conventional nutrition advice from doctors, dietitians, and major health organizations. If the definition of insanity is doing the same thing over and over again and expecting different results, then those who continue to espouse the same views on nutrition again and again, thinking something will change in the collective health of our society, belong in an asylum!

Whether these nutritional health experts realize it yet or not, there's a bona fide ketogenic revolution currently underway, and it's only going to gain strength in the years to come as more and more people embrace and adopt this way of living. We're already seeing it being embraced by significant numbers of people in countries like Sweden, South Africa, Australia, and New Zealand. The momentum for ketogenic diets is building all across the globe, as brave researchers conduct studies to look for the truth without an agenda, enlightened medical doctors see improved patient outcomes without the need for risky prescription medications, and journalists, bloggers, and enthusiastic laypeople carry the torch into every nook and cranny of our society. This book is yet another resource for people to turn to in order to learn more about how ketosis can help them get healthy.

So what is a ketogenic diet? At the most basic level, a ketogenic diet is one that relies on fat as the main source of energy. That may not sound like anything special, but it's actually quite profound. The vast majority of people today are walking around right now

### KETONES 101

The term *ketogenic* comes from the word *ketones*, which are what truly fuel your body when you're in ketosis. When you burn fat, your body produces ketones, and these are what your cells use for energy. There are three different kinds of ketones: beta-hydroxybutyrate, which is found in the blood; acetoacetate, which is found in the urine; and acetone, which is found in the breath.

burning glucose—sugar—for fuel and eating mostly carbohydrates to meet their daily energy needs. You've heard of marathon runners needing to "carb up" before a long run; that means they're loading their bodies with sugar to burn off during the race. But burning fat as fuel is much healthier and more efficient, and a ketogenic diet is a great metabolic tool for improving your health. In fact, ketogenic researchers Dr. Steve Phinney and Dr. Jeff Volek have noted that a sugar-burner has only about 2,000 calories' worth of energy stored in their body while a fat-burner has over 40,000 calories' worth of fuel—more than twenty times as much!

## ARE YOU IN KETOSIS?

A lot of people think a ketogenic diet is just a low-carb diet, but to be truly keto it needs to be low-carb, high-fat, and moderate-protein. And the only way to know if you're in ketosis—burning fat instead of sugar—is to test for ketones!

- **Blood:** Testing your blood is the gold standard in ketone testing. We recommend using the Precision Xtra (called Freestyle Optium outside the United States), which takes just a finger prick.

- **Urine:** You can measure acetoacetate in your urine with a product called Ketostix, but urine ketones are not a reliable sign of ketosis once you're fully keto-adapted.

- **Breath:** Acetone can currently be measured using a device called Ketonix. Other devices are in development.

Urine strips change color to indicate the general level of ketones (none, some, a lot), but if you test your blood or breath, look for ketone levels over 1 millimolar—that's when you're in ketosis!

To get your body to start using fat for fuel instead of sugar, it's necessary to restrict your intake of carbohydrates and moderate protein—and eat as much saturated and monounsaturated fats as it takes to feel full. That's the basic template for the ketogenic diet, and it launches your body into a two- to four-week period of keto-adaptation as you start to burn fat to produce ketones, the molecules your body uses for energy. Keep in mind that the amount of fat, protein, and carbohydrates in a ketogenic diet is going to vary widely from person to person, depending on their individual metabolic needs. People who are active and/or relatively healthy may be able to consume more carbohydrates and protein than those who are less active and/or metabolically challenged. Tinker with the amounts and test on your own to find the right levels to put your body into ketosis.

Once you're fully adapted to using fat for fuel, you're officially in nutritional ketosis (a term first coined in the mid-1980s by Dr. Phinney). It can take anywhere from two weeks to as much as two months to completely shift over to burning fat as the primary fuel source and experience the totality of the benefits that come from being in ketosis. We'll share more about the huge benefits to your health throughout the pages of this book. But for now, know that it is a completely normal, desirable physiological state and has been the default metabolic state throughout all of human history.

As you read, keep in mind that this book isn't a comprehensive guide to keto. Our focus here is on the recIpes and cooking for a delicious and healthy ketogenic diet. If you're interested in learning more, check out my earlier book *Keto Clarity* or any of the books, websites, and blogs listed in the resources section (page 359).

Coming up in the next chapter, we'll share a bit of the history behind the ketogenic diet, where it came from, why it disappeared from the public for a period of time, and how it is now reemerging as a major force in the nutritional conversation.

# The History of Keto

*The doctor of the future will no longer treat the human frame with drugs, but rather will cure and prevent disease with nutrition.*

—Thomas Edison

One of the hallmarks of a ketogenic diet is that it's low in carbohydrates, and of course the low-carb diet isn't new on the nutritional scene. The late, great Dr. Robert C. Atkins helped popularize it in the early 1970s and again in the early 2000s, but it actually goes back much further. Dr. Atkins based much of his nutritional philosophy on research conducted by Dr. Alfred Pennington, who published a landmark study in the October 1963 issue of the *Journal of the American Medical Association* in which he recommended treating obesity by cutting starch and sugar and replacing it with fat and protein. And we have to go back one hundred years earlier than that to find the real beginning of the advent of low-carb, high-fat diets in our culture.

## THE WORLD'S FIRST BESTSELLING DIET BOOK

Long before the name "Atkins" become synonymous with "low-carb," an overweight undertaker and coffin maker named William Banting helped popularize the low-carb, high-fat way of eating in the mid-nineteenth century. After losing forty-six pounds and improving his mobility, hearing, and vision by eating a diet that focused on meat and vegetables and eschewed starch and sugar, on the recommendation of a London surgeon named Dr. William Harvey, Banting became the world's first bestselling diet-book author when he published a booklet entitled *Letter on Corpulence* (read it online at www.lowcarb.ca/corpulence) in 1863. In this little book, which sold over 63,000 copies (astonishing for a book at that time), he extols eating more fat and restricting carbohydrates as the real key to losing weight and getting healthy.

Banting's *Letter on Corpulence* was so well received that his name quickly became synonymous with dieting. It was common to ask anyone who was attempting weight loss, "Do you Bant?" In fact, Banting was the recommended diet taught in medical schools until 1959, when it was replaced by the low-fat, high-carb diet popularized by researcher Ancel Keys (more on that in a moment).

## THE DISCOVERY OF KETONES

The scientific understanding of ketosis began in 1921, when nutritional researcher Dr. Rollin Turner Woodyatt was examining the role of starvation and carbohydrate restriction in metabolism and the impact these interventions had on patients with diabetes. Dr. Woodyatt discovered there were three specific molecules that became prevalent in the blood, urine, and breath of healthy study patients who were fasting for long periods or eating a low-carb, high-fat diet. He called them *ketone bodies,* and because they consistently appeared when sources of glucose (primarily carbohydrates and protein) were withheld, Dr. Woodyatt and his team knew they were being used as an alternative fuel source in the absence of glucose.

A few years later, in 1924, Dr. Woodyatt's discovery caught the attention of a nutritional health researcher named Dr. Russell Wilder. Dr. Wilder continued to examine the metabolic role of ketone bodies and coined the term *ketogenic diet* to describe the dietary approach that limits carbohydrates and increases dietary fat intake as a means of raising the level of ketones in the blood.

The goal of Dr. Woodyatt's research was to find a way to mimic the therapeutic effects of fasting for patients with epileptic seizures, without all the ill effects that come with not eating any food (a concept now commonly referred to in research as "fed starvation"). He noticed that the ketogenic diet allows the body to experience all of the healing properties of starvation while still, in fact, being fed. In other words, ketones can be produced in an unhealthy manner by not eating food at all, or in a healthy manner by eating a low-carb, moderate-protein, high-fat diet. This was a major, Nobel Prize–worthy breakthrough in our understanding of nutrition, though unfortunately very few of Dr. Woodyatt's contemporaries realized it at the time. But through his work, the ketogenic diet was now officially on the radar for the first time as a viable medical therapy.

The ketogenic diet was the primary and most effective treatment option for people with epilepsy until anticonvulsant drugs were developed beginning in the late 1930s. While this nutritional therapy wasn't a panacea that made everyone who tried it completely seizure-free, it certainly revealed the great potential of ketone bodies for improving health. The positive role of ketosis in treating epilepsy led medical professionals and researchers to begin seriously looking at how it could

*Dear Jimmy,*

*You have helped change my life more than you can imagine. I've read your books and listened to almost all of your wonderful podcasts. You and Maria Emmerich have helped changed my life so much. I feel fantastic and have endless energy now.*

*I'm a personal trainer and chef and I have changed my ways drastically and for the better. I've even competed in my first bodybuilding competition at the age of 44, with Maria's coaching. I'm helping spread the word about keto in the fitness community.*

*Thanks again Jimmy :)*

*Sincerely,*

*Lisa Colclasure*
*Denver, Colorado*

help treat a myriad of other conditions that are affected by the metabolic pathway of ketones. That research still continues to this day and is promoted through organizations like The Charlie Foundation.

## THE LOW-FAT FOLLY

The mainstream popularity of the ketogenic diet took a major hit when researcher Ancel Keys published his Seven Countries Study. The study examines the diets of middle-aged men in the United States, Europe, and Japan, and it began in 1958 and is still ongoing. The results published in the late 1950s showed that levels of blood cholesterol are directly related to the risk of heart attack and stroke. Keys hypothesized that eating high amounts of dietary saturated fat in foods like butter, lard, full-fat meats, and cheese increases blood cholesterol, which in turn he tied to an increased risk to cardiovascular health (widely referred to as the "diet-heart hypothesis"). Therefore he advocated eating a low-fat diet to prevent heart disease.

However, it has been well documented that the Seven Countries Study is seriously flawed because Keys left out data from countries with low saturated fat intake and higher levels of heart disease and from countries with high saturated fat intake and lower levels of heart disease. If you want to learn more about the faulty science that set the low-fat diet in motion, we highly recommend watching the documentary *Fat Head,* by Tom Naughton, and reading the *New York Times* bestselling books *Good Calories, Bad Calories,* by Gary Taubes, and *The Big Fat Surprise,* by Nina Teicholz. It's utterly amazing that what most Americans believe is the prudent way to eat healthy is all based on flawed science. But it is.

With his Seven Countries Study, Keys set in motion a proliferation of the low-fat, high-carb nutritional approach, which was embraced by major health organizations such as the American Heart Association and American Diabetes Association, quickly lending credibility to a diet that never had any credible research behind it. That didn't matter to Senator George McGovern, who himself followed the ultra-low-fat diet program developed by nutritionist Nathan Pritikin in the late 1970s. McGovern's heavy influence as the chairperson of the Senate Select Committee on Nutrition and Human Needs from 1968 to 1977 eventually led to the 1977 Dietary Goals for the United States, which recommended that Americans eat less fat and more complex carbohydrates. These government-sanctioned nutritional recommendations quickly spread around the world. However, as a

February 2015 study in the journal *Open Heart* showed, the recommendation to cut total fat in the diet to less than 30 percent of calories was completely arbitrary—even at the time, no data supported that position. And to this day, no study has ever found data to support that recommendation. None!

When fat-phobia came into full force during the 1980s, it led to the creation of low-fat and no-fat food products that dominated store shelves. SnackWell's low-fat treats, rice cakes, margarine, low-fat bagels, fat-free ice cream, and more became staples of the American diet, with tens of millions of us obediently cutting our consumption of fat, especially saturated fat, way down out of fear of having a heart attack. Then in 1992, when the food pyramid was introduced (it was replaced in 2011 by MyPlate), we were told to eat more carbohydrate-based foods like whole grains, fruits, and vegetables and less meat and fat. So we shifted our calorie intake dramatically toward carbohydrates, and in the following years there was an astronomic rise in the rates of obesity, type 2 diabetes, heart disease, and other chronic health problems. Coincidence? We think not.

## A WORLDWIDE KETOGENIC REVOLUTION IS UNDERWAY

Interestingly, the idea for a food pyramid was first developed in 1972 by Sweden's National Board of Health and Welfare, which wanted a way to communicate which foods were most nutritious and least expensive. This is ironic now as Sweden is one of the few countries leading the way back to a low-carb, high-fat diet (they refer to it as "LCHF") thanks to the leadership of some brave physicians willing to challenge the status quo on diet. In January 2008, Dr. Annika Dahlqvist, a Swedish physician who successfully treats her diabetes patients using LCHF, was sued by two dietitians who took her before the National Board of Health and Welfare (the equivalent of the United States' FDA) for putting her patients at "severe risk" by recommending a low-carb, high-fat diet. They attempted to have her medical license stripped, but she held firm in her belief this was the best approach for treating patients with obesity and diabetes. After investigating the evidence for LCHF, the board concluded that a low-carb diet is "in accordance with science and well-tried experience for reducing obesity and type 2 diabetes."

After that, interest in low-carb, high-fat exploded in Sweden. Another Swedish physician and blogger named Dr. Andreas Eenfeldt, author of the book *Low Carb High Fat Food Revolution,* has been a frequent guest in the media promoting reducing carbohydrate consumption and increasing dietary fat as a way to get healthy. The message of Dr. Dahlqvist, Dr. Eenfeldt, and other LCHF advocates seems to be taking hold in the Swedish population: a March 2011 poll found nearly one in four Swedes were on some kind of low-carb diet plan. That's huge! But the change to low-carb, high-fat isn't just happening in Sweden. Great things are also happening in South Africa.

The momentum for a low-carb, high-fat diet in South Africa—where it's referred to as "Banting" in tribute to William Banting—can be tied directly to the enthusiastic work being done there by a running legend named Tim Noakes, a professor emeritus of exercise science and sports medicine at the University of Cape Town whose 1991 classic book *Lore of Running* is still widely considered the bible for runners. In that book, Noakes advocated a high-carb diet for athletes. But after reading the 2010 book *The New Atkins for a New You,* by three respected nutritional health researchers, Dr. Stephen Phinney, Dr. Jeff Volek, and Dr. Eric Westman, Noakes realized he'd been mistaken about the role of carbohydrates in the diet, and he put his reputation on the line by publicly announcing he was wrong and encouraging his readers to tear out the pages in his book where he discusses nutrition.

Noakes has become such an influential voice in the diet debate in South Africa that his 2013 book with co-author Jonno Proudfoot, *The Real Meal Revolution,* was the number-two bestselling book in South Africa in 2014, beating out perennial fiction bestsellers such as *Fifty Shades of Grey.* The excitement about the "Noakes diet," "Banting," and low-carb, high-fat is so strong there you'd be hard-pressed to find anyone who hasn't heard about it. In February 2015, Noakes brought together sixteen of the world's foremost experts on low-carb, high-fat diets (including one of this book's coauthors, Jimmy Moore) in Cape Town for an international conference called the Old Mutual Health Convention, which was attended by 600 medical professionals and 300 laypeople. Similar events are planned for London in late 2015 and Washington, DC, in 2016.

The ketogenic diet isn't going away anytime soon, and for good reason. Coming up in the next chapter, we'll share how a ketogenic diet will heal your body and put you back on the course to optimal health.

# Why Going Keto
# Will Heal Your Body

*If diet is wrong, medicine is of no use.*
*If diet is correct, medicine is*
*of no need.*

—Ayurvedic proverb

For all the amazing deliciousness that a ketogenic diet offers, it would mean nothing if it failed to heal your body and give you the best health you've ever experienced. But the great news for you is that it does this in spades, and the health benefits are arguably the best part of going keto.

The amount of nutrients you receive from eating a low-carb, moderate-protein, high-fat diet composed of real, whole foods is greater than virtually any other dietary plan you could possibly choose. When you fully embrace this way of eating, you'll see some powerful results that you don't experience on any other diet. Making this a lifestyle change that you enjoy is all part of the joy of being on a ketogenic journey.

What exactly happens when you make the switch from burning sugar for fuel to burning primarily fat and ketones? Let's take a look at the incredible benefits you see almost immediately when you start eating this way:

No more sleepy afternoons following lunch

Clear skin

Improvements in chronic joint and muscle pain

No more hunger and cravings

Fat loss and appetite control

Calm mood and steady energy throughout the day

Sound, restful sleep

A feeling of contentment and gratitude about life

Markedly improved cardiovascular health markers

No more obsessing and worrying about food

Improved resistance to chronic diseases

Optimized brain health and improved memory

This brief list of the benefits of a ketogenic diet is merely the tip of the iceberg. In the decades since Dr. Woodyatt discovered that a ketogenic diet is beneficial for preventing epileptic seizures, scientific studies have shown that it can also help many of the most catastrophic neurodegenerative conditions, including autism, Alzheimer's, Parkinson's, amyotrophic lateral sclerosis (ALS, also known as Lou Gehrig's disease), narcolepsy, schizophrenia, bipolar disorder, traumatic brain injury, and stroke. Additionally, there is now strong evidence that other diseases can be improved with a ketogenic diet, such as type 2 diabetes, cardiovascular disease, polycystic ovary syndrome (PCOS), irritable bowel syndrome (IBS), heartburn (GERD), and nonalcoholic fatty liver disease (NAFLD). And we're now seeing emerging areas of research for the effects of a ketogenic diet on cancer (especially brain cancer), migraines, gum disease, acne, hair loss, and more. The ketogenic diet is indeed the real deal, and it's worth giving it a second look as a means for optimizing your overall health.

Most importantly, the ketogenic diet helps you control two critical aspects of health. Nope, not your weight or cholesterol, which many health professionals overly obsess about. The areas that are most important to zero in on are your blood sugar levels and inflammation. Your doctor may or may not have talked to you about these, but it's incumbent upon you as the number-one advocate for your health to know where you stand when it comes to these measures. Nutritional ketosis can help move both of them in the right direction.

## HOW THE BODY MAKES SUGAR FROM PROTEIN

Carbs aren't the only thing that your body gets sugar from. Believe it or not, protein can be a source of glucose, too. When the body gets more protein than it needs, the liver converts the excess protein into glucose through a process known as *gluconeogenesis*. That's why it's so important to moderate your protein intake—too much protein results in higher blood sugar levels and makes getting into nutritional ketosis next to impossible.

Blood sugar probably isn't even on your radar at the moment unless you have diabetes, but it's arguably the most important health marker there is, and literally anyone can test it at home. No one just wakes up one day with type 2 diabetes. It's a disease that develops from years upon years of uncontrolled high blood sugar levels as a direct result of consuming an unhealthy diet full of refined carbohydrates. This is what I like to refer to as "crappy carbage," and it literally destroys your natural ability to handle even real-food carbohydrates down the road.

Consuming foods that raise blood sugar (namely carbohydrates and, to a lesser degree, protein) causes the pancreas to release insulin, which pushes glucose out of the bloodstream and into cells, which use it for energy. In a healthy person, insulin keeps glucose levels steady between 80 and 100 mg/dL. The one-hour postprandial (after-eating) blood sugar reading never gets even close to 140 mg/dL, and the two-hour postprandial blood sugar reading comes back to the baseline fasting level. This indicates perfect beta-cell function, and people with these results are commonly referred to as "insulin-sensitive."

However, over time, eating excessive amounts of carbohydrates puts enormous stress on the pancreas to keep up with the demand for insulin. This is the beginning of a condition known as "insulin resistance," in which blood sugar can remain elevated well above the baseline reading for hours upon hours following a meal. When this happens, tolerance for carbohydrates and the glucose effects of eating protein becomes lower and lower, and the ultimate result is obesity, hyperglycemia, and, if left unchecked, type 2 diabetes. This is why a ketogenic diet is the perfect solution for people dealing with insulin resistance: it removes the burden on the pancreas to keep up with the insulin demands of a high-carb diet. In other words, going keto helps your pancreas chill out and not work as hard.

Even people who haven't suffered damage to their ability to make insulin may be overworking their pancreas by eating carbohydrates like there is no tomorrow. Unfortunately they will have to pay the piper someday if they remain oblivious to the direct role what they are eating can have on their health. They might get away with it while they are young and relatively healthy, but it will catch up to them eventually.

The most conservative estimates find that at least one-fourth of people in the United States (about 68 million) are already suffering from insulin resistance. This includes people with diabetes, prediabetes (elevated fasting blood sugar that's not quite at the level of diabetes), and fasting blood sugar levels consistently above 100 mg/dL—and if nothing is done to correct the last two, they're one-way tickets straight to type 2 diabetes. People with insulin resistance are also at a greater risk of developing heart disease, fatty liver disease, infertility, and more. Avoiding this fate should be the goal of everyone, and knowing where you stand can be as easy as pricking your finger a few times with a glucometer, available at any pharmacy or chemist around the world. Knowledge is power, and if you know that you're insulin-resistant, you can take a stand for your own health and proactively change your course.

The second health marker you should be aware of in your pursuit of optimal health is inflammation. That word makes a lot of people think of a time when you twisted your ankle and it swelled up and radiated heat. This is acute inflammation, and it's a temporary, necessary

*Hi Jimmy,*

*Thanks to a ketogenic diet, I have lost 65 of the 90 pounds I had to lose. But my biggest surprise was the health benefits, including total relief without a single drug from a severe case of PMS, mood swings, and other hormonal issues; mysterious disappearance of fungal nails; marked reduction in overall inflammation in the body; and recovery from many chronic injuries that I had no idea were related to a high-carb diet.*

*God bless!*

*Elizabeth Antony*

*Florida*

part of the healing process. But what I'm referring to is chronic inflammation caused by poor nutrition and lifestyle choices, which works slowly to cause damage to your body. When inflammation levels are higher, you are at a greater risk for heart disease and other health calamities.

Sadly, the medical profession prefers to look at cholesterol to determine your risk for heart disease, but it's inflammation that you should be much more concerned about. (We talk much more about this in *Cholesterol Clarity*.) Some inflammation can be a good thing because it can help you fight off bacteria, viruses, fungi, and toxins. But if left unchecked and chronically elevated over long periods, it can become a much more serious health problem. Nearly every chronic disease is linked to chronic systemic inflammation, including heart disease, cancer, diabetes, metabolic syndrome, obesity, polycystic ovary syndrome, autoimmunity, irritable bowel disease, and more. Want to take a wild guess at which foods raise inflammation levels the most? It's the twin villains for health—carbohydrates and vegetable oils.

Head down the center aisles of virtually any grocery store and grab any product off the shelf, and you're almost guaranteed to find some foodlike science experiment mixing sugar, grains, and highly processed vegetable oils like soybean oil, cottonseed oil, and even the so-called healthy canola oil. (If you think canola oil is healthy, go on YouTube, search for "how canola oil is made," and prepare to be shocked.) All these are disastrous for your health because they add more and more inflammation to your body. First, sugar and grains are carbohydrates, which the body needs insulin to process, and high insulin levels mean high inflammation. Second, the manmade fats in processed vegetable oils are loaded with omega-6 fatty acids, and when the body's ratio of omega-6 to omega-3 fatty acids becomes too lopsided, inflammation is the result. A desirable ratio is 4 to 1 or better. On the Standard American Diet, the ratio is closer to 20 to 1.

As inflammation increases, the quality of your health drops like a rock. Thus, a real foods–based ketogenic diet, which eliminates these foods from your diet completely, is an anti-inflammatory nutritional plan that will put you back on the road to health and healing. In fact, a February 2015 study from Yale researchers published in the journal *Nature Medicine* found that beta-hydroxybutyrate (the ketone body in the blood) inhibits the development of inflammation.

There's a simple blood test for the amount of inflammation in your body: the high-sensitivity C-reactive protein (hs-CRP) test, which looks at C-reactive protein, the primary marker for chronic inflammation in the body. Scientists have known about the importance of CRP for a long time, but doctors tend to focus on treating cholesterol because there are medications like statin drugs that can lower it. Unfortunately, lowering cholesterol has not resulted in lower rates of heart attacks and cardiovascular disease as the pharmaceutical companies had hoped for. That's because they ignored inflammation's critical role in the development of heart disease.

The healthy range of hs-CRP is anywhere from 0 to 3 mg/dL, but the ideal level is below 1 mg/dL. Cut out sugars, grains, and vegetable oils from your diet, and you are sure to get your inflammation down to levels that indicate you are healthier than you ever thought possible. Combine low inflammation with normal blood sugar, and you've found the recipe to healing your body and getting back on track in your pursuit of robust health. This is the power of nutritional ketosis that awaits you when you make this a permanent lifestyle change.

You may have noticed that I haven't shared much about what is perhaps the most well-known and ballyhooed benefit of a ketogenic diet—weight loss. We have the late, great Dr. Robert C. Atkins to credit for bringing ketosis to the masses with the overwhelming success of his series of bestselling books, which promoted the "k" word as a means for shedding pounds. He described it in *Dr. Atkins New Diet Revolution* as lipolysis, a fancy-schmancy way of saying that you are burning fat as your primary source of energy. And that's what ketosis is in a nutshell—utilizing fat for fuel. Some people mistake this to mean that if you are in ketosis, you'll automatically lose weight. Not necessarily.

Burning fat as your primary fuel source can indeed lead to a reduction in stored body fat. However, being in a state of nutritional ketosis is simply an indication that your body prefers to get its energy from fat, and that includes the fat you eat as well as your stored body fat. I hate to be the bearer of bad news, but simply eating ketogenic doesn't magically make you shed pounds. While many do see weight fall off very easily and rapidly when they shift from mainly burning sugar to burning fat, it's not a given, and you shouldn't expect it. If you experience weight loss on a ketogenic diet, it's merely a side effect of your healthier eating habits. And if you're still struggling with taking off the weight while you're on keto, the diet will help you optimize your health while you figure out what might be going on.

The problem with focusing solely on weight loss as your reason for getting into ketosis is that it ignores so many nondiet factors involved in weight regulation, including lack of sleep, stress, hormonal imbalances, metabolic syndrome, and so much more. Yes, we'd all love to be able to just eat a certain way to make our weight and health problems disappear for good. But each individual who begins a ketogenic diet comes into it with a unique history, lifestyle, and body. That's why we are big fans of tinkering and testing to figure out what works best for you and considering every aspect of your life that could be negatively contributing to your weight and health.

If you're thinking about getting into nutritional ketosis just to lose weight, don't. You'd be setting yourself up for failure and disappointment before you even got started. Try shifting your focus away from your weight and toward improving your health. When you start looking at key health markers such as blood sugar and insulin levels, inflammation markers such as C-reactive protein levels, the triglyceride-to-HDL ratio on your cholesterol panel, your energy level and mood, and other quality-of-life factors, the obsession over weight vanishes and your focus is readjusted to what matters most. The ketogenic diet is a whole-health approach designed to shift your body into becoming a fat-burning machine, whether your weight drops or not.

*Dear Jimmy,*

*Thank you, thank you, thank you!!! Today my fasting blood glucose was 87 and a few weeks ago I couldn't get it under 130. My ketones were at 1.4 this morning and I am feeling better than ever. I want to buy your new book for my mom and other family members. Just wanted to say how AWESOME you and your podcast are.*

*Blessings,*
*Amber Horton*

## DON'T CONFUSE KETOSIS AND KETOACIDOSIS!

Perhaps you've heard that ketosis can be dangerous. It's not—in fact, it's how the body survives during times of deprivation. So what's up with the scaremongering? *Ketosis* is often confused with *ketoacidosis*, a very serious, life-threatening condition that affects people who don't make any insulin, mostly type 1 diabetics and a few type 2 diabetics. Without insulin, the body may think that there is no glucose to be had and start producing ketones, even when there's lots of glucose in the bloodstream. This results in both high blood sugar levels (above 240 mg/dL) and high blood ketone levels (close to 20.0 mmol), and that's bad news. But this can never, ever happen in anyone (including type 1 diabetics) who is eating a low-carb diet—which is fundamental to a ketogenic diet. Ketosis is a healthy way to nourish and heal your body.

Coming up in the next chapter, we'll examine the nuts and bolts of a ketogenic diet. While the main principles are the same for everyone—eat more fat, less protein, and hardly any carbs—the exact amount of each that gets you into ketosis will vary from person to person. But everyone reading this book can fully experience the benefits that come from going keto with the proper diet.

# The Nuts and Bolts of Ketogenic Nutrition

*The nutritional composition of beef provides much-needed protein, vitamins, and iron.*

—Jayson Lusk

For the past four decades, the default "healthy" diet for most people has been fewer calories, smaller portions, lower fat intake, more whole grains, and limited meat consumption. As it turns out, there's a disturbing lack of evidence that eating this way is actually good for you. Fortunately, researchers are finally questioning the conventional wisdom and providing evidence-based data to help us decipher what's truly healthy.

A February 2015 study conducted by researcher Zoë Harcombe and published in the cardiology journal *Open Heart* found that when, in the late 1970s, the U.S. government recommended limiting saturated fat intake to no more than 10 percent of total calories and total fat intake to no more than 30 percent of calories, there was no "solid trial evidence to back it up." The study noted that randomized, controlled clinical trials conducted at the time actually showed that there was no difference in the number deaths from heart disease whether saturated fat was limited or not. Nevertheless, the government's recommendation to limit saturated fat eventually became part of the Dietary Guidelines for Americans and the food pyramid (now MyPlate).

The, in Harcombe's words, "arbitrary" advice to limit fat intake led Americans to dramatically increase their consumption of carbohydrates in the form of "healthy whole grains" and led food manufacturers to create low-fat and fat-free products full of added sugars to make them taste good. The rest, as they say, is history. Since the introduction of these flawed nutritional principles, obesity and chronic disease have become more prevalent than ever before. Now virtually everyone blindly believes that saturated fat is bad for you because the government said so, and its recommendations are parroted by doctors, dietitians, and all the so-called health experts in the media as the gospel truth. But it's all one big fat lie!

Thankfully, this conventional wisdom is now being exposed as a totally misguided approach that fails to take into account the way humans ate for thousands of years prior to the industrialization of the food supply. And despite what many "health experts" would have you believe, that nutritional approach of our ancestors most certainly wasn't a low-fat, high-carb diet with no animal products, even though that is often touted as the best diet for humans to consume. Not even close.

## THE MYTH OF FRUITS AND VEGETABLES

If you ask the average person on the street which foods are the most nutritious, they'll likely gravitate to the pat answer of "fruits and vegetables." You can hardly blame people for responding this way because we've been conditioned to believe that all that is good in the human diet comes from these foods almost exclusively. It's one of the reasons why some people gravitate to a vegetarian or vegan diet when they want to get healthy—the assumption is that it will make your diet the most nutrient-dense that it could possibly be. But this wrongly assumes that there is no nutrition in anything else.

To see how deeply seated the belief in the healthfulness of fruits and vegetables is, just watch television. Commercials frequently brag that their products are nutritious and wholesome simply because they contain these foods. Don't misunderstand what I'm saying here—fruits and vegetables can and should be part of your diet. But assuming that just eating fruits and vegetables is enough to be healthy is a shortsighted way to look at the nutritional value of the food you consume. For starters, not all fruits and vegetables are created equal, and the choices people make in this regard tend to be the worst.

At the American Society of Bariatric Physicians conference in Nashville, Tennessee, in 2007, a representative from the American Diabetes Association presented the results of a 1999 to 2000 survey of diabetic eating patterns. According to the report, the following is a breakdown of the kinds of vegetables consumed by adults age twenty and over, on average:

| | |
|---|---|
| Fried potatoes | 22% |
| Other potatoes | 13% |
| Tomatoes | 11% |
| Dark green/orange | 11% |
| Legumes/beans | 8% |
| Others | 35% |

As you can see, over one-third of the total vegetable consumption by adults consists of starchy, carbohydrate-based potatoes, mostly fried. Hmm, what could that be? Oh yeah, it's most assuredly french fries from fast-food restaurants like McDonald's, cooked in highly inflammatory, omega-6-rich vegetable oils. If you think that's bad, take a look at the vegetables that the same ADA dietary trends report says children ages two to nineteen are consuming (don't pass out when you see this!):

| | |
|---|---|
| Fried potatoes | 46% |
| Other potatoes | 10% |
| Tomatoes | 9% |
| Dark green/orange | 7% |
| Legumes/beans | 6% |
| Others | 22% |

Yes, you read that right! Almost two-thirds of the "healthy" vegetables that children consume is made up of potatoes. Say what?!

Although they're not sweet on the tongue, one carb-loaded potato packs a walloping sixty grams of carbohydrates, which could be problematic for people with blood sugar abnormalities, insulin resistance, and obesity because of its impact on blood sugar. Some people can eat potatoes and tolerate them well, of course. But if you're in ketosis, the blood sugar rise from consuming them will likely shift you back to being a sugar-burner again.

That's not to say that you won't be eating any vegetables at all on a ketogenic diet. On the contrary, you can get a lot of healthy vitamins and nutrients from green leafy vegetables like spinach and kale, as well as from nonstarchy vegetables such as broccoli, cauliflower, and asparagus. Going keto doesn't mean that you cut out all of your vegetable consumption. But it's important to be mindful that there are better choices than starchy vegetables—and the recipes in this book include a lot of great options.

Okay, that's great for veggies, but what about fruits? Surely those are healthy, right? Well, maybe not so much if your goal is to be in a state of nutritional ketosis. As we shared in *Keto Clarity*, my coauthor, Dr. Eric Westman, has a poster on the walls in his patient rooms that states, "Fruit is nature's candy." You may balk at this idea upon first hearing it, but think about it for a moment. When you consume sugar in any form, it forces your body to secrete insulin to deal with the rising blood sugar. In a healthy individual, the insulin kicks in just enough to

---

*Dear Jimmy,*

*I'm 36 years old, and I've spent the better part of my adult life as a workaholic. Eighty-hour workweeks at a high-stress career, getting my MBA at night, and raising two toddlers left very little time to focus on my health, or at least that's how I justified it. In May 2014, I fell apart, landing in the hospital and then being diagnosed with an autoimmune disease that doctors believe was triggered by stress. I was overweight, sick, and depressed. I had done low-carb diets for 15 years, losing and regaining weight on Atkins after I tired of the same food. When I did research on the benefits of a ketogenic diet to help ease symptoms of autoimmune disease, I found your book, which led me to your website and podcast. Thanks to going keto, since August 2014 I've lost 30 pounds and my autoimmune disease is in remission. I believe in real food, and I believe in myself, and you were a big part of helping me remember that.*

*With gratitude,*
*Darcy Rutzen*
*Chicago, Illinois*

push the sugar into the cells with no adverse effects on health. That's why some people with healthy metabolisms can consume fruit without any problem.

But what about someone who is insulin-resistant due to years of consuming highly processed carbohydrates? In these individuals, the pancreas still functions well enough to create a little bit of insulin to deal with carbohydrates, but the response is much more sluggish, resulting in elevated blood sugar levels—and over time, that can develop into type 2 diabetes. That's why it's so critically important to reduce your sugar consumption if you are insulin-resistant and why a ketogenic diet is the best way to manage insulin resistance.

The argument has been made that fruit is good for you because, along with natural sugars, it contains fiber and vitamins. And that's true. But for the vast majority of people dealing with insulin resistance, the body can't tell the difference between the sugar content in a can of Coca-Cola (thirty-nine grams in twelve ounces) and the sugar content in a banana (around thirty grams of carbohydrates, mostly sugar). An apple has close to twenty grams of carbohydrates, mostly sugar, and a quarter cup of the ever-popular raisins, which many parents think are a healthy snack for kids, contains about twenty-five grams of carbohydrates.

The same principle applies to fruit juice, which is much worse for you than whole fruit, although many people, especially parents, believe it's healthy. But because it's separated from the fiber in the whole fruit, the sugar in fruit juice hits the bloodstream fast and causes a spike in blood sugar. Eight and a half ounces of apple juice—the amount in one juice box—contains twenty-five grams of sugar. And that's real, unsweetened fruit juice. Even more insidious are popular drinks that are marketed as juice but contain very little real fruit juice and a ton of added sugar. And parents blindly buy these as a nutritious option for their kids, not realizing there's almost as much sugar in these products as in a can of Coke!

Again, if you're healthy and can tolerate the high levels of carbohydrates in fruit without seeing a negative impact on your blood sugar, then go for it. But the unfortunate reality is that for most of us, exposure to crappy carbage foods like Doritos, Twinkies, Coca-Cola, and more have distorted our natural response to the carbohydrates in real foods, to the point that even those cannot be consumed *ad libitum* without negative consequences. Unfortunately, the idea that all fruits and vegetables are freebies in your diet just isn't true.

So, as you can see, it's a big cop-out for health experts to tell people to "eat fruits and vegetables" for a more nutritious diet without a qualifying statement to explain exactly what they mean. So if the health halo on fruits and vegetables is now somewhat tarnished in your mind, which foods are truly nutritious? Great question.

## THE REAL NUTRIENT-DENSE FOODS

To examine which foods are truly nutritious a bit more closely, let's turn to Mathieu Lalonde, PhD, an organic chemist from Harvard University who gave a fantastic lecture called "Nutrient Density: Sticking to the Essentials" at the 2012 Ancestral Health Symposium (watch the entire presentation on YouTube at http://youtu.be/HwbY12qZcF4). In that talk, Lalonde ranked various foods according to their nutrient density—in other words, how many vitamins, minerals, and other vital nutrients are packed into each serving. Keeping in mind that mainstream nutritional health experts constantly say that fruits and vegetables are the most nutritious foods, his results were quite astonishing.

### NUTRIENT DENSITY SCORE RANKING

1. Organ meats and oils
2. Herbs and spices
3. Nuts and seeds
4. Cacao
5. Fish and seafood
6. Pork
7. Beef
8. Eggs and dairy
9. Vegetables (raw and unprepared)
10. Lamb, veal, and wild game
11. Poultry
12. Legumes (raw or cooked edible)
13. Processed meat
14. Vegetables (cooked, blanched, canned, pickled)
15. Plant fats and oils
16. Fruit
17. Animal skin and feet
18. Grains and pseudocereals (cooked)
19. Refined and processed fats and oils
20. Animal fats and oils
21. Grains (canned)
22. Processed fruit

As you can see, fruits and vegetables don't even come close to the top of the list. More nutritious are organ meats and oils, herbs and spices, nuts and seeds, cacao (used to make dark chocolate), fish and seafood, pork, beef, and eggs and dairy. Raw vegetables come in ninth, and you've got to go quite a ways down the list before you see fruit. It's no coincidence that the bottom of the list looks a lot like the Standard American Diet while at the top of the list are, conspicuously, the very foods consumed on a low-carb, high-fat, ketogenic diet composed of real-food ingredients, like those used in this cookbook.

## THE IMPORTANCE OF MACRONUTRIENTS

A well-formulated ketogenic diet is, by definition, one that is low in carbohydrates, moderate in protein, and high in fat. All of the recipes in this book fit this template, which helps shift your body from using primarily sugar as fuel to using fat. While you may have heard low-carb diets described as "high-protein," the fact is that a low-carb diet really needs to be high in fat. Your brain and other body cells are at least 60 percent fat, so it makes sense that you need to eat more fat to feed your body.

So, on a ketogenic diet, you need to cut carbs way down and eat a lot more fat. But what should you do about protein? Great question. It's best to moderate your intake of that macronutrient to your personal threshold level for it. You probably don't need as much protein as you think, and it's important to not eat too much of it because the body changes excess protein into glucose. That's a problem for two reasons: first, when you are trying to be ketogenic and burn fat for fuel, producing glucose is counterproductive; and second, if you're severely insulin-resistant and sensitive to carbohydrates, it stands to reason that you will also be sensitive to the glucose produced from excess protein. So avoid eating chicken breasts and protein powders and choose fattier cuts of meats to moderate your protein intake sufficiently to get into a state of nutritional ketosis.

Everyone is different, so it's impossible to say that if you eat fat, protein, and carbs in a certain proportion, you'll be in ketosis. But there are general ranges that it's good to shoot for:

> **Fat:** At least 60 percent, up to 85 percent (remember, this refers primarily to healthy saturated and monounsaturated fats)
>
> **Protein:** Around 15 percent is a good goal; if you're an athlete, perhaps 20 percent
>
> **Carbs:** From 0 to 20 percent

But again, you need to find the right proportion that gets you into ketosis. For me (Jimmy), that's 80 percent fat, 15 percent protein, and 5 percent carbs. For my wife, Christine, it's 60 percent fat, 25 percent protein, and 15 percent carbs—and at those levels, we produce about the same amount of ketones. For Maria, it's 70 to 80 percent fat, 15 to 20 percent protein, and 5 percent carbs or fewer. It's a highly individualized formula, and you need to experiment while testing your blood for ketones (see page 13) to find out what's right for you.

To figure out the proportion of macronutrients in the food you eat, you'll need to do a little math. Each gram of fat has nine calories, while each gram of protein and carbohydrate has four calories. So to calculate the proportion of each in a dish, here's the basic equation: (9 times grams of fat) + (4 times grams of protein) + (4 times grams of carbohydrate) = total calories. We've made it a little easier with the recipes in this book by providing the amount and percentage of fat, protein, and carbs in each recipe (including sauces and toppings). But whether you're doing the math on your own or following the recipes, keep testing your blood to make sure the ratio of macronutrients you're consuming is right for you.

### USING THE KETO METERS

**KETO** Dishes that are lower in carbs and protein and higher in fat tend to be more ketogenic, so if you're having trouble getting into ketosis, try looking for recipes with a "high" keto meter.

It's important to follow a ketogenic diet the right way, using real food as the basis for what you eat. There are a lot of products marketed as "low-carb" that are anything but. Coming up in the next chapter, we'll discuss why your ketogenic diet really needs to consist of real, whole foods for you to experience the most benefits to your health.

# Keto and Paleo Are a Match Made in Heaven

*Don't eat anything your great-grandmother wouldn't recognize as food.*

—Michael Pollan

On the list of most-Googled diet search terms, *ketogenic* landed at number five in 2013 and at number two in 2014. But guess what landed at number one both years? Paleo! You've probably heard of this term, which has soared in popularity through perennial *New York Times* bestselling books like *The Paleo Solution,* by Robb Wolf, and *Practical Paleo,* by Diane Sanfilippo, among many others. You may have read articles or seen television news stories that refer to Paleo as the "caveman" or "ancestral" diet. For our purposes, eating Paleo simply means choosing real, whole foods that our ancestors would have recognized as food. And you don't even have to go back as far as Paleolithic humans, either.

In his book *In Defense of Food,* Michael Pollan suggests imagining that you're grocery shopping in a twenty-first-century supermarket with your great-grandma. She would see Coca-Cola, breakfast cereal, Doritos, Hot Pockets, Little Debbie snack cakes, and all the other sugary, grainy, vegetable-oil-laden stealth bombs that litter grocery store shelves these days as merely foodlike products, not actual food. Real food to her meant full-fat meat from cows that ate grass on a family farm, wild game that Great-Grandpa hunted himself, whole eggs from chickens allowed to roam in the sun and forage in open areas, wild-caught fish, natural fats like butter and lard, some wild vegetation gathered during hunting expeditions, and perhaps some nuts and seeds and other vegetables grown in a garden. We've become so far removed from this concept of real food that we have to resort to using the word *real* to describe the kind of food we are talking about! It's crazy!

It is entirely possible to be ketogenic without adopting Paleo nutritional principles, and you can follow Paleo without necessarily being low-carb or ketogenic. But marrying keto with Paleo is a match made in heaven for your overall health.

---

*Hi Jimmy,*

*I am thrilled that I stumbled on your story and the ketogenic lifestyle. I am a 58-year-old woman who has been on every diet imaginable. I think the first one was at 11 years of age. Believe me when I say that keto is the easiest one of all. I actually lost 10 pounds this year between Thanksgiving and New Year's. I don't think I ever made it through the holidays without gaining at least 5.*

*I'm down 78 pounds overall and have 50 or so to go, but this time I can see the light at the end of the tunnel and am certain that I can live this way for the rest of my life. My blood pressure is back to normal, my joints no longer ache, I can take the stairs without groaning. I feel like I'm back in my thirties. I used to think I was destined for an early grave. You've given me my life back.*

*All I can say is thank you. Thank you. Thank you.*

*Sincerely,*

*Deborah Saddler*
*Hartford, Ohio*

If you're dealing with insulin resistance—including type 2 diabetes, prediabetes, and consistently elevated blood sugar levels, and obesity usually is a sign of one or more of these—it's especially important to keep your carbohydrate intake way down. These conditions make it impossible to handle even real-food carbohydrates as well as a healthy person does. Following a ketogenic diet is an excellent way to do that: it eliminates most carbs from your diet while providing enough healthy fats to keep you from getting hungry. And people with obesity, diabetes, insulin resistance, and chronic health problems tend to do best when they follow a ketogenic approach that fits within the basic Paleo principles, for the same reason that Paleo is better for everyone: it fits the way our bodies are designed to work.

The diet of our Paleolithic ancestors consisted of fish, all parts of the animals they hunted, eggs, fruits, vegetables, nuts, and seeds. Added to all this was one other key source of energy that came to the rescue when food was scarce and after a big animal kill, when they ate a lot of animal fat. Can you guess what sustained them during these times? You guessed it: ketones! Our Paleolithic ancestors spent most of their time in a state

of ketosis, and it kept them energized for hunts when food was scarce and after a big low-carb, high-fat meal. They didn't know it was ketones that provided them this benefit, but that's exactly what it was.

In fact, the traditional diet of the Inuit peoples is very likely a Paleo-style ketogenic diet. It's difficult to grow any vegetation in the sub-freezing, icy conditions of the Arctic, so the Inuit traditionally subsisted on whale blubber, fish, and other animal-based foods. Despite the lack of carbohydrates in their diet, they experienced no negative effects on their health. On the contrary, their health was robust, they were full of energy, and they were able to go long periods without food.

Getting into a state of nutritional ketosis by restricting carbohydrates, moderating protein, and increasing saturated and monounsaturated fats gives your body a long list of positive health effects. And following a Paleo ketogenic diet allows you to get the real, whole, nourishing foods that you want and need to thrive, perhaps for the first time in your life. Being ketogenic and being Paleo are not mutually exclusive. You can—and probably should—pursue both to reap the most benefits.

There is some controversy about a ketogenic diet among a small group of Paleo advocates, however. Some popular Paleo bloggers, podcasters, and authors like to refer to their way of eating as "macronutrient agnostic," by which they mean that they don't worry about the proportion of macronutrients—fat, protein, and carbohydrates—they eat. They believe that as long as you're eating real foods and not the foodlike products that are typical of the Standard American Diet, then you don't need to worry about how much of each macronutrient. As long as the carbohydrate-based foods you consume are whole—such as sweet potatoes and fruit—and not processed, they say, then there are absolutely no adverse consequences to your health, such as diabetes, obesity, or Alzheimer's disease. Some recommend eating up to seventy-five grams daily of starchy and sugary carbohydrates from whole foods—and adding in the carbs from nonstarchy vegetables likely pushes this figure above one hundred grams daily. With this carb intake, it's next to impossible to get into a state of nutritional ketosis for the vast majority of people who are attempting to lose weight or fix a problem associated with insulin resistance.

But many critics of the ketogenic diet do acknowledge that ketones are beneficial for certain diseases—it's been proven that Alzheimer's, epilepsy, and Parkinson's are all improved by raising the level of blood ketones. So some have suggested continuing to eat a lot of carbohydrates while consuming very high levels of medium-chain triglycerides (MCT) oil as well as coconut products, both of which can artificially raise ketones in the blood for a few hours. (To maintain a steady state of ketosis, you'd need to take these supplements every few hours.) Using these ketone-boosting supplements does force ketone production, but excessive consumption of MCT oil leads to major gastric distress and acid reflux problems. It's not a natural way to produce ketones in the body and doesn't fall within the definition of a "ketogenic diet" as we have outlined in this book.

The Paleo gurus who recommend this strategy generally have concerns that restricting carbohydrates is unhealthy. But this fear is much ado about nothing. I've interviewed hundreds upon hundreds of medical and nutritional health practitioners who use a ketogenic approach with patients on a daily basis, and none of them report any negative health effects. There are no scientific studies showing ill effects from a ketogenic diet that includes adequate calories. In fact, studies show just the opposite: a ketogenic way of eating is incredibly effective in treating health problems. It's unfortunate that these misconceptions about keto persist because they're excluding a large segment of the community who could stand to benefit from a Paleo-style ketogenic diet.

The reality is that most people interested in a Paleo diet are overweight and/or dealing with some sort of health problem, and they could benefit from getting into nutritional ketosis as well as eating the real, whole foods that a Paleo diet emphasizes.

**It's one thing to know that you're pursuing nutritional ketosis in order to improve your health. But what does a ketogenic diet really look like? Any healthy diet should let you eat great-tasting food that nourishes your body and keeps you disease-free. We'll explain more thoroughly why cooking is a vital part of your ketogenic success in the next chapter.**

# Cooking Keto

*One should eat to live, not live to eat.*

—Benjamin Franklin

It's a well-known fact that humans can survive only a few days without water and a few weeks to, at most, a few months without food. What we decide to put in our mouths is what will nourish our bodies, give us energy, and keep us healthy, so no matter what kind of diet we choose to follow, we need to be deliberate and purposeful about what we eat.

Cooking has unfortunately become a lost art in the twenty-first century. Instant, ready-to-eat foods are in great abundance everywhere you look in the Western world at the myriad of fast-food joints, grocery stores, restaurants, and all the little corner convenience stores. We've become a grab-and-go society with very little regard for food quality, and that might explain why we are dealing with massive epidemics of obesity, diabetes, and other chronic health conditions. One of the primary purposes of this cookbook is to get you excited about the art of cooking the way your great-grandmother used to not that long ago. And despite the image that may conjure up in your head of a messy, flour-dusted kitchen strewn with pots and pans, it's really not as complicated as you might think.

Part of the problem with the kind of "food" ("food-like products" might be more appropriate) that most Americans eat these days is that it is generally highly processed, loaded with inflammation-inducing carbohydrates and vegetable oils, and not very satisfying at all. That's why we are constantly thinking about food to such an absurd level that while we are eating breakfast, we think about what we'll be eating for lunch. And while we're eating lunch, we think about what we'll be having for supper. Plus, the endless snacking that takes place between meals is proof positive that we have become completely disengaged with the way our bodies are supposed to be fed. A ketogenic diet returns the body to a more normal feeling of satiation and satisfaction.

While we all like the convenience of grabbing a frozen dinner or packaged food, the reality is that we were never intended to eat this way. Think about it: before packaged, processed foods emerged at the end of World War II (interestingly, they were created to mimic the military's food rations), what did we eat? Good old-fashioned food that was made at home with ingredients purchased from local farms. In the decades since, we've gotten further and further away from the real food that our grandparents and great-grandparents ate. It's no surprise that obesity and disease rates have skyrocketed alongside this trend.

Who doesn't enjoy going out to eat every now and then? But the problem is that too many people stop by

---

*Dear Jimmy,*

*Thanks for changing my life and my husband's life. I am managing my prediabetes thanks to keto. My blood glucose this morning was 4.3 and my ketones 3.9. Yesterday I ate bolognese, zucchini, cabbage, fatty lamb cutlets, and 3 eggs. I drove for 8 hours and swam at Bondi Beach for an hour. I had tons of energy, slept well, and now am ready for a new day :-)*

*My husband has lost 11 kgs [about 24 pounds] and is now down to 68 kgs [about 150 pounds]. He can't remember ever weighing this low. He is 65, I am almost 60, and we are happy and in control of our health...thanks to you!*

*Anne-Marie Barbour*

*Canberra, Australia*

McDonald's on the way to work for breakfast, grab some Taco Bell for lunch, and then go by the supermarket to get a rotisserie chicken and potato salad for supper. Can I get a witness, anyone? Hey, we've all done it, and it is such a normal part of American culture now that nobody even bats an eye at it anymore. And while eating this way on occasion isn't going to have long-term consequences, when it becomes a daily routine, the health effects can add up very quickly. Unfortunately, this is the Standard American Diet that is plaguing our collective weight and health today.

The saddest part of the way we look at food these days is the fact that we're often totally oblivious to what is actually in the foods we are eating because we never read the ingredients list horror show. (Virtually all packaged foods contain disastrously processed versions of sugar, grains, vegetable oils, and some derivative of corn, all damaging to our health.) And even if we do take the time to read the nutrition information, we're often only looking to see if it's low in fat, which usually means that the fat has been replaced with more and more carbohydrates and other added junk—it's not an indication that the food is good for us by any means. Is this really the best we can do for feeding ourselves? Absolutely not. We can and should do better.

Just recognizing how propaganda has led us to fear fat and embrace packaged foods should be motivation enough to get us back into our kitchens again. But far too many people are scared to cook without dumping ingredients out of a box. They don't feel adequately equipped to make delicious and nutritious food for their families as matriarchs did on a regular basis just two generations ago. With this book, we are committed to giving you the tools to reinvigorate your meals with healthy dishes that everyone in the family will enjoy eating.

But what exactly do you eat on a ketogenic diet? I often get this question over e-mail or via social media, and it always makes me laugh. My pat snarky answer usually sounds a little something like this: "It's this mysterious substance known as real food!" Eating real, whole foods is like a foreign concept to so many people. When you strip away prepackaged foods that come with a barcode, food you zap in the microwave for a few minutes before eating, and fast food emanating that disgusting smell of burnt cooking oil, people are left at loose ends when it comes to feeding themselves. That's why a cookbook like this one for people following a

ketogenic diet is so incredibly necessary, now more than ever before.

So what kind of foods do you get to eat when you are pursuing nutritional ketosis? It's a great question, and the list is a lot longer than you probably realize. Keep in mind that the foods that help one person get into ketosis may not necessarily work for everyone. You need to find your individual carbohydrate tolerance level and your personal protein threshold (keep testing your ketone levels to make sure you're in ketosis—see page 13), and then eat mostly saturated and monounsaturated fats to satiety. Let's look at the wide array of yummy foods you have at your disposal to make truly extraordinary meals. We'll break it down by macronutrients, starting with carbohydrates, then healthy fats, then proteins.

## CARBOHYDRATES

| | |
|---|---|
| Arugula | Lime |
| Artichokes | Mushrooms |
| Asparagus | Okra |
| Blackberries | Onions |
| Blueberries | Parsley |
| Bok choy | Peppers |
| Broccoli | Pumpkin |
| Brussels sprouts | Radicchio |
| Cabbage | Radishes |
| Cauliflower | Raspberries |
| Celery | Rhubarb |
| Chicory greens | Scallions |
| Cranberries | Shallots |
| Cucumbers | Snow peas |
| Eggplant | Spaghetti squash |
| Garlic | Spinach |
| Green beans | Strawberries |
| Jicama | Summer squash |
| Kale | Tomatoes |
| Leeks | Watercress |
| Lemon | Wax beans |
| Lettuce | Zucchini |

## HEALTHY FATS

Almonds

Almond butter

Almond milk, unsweetened

Almond oil

Avocado

Avocado oil

Beef tallow

Blue cheese

Brazil nuts

Butter (Kerrygold is a high-quality brand)

Cheese (cheddar, Colby, feta, mozzarella, provolone, ricotta, Swiss, and others)

Chia seeds

Chicken fat

Coconut

Coconut cream

Coconut milk, unsweetened

Coconut oil

Cream cheese

Dark chocolate (80 percent or higher)

Fish oil (Carlson brand is a fabulous cod liver oil)

Ghee

Greek yogurt

Heavy whipping cream

Lard

Macadamia nut oil

Macadamia nuts

Mayonnaise

Olive oil

Pecans

Pili nuts

Pistachios

Sour cream

Sunflower seeds

Walnuts

## PROTEINS

Bacon (not turkey bacon)

Beef jerky (watch out for added sugars)

Beef ribs

Beef roast

Bratwurst

Chicken (choose the darkest cuts, skin on)

Duck

Eggs (whole)

Fish (bass, carp, flounder, halibut, mackerel, salmon, sardines, trout, tuna)

Ground beef (not lean)

Goose

Ham

Hot dogs (Nathan's brand is the best)

Kielbasa

Pepperoni

Pheasant

Pork chops

Pork ribs

Pork rinds

Pork roast

Quail

Salami

Sausage

Shellfish (crab meat, mussels, oysters, scallops, shrimp)

Steak (the fattier the better)

Turkey (darker pieces are best)

Veal

As you can see, you have a plethora of incredible food choices to enjoy on a ketogenic diet. It's just a matter of putting them all together in a cohesive way to create the magic in your kitchen that makes mealtimes something to look forward to each and every day. And that's why we created this cookbook: to empower you, the home cook, to make spectacular dishes that tantalize your taste buds while giving you the nourishment you want and need for optimal health.

There's no need to make it complicated. The sumptuous food you get to eat on a ketogenic diet—like the dishes you'll enjoy in this book—is what makes it so desirable. We hope that you've come hungry and salivating for delicious recipes, because we're loaded for bear in the coming pages.

# Specialty Ingredients

*Moving away from the Standard American Diet, with all its carbs and sugar, to a healthy, real foods–based, ketogenic diet can mean using some less-familiar ingredients. Below you'll find my notes on these ingredients and where to find them.*

*A few of the keto-friendly ingredients used in this book can be hard to find locally or not competitively priced. To help you gather what you need, I've created an online store where you can find these ingredients at the best prices I have found. To access it, go to my site, mariamindbodyhealth.com, and click on Maria's Amazon Store. Or go directly to the following URL: http://astore. amazon.com/marisnutran05-20.*

## ALOE VERA

I often add aloe vera to shakes as a supplement. It's well known for healing external cuts, but it's also a great remedy for esophageal erosions. Even if acid reflux has subsided, most people still have damage to the lining of the esophagus and can experience erosions every so often. The plant's extract puts a protective coating on the esophagus and helps control reflux from the stomach. You can find quality aloe vera at most health food stores.

## BUTTER, UNSALTED

It's important to use unsalted butter rather than salted butter so that you can control the exact amount of salt in a dish. It also, as recently discussed on KCRW's *Good Food* podcast, gives you better results when frying vegetables in butter. Because salt releases moisture in food, frying vegetables in salted butter will actually result in them being steamed rather than fried. Unsalted butter gives you a crispier result.

## COCOA BUTTER

Cocoa butter is made from cacao beans that are melted and pressed. It has a lovely, rich fragrance of dark chocolate and many natural antioxidants, and it has a long shelf life—over three years.

I like to use cocoa butter for making the perfect sugar-free chocolate bars and other treats. You can eat it plain or add a bit of natural sweetener. Melting cocoa butter takes longer than melting traditional fats, but unlike most chocolates, it is very forgiving and heats well without separating.

## COCONUT AMINOS

Coconut aminos is a great soy sauce replacement. Conventional soy sauces are made with nonorganic, genetically modified (GMO) soybeans. Because unfermented soy contains compounds that affect estrogen receptors in the body, it can disrupt hormones, so it's best to avoid it.

Although coconut aminos has the flavor profile of traditional soy sauce, it is made solely from raw coconut tree sap and sun-dried sea salt, which is then naturally aged. Coconut aminos has seventeen amino acids and is filled with minerals, vitamin C, and B vitamins.

I use coconut aminos in my dressings, marinades, and sautés, and I serve it with rice-free sushi (pages 92 and 238). You can find it at some health food stores or online at Amazon.com.

## COCONUT VINEGAR

Coconut vinegar has more vitamins and minerals than other vinegars, and it's an excellent source of fructo-oligosaccharides, a prebiotic that promotes digestive health. It's a delicious vinegar that doesn't have a coconut-y flavor, making it great for your favorite dressings and marinades. Coconut vinegar may also be used instead of apple cider vinegar for skin care.

## EXTRACTS AND FLAVORS

To add certain flavorings without altering a dish's proportions of fat, protein, and carbs, I often use extracts and flavors—from the common vanilla and almond extracts to Kahlúa, apple, peppermint, and cherry flavors, and more. Although the difference between extracts and flavors can get technical, in a nutshell, extracts are more concentrated than flavors. Another option is to use flavor oils, which are even more concentrated than extracts. If a recipe calls for a teaspoon of a flavor or extract, use only a few drops of a flavor oil.

Look for brands free of polyglycol and added coloring. I prefer the Frontier brand, which is free of any additives. You may be able to find it at your local health food store, but it's also available online: www.frontiercoop.com. Best Flavors is another good brand for organic extracts: www.bestflavors.com.

## FISH SAUCE

One staple that every cook should have in the fridge is fish sauce, which can take a dish from good to amazing. Like mushrooms and aged cheese, fish sauce adds umami, a pleasant, savory taste. Umami is subtle, but it intensifies and enhances other flavors—in other words, it makes food delicious.

I recommend the Red Boat brand of fish sauce, which contains only anchovies and sea salt. A bottle of fish sauce will last you a long time—it's strong stuff, so you need only a few drops per dish.

## GUAR GUM AND XANTHAN GUM

In gluten-free baking, xanthan gum and guar gum are essential for replacing certain properties of gluten.

The gluten in white flour creates a paste when you mix it with water. (Fun fact: In Poland, they use this paste to hang wallpaper!) Guar gum and xanthan gum do the same thing in gluten-free baking, creating that chewy texture we love in breads and baked goods. And just as the gluten in wheat thickens dough and traps air bubbles created by yeast to make baked goods light and fluffy, xanthan gum helps starches combine to trap air, while guar gum helps keep large particles suspended in the batter (like blueberries in coffee cake). Xanthan gum and guar gum also help keep mixes from separating.

Xanthan gum and guar gum also make excellent thickeners for liquids, such as soups, syrups, and shakes. However, in foods with a high acid content, such as those containing lemon juice or vinegar, guar gum can lose its

thickening abilities. If you're making a citrus-flavored baked good and all you have is guar gum, just increase the amount you use.

I purchase xanthan and guar gum online at Amazon. com. I recommend the NOW brand (www.nowfoods.com).

*NOTE: If you have severe allergies, do not use xanthan gum; use guar gum instead.*

| | GUAR GUM per cup gluten-free flour | XANTHAN GUM per cup gluten-free flour |
|---|---|---|
| Cookies | ¼ tsp | ¼ tsp |
| Cakes and pancakes | ¾ tsp | ½ tsp |
| Muffins | 1 tsp | ¾ tsp |

| | GUAR GUM per quart | XANTHAN GUM per quart |
|---|---|---|
| Hot liquids (like soups) | 1–2 tsp | 2 tsp |
| Cold liquids (like pancake syrup) | 1–2 tsp | 2 tsp |

**TIP:** *Add xanthan gum and guar gum to the oil in a recipe first and mix them together completely before adding the mixture to the rest of liquid ingredients. Using a blender or food processor helps them dissolve properly; clumps will make a big unappetizing bite in foods.*

## HEAVY CREAM

I once thought whipping cream and heavy cream were the same and always grabbed whichever was on sale. Turns out, there is a difference.

Heavy cream has a fat content of between 36 and 39 percent. Whipping cream, on the other hand, is between 30 and 36 percent fat. The higher fat content makes whipped cream made from heavy cream denser and more stable. It's also more ketogenic, which is why I prefer to use it on desserts. I've also found that heavy cream gives soups and sauces a better mouthfeel.

## HOT SAUCES

When choosing a hot sauce, always check the ingredients for added sugar and harmful additives. I prefer Dark Star Sriracha Hot Chili Sauce. Its only ingredients are peppers, garlic, herbs, spices, and balsamic vinegar. I also recommend Xyla brand Buffalo wing sauce, which is sugar-free and uses coconut oil instead of vegetable oils.

## KELP NOODLES

Kelp noodles are simply noodles made from kelp. They have a crunchy texture that is different than that of traditional pasta if you do not cook them long enough. My favorite way to use kelp noodles is in a slow cooker, where they have time to break down and get soft. These can be found in Asian markets or online at Amazon.com.

## L-GLUTAMINE POWDER

L-glutamine is a great nutritional supplement that I like to add to shakes. It plays a major role in DNA synthesis and serves as a primary transporter of nitrogen into the muscle tissues. It also decreases sugar, carbs, and alcohol cravings and helps heal the intestinal lining. I prefer the NOW brand, which can be purchased online at Amazon.com.

## LIQUID SMOKE

I love to use our smoker, but if I am craving that smoky flavor and don't have the time to smoke something, adding a teaspoon of liquid smoke has a similar effect and enhances the flavor of a dish.

When purchasing liquid smoke, be sure to check for artificial flavors and colors. I prefer Wright's brand, which does not contain gluten, soy, or artificial flavors or colors. You can find Wright's brand at most grocery stores and online.

## MCT OIL

MCT stands for "medium-chain triglycerides," which are chains of fatty acids. MCTs are found naturally in coconut oil, palm oil, and dairy; MCT oil is extracted from coconut or palm oil and contains higher, concentrated levels of MCTs. Unlike coconut oil, it stays liquid even when refrigerated.

MCT oil can be found at most health food stores, but if you have trouble finding it, you can use macadamia nut oil, avocado oil, or a quality olive oil instead. I prefer cooking with the SKINNYFat brand of MCT oil because it doesn't have a distinct coconut taste that can overwhelm dishes. I also use SKINNYFat because I've found that, unlike other MCT oils, it does not cause the stomach upset that can occur when first adding MCT oil to your diet. If you buy SKINNYFat MCT oil from their website (www. caltonnutrition.com/skinnyfat), get five dollars off your purchase with this coupon code: $5KetoOil.

## MIRACLE NOODLES

Miracle Noodles are composed of a dietary fiber called *glucomannan* and contain very few calories and close to zero carbohydrates. They are fun to cook with because they do not have much flavor on their own but are amazing at absorbing the flavors you use them with. You can find Miracle Noodles online on Amazon.com, but if you prefer, zucchini noodles and cabbage noodles are good substitutes.

## PROTEIN POWDERS

It is often difficult to make baked goods without adding the carbohydrates of flours—even nut flours, which are often used in Paleo cooking, are full of carbs. Cooking with protein powders is a great way to make breadlike items without the carbs that can take people who are extremely carbohydrate-sensitive out of ketosis. Protein powders are also a great way of getting the right amount of nutrients; just make sure that you aren't getting too much protein, which can kick you out of ketosis.

If you are dairy-sensitive, egg white protein powder is a great substitute for whey protein powder. But consider using only an unflavored version. Other flavors may have sweeteners such as xylitol, which may cause some people's blood sugar to increase. And when you're cooking with egg white protein powder, it's helpful to be able to add your own sweetener and better control the exact amount in your dish.

When choosing a protein powder, always look at the ingredients. If you see "sugar" or other names for sugar—sucrose, glucose, or other words ending in "-ose"—find a new brand. I personally love Jay Robb brand, which is completely sugar-free and uses whey from farm-raised, grass-fed cows not treated with the synthetic bovine growth hormone rBGH. You can find Jay Robb brand protein powders at most health food stores and online.

If you use a different brand, make sure that there is no fat in the protein powder. Yes, we love fat on the ketogenic diet, but if you add fat to whipped egg whites, they will fall and the baked good you are making will likely fall.

## SALT

When you first adopt a ketogenic lifestyle, one of the first side effects is a rapid improvement in insulin sensitivity, which causes insulin levels to fall. And as insulin falls, the kidneys begin to release excess fluid. It's common to be up in the middle of the night urinating more than usual. This will go away eventually, but as the extra water goes, it also removes essential sodium and electrolytes.

When sodium levels fall below a certain level, which can happen quite fast, there are some side effects such as headaches, low energy, dizziness, and cramping. It's important to add sodium to your diet to replace what you've lost. You can add more salt to your food, drink bone broth, or take sodium tablets.

**What type of sea salt should I use?** Not all salts are created equal. Most ordinary table salts are refined, bleached, and processed to the point that they lose nearly all their minerals, and often anticaking agents—including sugar!—are added. I recommend cooking with Himalayan or Celtic sea salt, which are either harvested from ancient sea beds or made by evaporating sea water with high mineral content. About 70 percent of their nutritional content is sodium—they contain about the same amount as table salt. The other 30 percent is made up of minerals and micronutrients (including iodine) found in mineral-rich seas.

In addition to prizing sea salts for their nutritional value, I greatly prefer their taste to that of table salt, which can taste like chemicals. (Incidentally, do not mistakenly use Morton's "sea salt," which is devoid of iodine and nutrients.)

## TOMATOES

I was shocked when I found that green tomatoes are highest in carbs! I thought they would be lower since they are less ripe and less sweet.

Here is the breakdown per cup:

|  | Carbs | Fiber |
|---|---|---|
| Yellow tomatoes | 4.1 g | 1 g |
| Orange tomatoes | 5 g | 1.4 g |
| Red tomatoes | 7 g | 2.2. g |
| Green tomatoes | 9.2 g | 2 g |

It's so easy to lower your carbs by using yellow tomatoes, and as I tell my clients, whenever you can easily lower sugar or carbs, do it! For example, change the marinara sauce you use if you find one with one fewer carbs. In my college days I used Prego marinara sauce, which has about 12 grams of carbs per serving. Now I use homemade marinara, which has only 3 grams per serving because I use yellow tomatoes.

If you are using store-bought tomato products, purchase them in glass jars instead of cans because cans can leach bisphenol A (BPA), an endocrine disruptor,

into tomatoes; the acid in tomatoes really sucks in the BPA at a high rate. Also check the ingredients in marinara sauces for soybean oil and added sugars or corn syrup, all of which you want to avoid.

## SWEETENERS

If you crave sweets, these nonsugar natural sweeteners can help fulfill those cravings without playing havoc with your weight and blood sugar. Here are the natural sweeteners I use and why:

|  | Calories | Sweetness | Conversion per cup of sugar |
|---|---|---|---|
| Stevia glycerite | 0 | 300% as sweet as sugar | 1 teaspoon |
| Erythritol | 0 to 0.2 per gram | 70% as sweet as sugar | 1 cup (plus 1 teaspoon stevia glycerite for sweetness) |
| Yacón syrup | 1.5 calories per gram | 50% as sweet as sugar | 2 cups |
| Xylitol | 2.4 calories per gram | 100% as sweet as sugar | 1 cup |

### Stevia Glycerite

Stevia is an herb that has been used as a sweetener in South America for hundreds of years. Stevia glycerite is a thick liquid form of the sweetener that's almost like honey. Unlike the powdered version, it has no bitter aftertaste. None of my recipes use powdered stevia, but if you purchase it for something else, make sure to check for additional ingredients such as maltodextrin, which is a corn derivative that raises blood sugar.

Stevia glycerite is great for cooking because it maintains flavor that many other sweeteners lose when heated. However, when used for baking it usually needs to be combined with another sweetener because it doesn't caramelize or create bulk. I purchase mine on Amazon.com, and I recommend the NOW brand (www.nowfoods.com).

### BENEFITS OF STEVIA

1. DOESN'T AFFECT BLOOD SUGAR: Since stevia doesn't affect blood glucose levels, it keeps your body in a ketogenic state.

2. LOWERS BLOOD PRESSURE: Studies show that a mix of hot water and stevia extract lowers both systolic and diastolic blood pressure.

3. HAS ZERO CALORIES: Stevia has no calories, which helps with weight loss.

## Erythritol

Erythritol is a naturally derived sugar substitute that looks and tastes very much like sugar, yet has almost no calories. Small amounts of erythritol are found naturally in grapes, melons, mushrooms, and fermented foods such as wine, beer, cheese, and soy sauce. Erythritol is usually made from plant sugars, which are mixed with water and then fermented. It is then filtered, allowed to crystallize, and dried. The finished product resembles table sugar and can be powdered or granulated.

When in granulated form, erythritol doesn't dissolve well in all foods (like salad dressings or caramel). That's why I almost always use powdered erythritol in my recipes. If you can find only the granulated kind, you can powder it yourself in a coffee grinder.

I prefer Swerve brand confectioners'-style sweetener, which uses non-GMO sources and is produced without solvents or synthetic chemical processes. I've found that it doesn't have the mouth-cooling sensation that other brands of erythritol do. Wholesome Sweeteners Zero is also a good brand; it is produced from organic sugar cane juice, which is naturally fermented and crystallized to create erythritol. Both brands are available on Amazon.com.

---

**BENEFITS OF ERYTHRITOL**

1. CRYSTALLIZATION: Because erythritol crystallizes, its final form is very similar to sugar, making it perfect for baking.

2. DOESN'T AFFECT BLOOD SUGAR: Like stevia, erythritol does not affect blood glucose or insulin levels, making it a great sweetener for diabetics. It also helps you stay in ketosis.

3. GOOD FOR ORAL HEALTH: Erythritol isn't metabolized by oral bacteria, which means that it doesn't contribute to tooth decay the way sugar does.

4. EASILY DIGESTED: Erythritol is mostly absorbed in the small intestine—hardly any of it reaches the colon—which helps prevent the digestive problems that can occur with other sugar alcohols.

---

## Yacón Syrup

Yacón syrup is a great low-glycemic sweetener that is pressed from the yacón root. It is a very thick syrup that is reminiscent of molasses, making it perfect for ketogenic gingerbread. I suggest using yacón syrup in place of honey, agave, maple syrup, or molasses. Since it is quite expensive, I use it only for special occasions. You can typically find the best prices for yacón syrup on Amazon.com. Sunfood is the brand I suggest.

| GLYCEMIC INDEX OF SWEETENERS | |
|---|---|
| Stevia glycerite | 0 |
| Erythritol | 0 |
| Yacón syrup | 0.5 |
| Xylitol | 7 |
| Maple syrup | 54 |
| Honey | 62 |
| Table sugar | 68 |
| High fructose corn syrup | 87 |

# VANILLA

Vanilla beans are high in phenolic compounds, which are potent antioxidants. Most people use vanilla extract rather than vanilla beans because it is easy to find and affordable. But if you are sidestepping using real vanilla beans, you are missing out on the benefits of all those phenolic compounds, which are lost during the process of making the extract. I purchase mine for a great price on Amazon.com.

---

**MAKING SUBSTITUTIONS**

If you want to use a different kind of fish or cut of steak than a recipe calls for, keep in mind that it may change the dish's fat ratio. A chart comparing the amount of fat in different fish and cuts of steak is available on my website at www.mariamindbodyhealth.com/charts.

Keep in mind that grass-fed beef has a different fat content than grain-fed beef. And remember, eating fish broiled with lemon and no fatty sauce would not be a ketogenic meal. My favorite part of eating fish is the tasty fatty sauces you get to use to make the meal ketogenic.

---

# condiments, dressings, broth, and other basics

# slow cooker bone broth

**■□□**
**KETO**　**NUT FREE**　**DAIRY FREE**

**PREP TIME:** 12 minutes

**COOK TIME:** 1 to 2 days

**YIELD:** 4 quarts (1 cup per serving)

3½ pounds beef, chicken, ham, or fish bones

2 stalks celery, chopped

1 medium yellow onion, chopped

7 cloves garlic, smashed with the side of a knife

2 bay leaves

2 teaspoons fine sea salt

¼ cup coconut vinegar

Cold filtered water

¼ cup fresh herbs or 1 teaspoon dried herbs of your choice (optional)

**SPECIAL EQUIPMENT**

Slow cooker　　Strainer

**VARIATION: VEGETABLE BROTH.**
*For a vegetarian-friendly broth, simply omit the bones. You can also add more vegetables, such as carrots and leeks.*

BUSY FAMILY TIP: *I make a huge batch and store portions in mason jars in the freezer for easy use in recipes.*

*When making bone broth, using an acid like organic vinegar helps extract more minerals from the bones. The extracted minerals, in turn, neutralize the acidity of the vinegar, so it doesn't affect the overall flavor of the broth. I use coconut vinegar, which exceeds all other vinegars in amino acid, vitamin, and mineral content. It is also a prebiotic that promotes digestive health. Don't worry, it doesn't taste like coconut!*

1. Place the bones, veggies, garlic, bay leaves, salt, and coconut vinegar in a 6-quart slow cooker, and add enough cold filtered water to cover everything.

2. Add the herbs of your choice, if using.

3. Set the slow cooker to high and cook for about 30 minutes, then reduce the heat to low. Skim off any scum or foam that appears on the surface.

4. Cook on low for 1 to 2 days. The long cooking time allows more gelatin and minerals to be extracted from the bones. When the broth is done, pour it through a strainer and discard the solids.

5. The broth will keep in the fridge for about 5 days or in the freezer for several months. When needed for recipes or for a cup of healing broth, scoop the meaty substance into a mug and warm it to make it a nice, thick liquid again.

## TIPS FOR MAKING THE BEST BONE BROTH

*1. Roast beef, lamb, pork, and chicken bones beforehand. Why? It adds color and flavor. Roast large bones at 375°F for 50 to 60 minutes, smaller bones for 30 to 40 minutes.*

*2. Start by covering the roasted bones with cold filtered water. Why? Certain proteins, particularly albumin, will dissolve only in cold water. Albumin helps clarify broth, so if you start with cold water, you will end up with a nice, clear broth. And because a substantial part of making broth comes down to eliminating impurities, it makes sense to start with the purest water you are able to use.*

*3. Do not skip the vinegar. Why? It draws the minerals out of the bones.*

*4. Use chicken feet when making chicken bone broth. Why? They add more collagen and create a thicker broth.*

*5. Add your favorite herbs. Not only do they add flavor, they also add nutrition. Rosemary, in particular, helps extract extra calcium from the bones.*

*6. Save leftover bones. Whenever you make beef, chicken, or fish dishes, store the leftover bones in the freezer until you have enough bones and time to make broth.*

### NUTRITIONAL INFO (per serving)

| calories | fat | protein | carbs | fiber |
|---|---|---|---|---|
| 13 | 0 g | 1.5 g | 1.7 g | 0 g |
|  | 0% | 46% | 52% |  |

## WHY BONE BROTH?

From a culinary standpoint, bone broth is superior to store-bought chicken or beef broth. It has the best flavor, and the collagen that leaches from the bones makes it a natural thickener, ideal for creating nice, thick sauces. If you substitute a store-bought broth in these recipes, you likely will not get a thick consistency.

From a health standpoint, bone broth is beyond compare. It is incredibly nourishing and so good for you that if it could be sold in pill form, the pharmaceutical companies would go broke. Its medicinal benefits are attributed to the exceptionally high levels of minerals and amino acids it gets from the bones. In fact, bone broth can be considered a high-quality mineral and protein supplement. Here are some of bone broth's most remarkable benefits.

**1. Attracts digestive juices:** The gelatin in bone broth is a hydrophilic colloid, which is a fancy way of saying that it attracts liquids. This is important because it means that it attracts digestive juices for rapid and effective digestion.

**2. Heals the gut:** The gelatin in broth works amazingly well as a treatment for intestinal disorders, including hyperacidity, colitis, and Crohn's disease, because it helps heal the intestinal wall and its many nutrients are easily absorbed, which can be a problem with these disorders. It also helps many people digest dairy products more easily, and strengthening the intestinal wall also supports the immune system. Bone broth should be the first therapeutic food for anyone suffering from digestive conditions affecting the intestines.

**3. Helps heal other illnesses:** The gelatin in bone broth is also useful for the treatment of anemia, diabetes, muscular dystrophy, and even cancer.

**4. Increases protein absorption:** Although gelatin isn't a complete protein itself (it only has the amino acids arginine and glycine in large amounts), it allows the body to fully utilize the complete proteins that are consumed. If you can't afford large amounts of meat in your diet, gelatin-rich broths are a great way to boost protein absorption.

**5. Contains lots of minerals:** Healthy bone tissue is naturally high in calcium, magnesium, phosphorus, and potassium, which are needed for a healthy bone structure, nervous system, and hormone balance. Broths made from fish bones also contain iodine, which is essential for a healthy thyroid.

**6. Improves joint health:** Because gelatin is derived from cartilage, bone broth is an awesome source of glucosamine and chondroitin, nutrients that are essential for joint health.

# HERB-INFUSED
## compound "butter"

■■■ NUT DAIRY
KETO FREE FREE

**PREP TIME:** 8 minutes, plus 3 hours to chill

**YIELD:** 1 cup (1 tablespoon per serving)

½ cup beef tallow or leaf lard, softened (see Note)

½ cup duck fat, softened (see Note)

1 head roasted garlic (see page 46)

1 tablespoon finely chopped fresh rosemary

1 tablespoon finely chopped fresh oregano

1 tablespoon finely chopped fresh chives

Fine sea salt and fresh ground black pepper to taste

**NOTE:** *I mix beef tallow (or leaf lard) and duck fat because at room temperature beef tallow and leaf lard are very solid while duck fat is almost liquid. Together they give an amazing flavor as well as a buttery texture. If you are not dairy-sensitive, you can use 1 cup of room-temperature unsalted butter instead of beef tallow and duck fat.*

*Many times when I ask clients to cut dairy, they can't imagine a life without butter. Using healthy natural animal fats, such as beef tallow and duck fat, is a great way to add flavor and satisfy cravings for that creamy, buttery texture. This compound "butter" tastes amazing on vegetables and grilled meats. I also love to give it as a gift!*

*You are welcome to mix up the flavors of the "butter" by using your favorite flavor profiles. (See the ideas below.)*

1. In a medium-sized bowl, mix together all of the ingredients. Place the mixture on a piece of parchment paper. Roll into a log shape and twist the ends of the paper to seal.

2. Refrigerate the "butter" until firm, about 3 hours. Slice into coins to serve.

**VARIATIONS.** *Though the above recipe is my go-to "butter" flavor, I've tried lots of combinations over the years, all of them delicious. If you're looking for some new flavor combinations, try the following:*

- *1 tablespoon each of finely chopped fresh rosemary, finely chopped fresh mint, and grated lemon zest*

- *1 tablespoon each of finely chopped fresh cilantro, grated lime zest, and ground cumin*

- *1 tablespoon each of finely chopped fresh thyme, finely chopped fresh rosemary, and finely chopped fresh sage*

- *1 tablespoon each of finely chopped fresh lemongrass and turmeric powder*

- *1 tablespoon each of finely chopped fresh lemongrass, finely chopped fresh tarragon, and Dijon mustard*

| NUTRITIONAL INFO (per serving) | | | | |
|---|---|---|---|---|
| calories | fat | protein | carbs | fiber |
| 123 | 13 g | 0.2 g | 1.4 g | 0 g |
| | 95% | 1% | 4% | |

# roasted garlic

■□□ **KETO**  **NUT FREE**  **DAIRY FREE**

**PREP TIME:** 5 minutes
**COOK TIME:** 40 minutes
**YIELD:** 12 heads

12 heads garlic
¼ cup MCT oil
½ teaspoon fine sea salt

**BUSY FAMILY TIP:** *I keep roasted garlic in my freezer at all times for easy use in recipes.*

1. Preheat the oven to 350°F.

2. Slice ⅛ inch off the top of the garlic to expose the cloves and place the garlic in a baking dish. Pour the MCT oil over the tops of the heads of garlic, letting the oil sink down into the cloves, and sprinkle the tops with the salt. Cover the baking dish with foil and place in the oven to bake.

3. The garlic is done when a center clove is completely soft when pierced with a paring knife. Even after it's soft, you can continue roasting until deeply golden for a more caramelized flavor—check the garlic every 10 minutes. Exact roasting time will depend on the size of your head of garlic, the variety, and its age.

4. Allow to cool and squeeze the garlic cloves from the skins as needed. Store unused roasted garlic in their skins in the freezer for up to 3 months.

| NUTRITIONAL INFO (per head) | | | | |
|---|---|---|---|---|
| calories | fat | protein | carbs | fiber |
| 97 | 4.8 g | 2.3 g | 11.5 g | 0.8 g |
| | 45% | 9% | 47% | |

# *dairy-free hollandaise*

**PREP TIME:** 5 minutes

**COOK TIME:** 5 minutes

**YIELD:** 2 cups (about 2½ tablespoons per serving)

6 large egg yolks

¼ cup lemon juice

2 tablespoons Dijon mustard (page 49)

1½ cups bacon fat, lard, or duck fat, melted (but not too hot)

½ teaspoon cayenne pepper

½ teaspoon fine sea salt

⅛ teaspoon fresh ground black pepper

**NUTRITIONAL INFO (per serving)**

| calories | fat | protein | carbs | fiber |
|----------|-----|---------|-------|-------|
| 241 | 26 g | 1.4 g | 0.6 g | 0 g |
|  | 97% | 2% | 1% |  |

1. In the bottom of a double boiler or in a medium-sized saucepan, bring 1 inch of water to a simmer over high heat, then adjust the heat to maintain a simmer. Put the egg yolks, lemon juice, and mustard in the top of the double boiler or in a heatproof bowl that fits over the saucepan with the simmering water.

2. Whisk the yolk mixture to blend, then, while whisking constantly, add the melted fat in a slow, steady stream (it should take about 90 seconds). Cook the sauce, while whisking, until it reaches 140°F.

3. Add the cayenne, salt, and pepper and continue whisking until thick, about 3 minutes, adjusting the heat to maintain the temperature of 140°F (remove from the simmering water if necessary). Adjust the seasonings to taste.

**VARIATION: TRADITIONAL HOLLANDAISE.** *If you are not dairy-sensitive, use melted unsalted butter as the fat (in place of the bacon fat, lard, or duck fat) to create a traditional hollandaise.*

# homemade mustards

**TIP:** *To make mustard more keto-friendly, I like to add a few tablespoons of Brown Butter (page 68).*

*Mustard seeds or mustard powder? It is kind of like asking, "Do you like crunchy or creamy peanut butter?"*

*I suggest using seeds when you want a crunchy texture. Keep in mind that the darker seeds are much stronger in flavor. There are three types of seeds:*

- *Yellow, also known as white, which have the mildest flavor. They are used mainly in American-style mustards and for pickling.*

- *Brown, which are quite a bit zestier than yellow and are used in European-style mustards (like Dijon) and for pickling when you want a deeper flavor. They are also used in Indian cooking.*

- *Black, which have a flavor that's similar to brown seeds and are also used in Indian cooking.*

*If you decide to make mustard from seeds, you need to soften them in liquid for 1 to 2 days beforehand.*

*I suggest using mustard powder if you desire a silky-smooth mustard. Mustard powder is made of finely ground white and brown mustard seeds. If you use powder, all you have to do is mix it with a liquid (like water or bone broth...not beer!) and let it sit overnight to fully hydrate and develop flavor. Don't let it sit longer, though, or it will taste harsh.*

## SWEET-N-SPICY MUSTARD

■■□ KETO  NUT FREE  DAIRY FREE

**PREP TIME:** 5 minutes, plus 8 hours to chill

**YIELD:** 1 cup (about 1 tablespoon per serving)

⅓ cup coconut vinegar or apple cider vinegar

⅓ cup white wine vinegar

⅓ cup powdered erythritol

3 tablespoons yellow mustard seeds

2½ tablespoons brown mustard seeds

2 tablespoons minced shallot

¾ teaspoon fine sea salt

¼ teaspoon ground white pepper

¼ teaspoon fish sauce (optional; for umami)

Pinch of ground allspice

1. In a medium-sized glass or nonreactive metal bowl, combine all of the ingredients, cover, and refrigerate overnight.

2. Transfer the mixture to a blender and puree until the mustard has reached the desired texture and thickness. I prefer to keep it chunky, but you can make it smooth if you prefer.

3. Store in an airtight glass container in the refrigerator for up to 2 weeks.

**SPECIAL EQUIPMENT**

Blender

| NUTRITIONAL INFO (per serving) | | | | |
|---|---|---|---|---|
| calories | fat | protein | carbs | fiber |
| 21 | 1.1 g | 1 g | 1.7 g | 0.6 g |
| | 47% | 19% | 32% | |

# DIJON MUSTARD

KETO · NUT FREE · DAIRY FREE

**PREP TIME:** 5 minutes, plus 2 days to chill

**YIELD**: 1 cup (about 1 tablespoon per serving)

⅓ cup brown mustard seeds

⅓ cup white wine vinegar

⅓ cup beef bone broth (page 42), plus more if needed

1 tablespoon powdered erythritol

1 teaspoon ground turmeric

½ teaspoon fine sea salt

⅛ teaspoon cayenne pepper

⅛ teaspoon stevia glycerite

1 to 2 teaspoons prepared horseradish (optional)

1. In a medium-sized glass or nonreactive metal bowl, combine all of the ingredients except the horseradish. Cover and refrigerate for 2 days.

2. Transfer the mixture to a blender and puree until the mustard is as smooth as desired. Add 2 to 4 tablespoons more beef broth if the mustard is too thick.

3. If you prefer a spicy mustard, add the horseradish.

4. Store in the refrigerator for up to 1 month.

**SPECIAL EQUIPMENT**

Blender

**NUTRITIONAL INFO (per serving)**

| calories | fat | protein | carbs | fiber |
|---|---|---|---|---|
| 18 | 1 g | 0.9 g | 1.4 g | 0.5 g |
| | 50% | 20% | 31% | |

## ROSEMARY THYME MUSTARD

■■□ KETO  NUT FREE  DAIRY FREE

**PREP TIME:** 5 minutes, plus 2 days to chill

**YIELD:** 1 cup (about 1 tablespoon per serving)

⅓ cup water or beef bone broth (page 42)

⅓ cup coconut vinegar or apple cider vinegar

3 tablespoons yellow mustard seeds

1 tablespoon brown mustard seeds

1 tablespoon powdered erythritol or ⅛ teaspoon stevia glycerite

2 teaspoons minced fresh thyme

2 teaspoons minced fresh rosemary

¾ teaspoon fine sea salt

¼ teaspoon fish sauce (optional; for umami)

1. In a medium-sized glass or nonreactive metal bowl, combine all of the ingredients. Cover and refrigerate for 2 days.

2. Place the mixture in a blender and puree until the mustard is thick but still coarse-textured.

3. Store in the refrigerator for up to 1 month.

**SPECIAL EQUIPMENT**

Blender

| NUTRITIONAL INFO (per serving) | | | | |
|---|---|---|---|---|
| calories | fat | protein | carbs | fiber |
| 15 | 0.8 g | 0.7 g | 1.2 g | 0.5 g |
| | 48% | 19% | 32% | |

## BBQ MUSTARD

■■□ KETO  NUT FREE  DAIRY FREE

**PREP TIME:** 5 minutes, plus 8 hours to chill

**COOK TIME:** 40 minutes

**YIELD:** 2 cups (about 1 tablespoon per serving)

1 cup Sweet-n-Spicy Mustard (page 48) or other prepared yellow mustard

¼ cup powdered erythritol or ¼ teaspoon stevia glycerite

¾ cup coconut vinegar or apple cider vinegar

1 tablespoon chili powder

1 teaspoon fresh ground black pepper

1 teaspoon ground white pepper

¼ teaspoon cayenne pepper

½ teaspoon wheat-free tamari or coconut aminos

2 tablespoons unsalted butter or coconut oil

1 teaspoon liquid smoke

1. In a saucepan over medium heat, stir together the mustard, erythritol, vinegar, chili powder, black pepper, white pepper, and cayenne pepper. Simmer for 30 minutes.

2. Stir in the tamari, butter, and liquid smoke and simmer for 10 more minutes. Let cool completely and transfer to a glass jar. Refrigerate overnight to blend the flavors before using.

3. Store in the refrigerator for up to 4 weeks.

| NUTRITIONAL INFO (per serving) | | | | |
|---|---|---|---|---|
| calories | fat | protein | carbs | fiber |
| 19.5 | 1.4 g | 0.6 g | 1.2 g | 0.3 g |
| | 62% | 12% | 24% | |

# tartar sauce

KETO · NUT FREE · DAIRY FREE

**PREP TIME:** 5 minutes

**YIELD:** ¾ cup (2 tablespoons per serving)

½ cup mayonnaise

2 tablespoons finely diced dill pickles

1 tablespoon coconut vinegar or white wine vinegar

¼ teaspoon fine sea salt

⅛ teaspoon fresh ground black pepper

**SPECIAL EQUIPMENT**

Food processor

Place all of the ingredients in a food processor and pulse until well combined but not yet pureed. Store in an airtight container in the fridge for up to 2 weeks.

| NUTRITIONAL INFO (per serving) | | | | |
|---|---|---|---|---|
| calories | fat | protein | carbs | fiber |
| 121 | 13.3 g | 0 g | 0.5 g | 0 g |
| | 99% | 0% | 2% | |

# "honey" dressing

**KETO**

**PREP TIME:** 2 minutes

**COOK TIME:** 15 minutes

**YIELD:** 1½ cups (2 tablespoons per serving)

½ cup (1 stick) unsalted butter

1 ounce cream cheese (about 2 tablespoons)

¼ cup powdered erythritol

½ cup unsweetened almond milk

*Before you begin, make sure you have everything ready to go. You need to work fast or the sweetener will burn.*

1. In a heavy-bottomed 2- or 3-quart saucepan, heat the butter on high heat. As soon as it comes to a boil, watch for specks of brown (this is brown butter—so good on veggies!). Immediately add the cream cheese and whisk until smooth and no chunks of cream cheese remain.

2. Add the erythritol and almond milk and whisk until smooth. Let cool in the pan for a couple minutes, and then pour into a glass mason jar and let cool to room temperature.

3. Store in the refrigerator for up to 2 weeks. To reheat, place in a small saucepan and heat on low for a minute, until liquefied.

**NUTRITIONAL INFO (per serving)**

| calories | fat | protein | carbs | fiber |
|---|---|---|---|---|
| 78 | 8.5 g | 0.3 g | 0.1 g | 0 g |
|  | 98% | 2% | 1% |  |

# DAIRY-FREE
## *avocado ranch dressing*

**■■□ KETO** **NUT FREE** **DAIRY FREE**

**PREP TIME:** 5 minutes

**YIELD:** 2 cups (2 tablespoons per serving)

1 avocado, halved and pitted

1 head roasted garlic (see page 46)

½ cup chicken or beef bone broth (page 42), plus more if desired

½ cup Copycat Baconnaise (page 65) or mayonnaise

2 tablespoons chopped fresh flat-leaf parsley

2 tablespoons chopped fresh dill

½ teaspoon coconut vinegar

½ teaspoon smoked paprika

¼ teaspoon onion powder

¼ teaspoon fine sea salt

¼ teaspoon fresh ground black pepper

½ teaspoon fish sauce (optional; for umami)

Place all of the ingredients in a blender or food processor and puree until smooth. Add more broth to thin the dressing, if desired. Place in a mason jar, cover, and store in the refrigerator for up to 2 weeks.

**SPECIAL EQUIPMENT**

Blender or food processor

**NUTRITIONAL INFO (per serving)**

| calories | fat | protein | carbs | fiber |
|----------|-----|---------|-------|-------|
| 86 | 8 g | 1.8 g | 2.6 g | 1.1 g |
| | 82% | 8% | 11% | |

# *ranch dressing*

**KETO**  **NUT FREE**

**PREP TIME:** 5 minutes, plus 2 hours to chill

**YIELD:** 1½ cups (2 tablespoons per serving)

8 ounces cream cheese (about 1 cup), softened

½ cup chicken or beef bone broth (page 42)

½ teaspoon dried chives

½ teaspoon dried parsley

½ teaspoon dried dill weed

¼ teaspoon garlic powder

¼ teaspoon onion powder

⅛ teaspoon fine sea salt

⅛ teaspoon fresh ground black pepper

In a blender or large bowl, mix together all of the ingredients. Transfer to a mason jar, cover, and refrigerate for 2 hours before serving (it will thicken up as it rests). Store in the fridge for up to 2 weeks.

**SPECIAL EQUIPMENT**

Blender

**NUTRITIONAL INFO (per serving)**

| calories | fat | protein | carbs | fiber |
|----------|-----|---------|-------|-------|
| 69 | 6.6 g | 1.7 g | 0.7 g | 0 g |
| | 86% | 10% | 4% | |

# DAIRY-FREE
## thousand island dressing

**KETO** ■■□ **NUT FREE** **DAIRY FREE**

**PREP TIME:** 2 minutes

**YIELD:** 1¼ cups (2 tablespoons per serving)

¾ cup Copycat Baconnaise (page 65) or mayonnaise

¼ cup chopped dill pickles

¼ cup tomato sauce, homemade (page 59) or store-bought

2 tablespoons powdered erythritol or a drop of stevia glycerite

⅛ teaspoon fine sea salt

⅛ teaspoon fish sauce

Place all of the ingredients in a jar and shake well. Store in the fridge for up to 2 weeks.

**NUTRITIONAL INFO (per serving)**

| calories | fat | protein | carbs | fiber |
|---|---|---|---|---|
| 59 | 4.9 g | 0.2 g | 3.8 g | 1.2 g |
| | 75% | 1% | 24% | |

# fat-burning salad dressing

■■■ **KETO**  **NUT FREE**  **DAIRY FREE**

**PREP TIME:** 2 minutes

**YIELD:** ¾ cup (2 tablespoons per serving)

½ cup MCT oil

¼ cup coconut vinegar or apple cider vinegar

1 teaspoon fine sea salt

½ teaspoon fresh ground black pepper

½ teaspoon stevia glycerite

½ teaspoon fish sauce

*This is a great way to add fat to a meal—just drizzle onto coleslaw or salad greens.*

Place all of the ingredients in a jar and shake well. Store in the fridge for up to 6 weeks.

**NUTRITIONAL INFO (per serving)**

| calories | fat | protein | carbs | fiber |
|---|---|---|---|---|
| 174 | 18.7 g | 0.1 g | 0.1 g | 0 g |
|  | 98% | 1% | 1% |  |

# greek salad dressing

**KETO** **NUT FREE** **DAIRY FREE**

**PREP TIME:** 8 minutes

**YIELD:** ½ cup (2 tablespoons per serving)

Juice of 1 lemon or lime

¼ cup MCT oil

1 clove garlic, minced

2 tablespoons finely chopped fresh oregano

1 tablespoon finely chopped fresh basil

½ teaspoon fine sea salt

½ teaspoon fresh ground black pepper

⅛ teaspoon fish sauce (optional; for umami)

1. Place the lemon juice, MCT oil, garlic, oregano, and basil in a blender or food processor. Mix to combine well. Add the salt, pepper, and fish sauce, if using, and pulse to combine.

2. Store in a glass jar in the refrigerator for up to 2 weeks.

**SPECIAL EQUIPMENT**

Blender or food processor

| NUTRITIONAL INFO (per serving) | | | | |
|---|---|---|---|---|
| calories | fat | protein | carbs | fiber |
| 139 | 14.3 g | 0.5 g | 2.1 g | 1.1 g |
| | 93% | 1% | 6% | |

# tomato sauce

■■□ | NUT | DAIRY
KETO | FREE | FREE

**PREP TIME:** 10 minutes

**COOK TIME:** 25 minutes

**YIELD:** About 2 cups (¼ cup per serving)

2 tablespoons MCT oil

½ cup diced yellow onion

1 head roasted garlic (see page 46) or 3 cloves raw garlic, minced

2 large tomatoes, pureed (about 2 cups)

¼ cup chopped fresh basil

¼ teaspoon stevia glycerite (optional)

½ teaspoon fine sea salt

⅛ teaspoon fresh ground black pepper

1. Heat the MCT oil in a large saucepan over medium-high heat. Add the onion and garlic and cook until the onion is translucent and starting to turn golden, stirring often.

2. Add the rest of the ingredients and simmer on low until the sauce thickens and coats a spoon, about 20 minutes.

**VARIATION: PIZZA SAUCE.** *To make this into pizza sauce, simmer for an extra 30 minutes to thicken it further and then puree it in a blender until smooth.*

**NUTRITIONAL INFO (per serving)**

| calories | fat | protein | carbs | fiber |
|---|---|---|---|---|
| 46 | 3.6 g | 0.6 g | 2.9 g | 0.7 g |
| | 70% | 5% | 25% | |

# yellow marinara sauce

**PREP TIME:** 5 minutes

**COOK TIME:** 3½ hours

**YIELD:** 2 quarts (about ⅓ cup per serving)

5 pounds yellow tomatoes

¼ cup beef tallow or coconut oil (or unsalted butter if not dairy-sensitive; see Note)

1 cup diced yellow onion

1 teaspoon plus 1 pinch fine sea salt

1 cup sliced button mushrooms (see Note)

2 heads roasted garlic (see page 46) or 8 cloves raw garlic, minced

⅓ cup finely chopped fresh basil

2 sprigs fresh flat-leaf parsley or 1 teaspoon dried

1 sprig fresh oregano or 1 teaspoon dried

1 sprig fresh thyme or ½ teaspoon dried

2 bay leaves

2 teaspoons red pepper flakes (optional)

½ teaspoon stevia glycerite (optional)

**NOTE:** *Butter cuts the acidic taste of the tomatoes, as do mushrooms.*

*A great tomato sauce has a balance of sweetness and acidity, but making the perfect sauce can be challenging. This recipe uses a couple tricks to counter the natural acidity of tomatoes, starting with the choice of tomatoes: yellow tomatoes are less acidic than red tomatoes. Plus, taking the time to caramelize the onions creates a natural sweetness that helps balance the acidic taste.*

1. Bring a large pot of water to a boil. Prepare an ice bath in a large bowl.

2. Cut a small "X" on the top of each tomato and drop them into the boiling water, a few at a time, for 10 seconds. Remove with a slotted spoon and drop into the ice bath. Peel the tomatoes—the skin will peel off easily—and quarter them. Scoop out the seeds with a small spoon and roughly chop the tomato quarters.

3. Place the beef tallow in a large stockpot over medium heat. Add the onion and sauté for 15 to 20 minutes, until the onion is dark brown, stirring often to avoid burning. Add a pinch of salt to the onion as it cooks. (This speeds up the caramelizing process; the salt will suck moisture out of the onion.) Continue stirring and watch as the onion turns darker and darker. If you feel that the onions are sticking to the bottom of the pan too much, add a very small amount of water or broth and stir vigorously to deglaze the pan.

4. Add the mushrooms and garlic to the caramelized onions and sauté for 8 minutes, or until the mushrooms are tender. Add the tomatoes, herbs (leave the fresh sprigs whole), red pepper flakes, if using, and 1 teaspoon of salt. Simmer on low heat for 2 to 3 hours, or until cooked down and starting to darken. Remove the sprigs of herbs and bay leaves. Stir in the stevia if desired.

5. Optional: Use an immersion blender to puree the sauce until smooth. For a thicker sauce, skip this step.

6. Store in the fridge for up to 7 days, or can it according to your canner's instructions for tomato products. Just before serving, add flavor enhancers if desired (see below).

**OPTIONAL FLAVOR ENHANCERS AND ACID NEUTRALIZERS**

*Heavy cream: Add a splash and let the sauce simmer for a few minutes to thicken.*

*Hard cheeses: Add ½ cup of grated Parmesan, pecorino, or another hard cheese to give the sauce a deep savory note.*

*Fresh cheeses and other fermented dairy products: Add a scoop of mascarpone, cream cheese, or crème fraîche.*

| NUTRITIONAL INFO (per serving) | | | | |
|---|---|---|---|---|
| calories | fat | protein | carbs | fiber |
| 48 | 2.5 g | 0.9 g | 5.5 g | 0.9 g |
| | 47% | 8% | 46% | |

# keto ketchup

■□□ KETO  NUT FREE  DAIRY FREE

**PREP TIME:** 2 minutes

**COOK TIME:** 45 minutes

**YIELD:** 2 cups (2 tablespoons per serving)

1½ cups beef or chicken bone broth (page 42) or water

1 (7-ounce) jar tomato paste

2 tablespoons apple cider vinegar or coconut vinegar

1 tablespoon powdered erythritol or 1 drop of stevia glycerite

1 teaspoon garlic powder

1 teaspoon onion powder

1 teaspoon fine sea salt

1. Combine all of the ingredients in a medium-sized saucepan. Bring to a boil, then reduce heat and simmer for 45 minutes.

2. Store in an airtight container in the refrigerator for up to 2 weeks.

| NUTRITIONAL INFO (per serving) | | | | |
| --- | --- | --- | --- | --- |
| calories | fat | protein | carbs | fiber |
| 17 | 0.2 g | 1 g | 2.7 g | 0.5 g |
| | 11% | 24% | 64% | |

# keto bbq sauce

■□□ **KETO**  NUT **FREE**  DAIRY **FREE**

**PREP TIME:** 3 minutes

**YIELD:** 2½ cups (about 1½ tablespoons per serving)

2 cups Keto Ketchup (page 62)

¼ cup powdered erythritol or 1 teaspoon stevia glycerite

2 tablespoons coconut vinegar or apple cider vinegar

1½ teaspoons liquid smoke

½ teaspoon onion powder

½ teaspoon garlic powder

½ teaspoon fresh ground black pepper

⅛ teaspoon fine sea salt

Place all of the ingredients in a large bowl and mix well. Store in an airtight container in the refrigerator for up to 2 weeks.

**NUTRITIONAL INFO (per serving)**

| calories | fat | protein | carbs | fiber |
|---|---|---|---|---|
| 15 | 0 g | 0 g | 3.7 g | 0 g |
| | 0% | 0% | 100% | |

## DAIRY-FREE
# *nacho cheese sauce*

**KETO** ■■■ | **NUT FREE** | **DAIRY FREE**

**PREP TIME:** 2 minutes

**COOK TIME:** 5 minutes

**YIELD:** 2 cups (about ¼ cup per serving)

6 large egg yolks

¼ cup lime or lemon juice

1 tablespoon Dijon mustard (page 49)

1½ cups bacon fat or duck fat, melted (but not too hot)

¼ cup nutritional yeast

½ teaspoon fine sea salt

¼ teaspoon Taco Seasoning (page 74)

1. Making this cheese sauce is like making hollandaise. In the bottom of a double boiler or in a medium-sized saucepan, bring 1 inch of water to a simmer over high heat, then adjust the heat to maintain a simmer. Put the egg yolks, lime juice, and mustard in the top of the double boiler or in a heatproof bowl that fits over the saucepan with the simmering water.

2. Whisk the yolk mixture to blend, then, while whisking constantly, add the melted fat in a slow, steady stream (it should take about 90 seconds). Cook the sauce, while whisking, until it reaches 140°F.

3. Add the nutritional yeast, salt, and taco seasoning and continue whisking until thick, about 3 minutes, adjusting the heat to maintain the temperature of 140°F (remove from the simmering water if necessary). Adjust the seasonings to taste. Remove from the stove and keep warm until serving.

4. Store in an airtight container in the refrigerator for up to 2 weeks. Reheat gently on the stovetop over low heat.

| NUTRITIONAL INFO (per serving) | | | | |
|---|---|---|---|---|
| calories | fat | protein | carbs | fiber |
| 416 | 42.4 g | 4.7 g | 3.9 g | 1.4 g |
| | 92% | 5% | 4% | |

# copycat baconnaise

 NUT FREE  DAIRY FREE
**KETO**

**PREP TIME:** 5 minutes

**YIELD:** 1¼ cups (1 tablespoon per serving)

2 large egg yolks

3 teaspoons lemon juice, divided

1 cup bacon fat, melted (but not too hot)

Fine sea salt (if needed)

**SPECIAL EQUIPMENT**

Food processor

1. Place the yolks in a small food processor with 1 teaspoon of the lemon juice and mix until well combined.

2. Turn the food processor on low and slowly drizzle the melted bacon fat into the yolk mixture, drop by drop in the beginning. If you add too much oil at once, it will separate.

3. As you add more bacon fat, the mixture will start to emulsify and thicken, and then you can begin pouring the fat in a steady stream.

4. Once you've added all the bacon fat, mix in the remaining 2 teaspoons of lemon juice. Taste and add salt if needed.

5. Store in the refrigerator and use within 5 days.

| NUTRITIONAL INFO (per serving) | | | | |
|---|---|---|---|---|
| calories | fat | protein | carbs | fiber |
| 120 | 13.3 g | 0 g | 0 g | 0 g |
| | 100% | 0% | 0% | |

# brown butter béarnaise

**KETO** **NUT FREE**

**PREP TIME:** 5 minutes

**COOK TIME:** 20 minutes

**YIELD:** 3 cups (3 tablespoons per serving)

1 recipe Brown Butter (page 68)

¼ cup chopped fresh tarragon or sage

2 shallots, minced

¼ cup coconut vinegar or white wine vinegar

12 large egg yolks

Fine sea salt

**SPECIAL EQUIPMENT**

Blender

*This recipe uses brown butter instead of regular butter for richer flavor. I recommend keeping a jar of brown butter in your fridge for easy use in recipes. It's a great staple!*

1. Place the brown butter in a medium-sized saucepan and melt over medium heat. Add the tarragon, shallots, and vinegar and bring to a simmer. Cook for 15 minutes. Remove from the heat and set aside to cool slightly.

2. Place the yolks in a blender. With the blender running on medium speed, add one-third of the brown butter mixture in a slow steady stream. Once it emulsifies, turn the blender speed up to high and add the remaining butter in a slightly quicker pour. Season with salt to taste.

**TIP:** *To make this sauce by hand, whisk the yolks in a large bowl. Then, while whisking vigorously, slowly add the brown butter reduction in a slow, steady stream. Once it emulsifies, you can pour the reduction in faster. Season with salt to taste.*

**VARIATION: DAIRY-FREE BÉARNAISE.** *Instead of brown butter, use ½ cup lard or bacon fat.*

| NUTRITIONAL INFO (per serving) | | | | |
|---|---|---|---|---|
| calories | fat | protein | carbs | fiber |
| 93 | 9.1 g | 2.2 g | 0.9 g | 0 g |
| | 88% | 9% | 4% | |

# brown butter

**KETO** **NUT FREE**

**COOK TIME:** 5 minutes

**YIELD:** ½ cup (2 tablespoons per serving)

½ cup (1 stick) unsalted butter

¼ teaspoon fine sea salt

*In France, brown butter is called* beurre noisette, *which means "hazelnut butter," referring to the brown color of hazelnut skins. It's simply butter that's been heated until the milk proteins are browned and some of the water evaporates. It adds a rich, nutty flavor to recipes that call for butter, and it can be used on its own as a warm sauce to accompany many foods, such as vegetables, faux pastas (like Zucchini "Pasta," page 284, or Slow Cooker Cabbage "Pasta," page 282), fish, omelets, and chicken. I even put a touch in homemade mustards to make them more keto. If you are a visual learner like me, check out the video tutorial here: https://vimeo.com/137512394*

Place the butter in a saucepan and heat on high for about 5 minutes. The butter will start to sizzle and foam up. Watch closely for brown flecks, and once you see them, remove the pan from the heat and whisk vigorously. Be careful that the flecks don't turn black—that means it's started to burn and has turned into black butter, or *beurre noir* (it is common in French cuisine, but it just tastes burnt to me). Add a touch of salt to taste.

**NUTRITIONAL INFO (per serving)**

| calories | fat | protein | carbs | fiber |
|---|---|---|---|---|
| 208 | 23 g | 0.3 g | 0 g | 0 g |
| | 99% | 1% | 0% | |

# fat-burning chimichurri sauce

 **KETO** | **NUT FREE** | **DAIRY FREE**

**PREP TIME:** 5 minutes, plus 1 hour to set

**YIELD:** 2 cups (about 2 tablespoons per serving)

1 head roasted garlic (see page 46) or 3 cloves raw garlic, peeled

1 packed cup fresh flat-leaf parsley

½ cup MCT oil

⅓ cup coconut vinegar

¼ packed cup fresh cilantro

¾ teaspoon red pepper flakes

½ teaspoon ground cumin

½ teaspoon fine sea salt

**SPECIAL EQUIPMENT**

Food processor

*Sauces and salad dressings are an easy and tasty way to turn a "low-carb" meal into a "ketogenic" one by adding healthy and flavorful fats. A steak on its own would not have enough fat to constitute a ketogenic dinner, but adding a flavorful, high-fat sauce transforms it into a satisfying ketogenic meal. This herb-infused, garlicky sauce from Argentina is great to serve not only with steak but also with chicken, fish, or seafood. It also makes a great sauce for zucchini noodles.*

1. Squeeze the roasted garlic cloves from the head into a food processor (or place the raw garlic cloves in the food processor). Add the rest of the ingredients and puree until smooth. Transfer to a serving bowl.

2. Cover and let stand at room temperature for up to an hour to allow the flavors to meld. Store in an airtight container in the refrigerator for up to 2 weeks.

**NUTRITIONAL INFO (per serving)**

| calories | fat | protein | carbs | fiber |
|---|---|---|---|---|
| 67 | 7.1 g | 0.2 g | 0.5 g | 0 g |
|  | 95% | 1% | 3% |  |

# enchilada sauce

**KETO** ■■□  **NUT FREE**  **DAIRY FREE**

**PREP TIME:** 10 minutes

**COOK TIME:** 15 minutes

**YIELD:** About 3 cups (¼ cup per serving)

2 cups chicken or beef bone broth (page 42)

1 cup diced yellow tomatoes

½ cup chopped avocado (about ½ avocado)

1 head roasted garlic (see page 46)

5 tablespoons chili powder

2 tablespoons fresh oregano or ½ teaspoon dried

2 tablespoons lard, duck fat, or other fat, melted

1 tablespoon coconut vinegar

½ teaspoon ground cumin

**SPECIAL EQUIPMENT**

Food processor

*I've had many recipe testers try multiple enchilada sauce recipes, and this one was the winner time and time again! Using homemade bone broth is the key to creating a thick and flavorful sauce. Store-bought broth will work, but the end result will not be as thick. It is also important to check the ingredients in store-bought broths; many contain MSG and other harmful ingredients.*

Place all of the ingredients in a food processor and pulse until very smooth. Pour the sauce into a small pot and heat slowly for about 15 minutes to thicken.

**BUSY FAMILY TIP:** *This recipe doubles well, so make extra for leftovers or to freeze in pint jars.*

| NUTRITIONAL INFO (per serving) | | | | |
|---|---|---|---|---|
| calories | fat | protein | carbs | fiber |
| 59 | 4.2 g | 1.6 g | 3.7 g | 2 g |
| | 64% | 11% | 25% | |

# taco seasoning

■□□ **KETO**  NUT **FREE**  DAIRY **FREE**

**PREP TIME:** 2 minutes

**YIELD:** ½ cup (1 tablespoon per serving)

2 tablespoons chili powder

1 tablespoon ground cumin

2 teaspoons fine sea salt

2 teaspoons fresh ground black pepper

1 teaspoon paprika

1 teaspoon ground coriander

½ teaspoon garlic powder

½ teaspoon onion powder

½ teaspoon red pepper flakes

½ teaspoon ground dried oregano

2 teaspoons powdered erythritol (optional)

*When I use spice blends, I expect them to consist of spices. Doesn't seem like too much to ask, is it?*

*Look at the following list of ingredients in store-bought taco seasoning: yellow corn flour, salt, maltodextrin, paprika, spices, modified corn starch, sugar, garlic powder, citric acid, autolyzed yeast extract, natural flavor, caramel color (sulfites).*

*They don't even list a spice until the fourth ingredient! But there are other problems, too. First, caramel coloring is a food dye that's been linked to increased risk of cancer. Another issue is maltodextrin. Sugar has a glycemic index of 52, while maltodextrin's is 110!*

*I'll stick to making a triple batch of my own taco seasoning and keeping it in my pantry.*

In a bowl, mix together all of the ingredients until well combined. Store in an airtight container away from heat and light for up to 2 months.

**NUTRITIONAL INFO (per serving)**

| calories | fat | protein | carbs | fiber |
|---|---|---|---|---|
| 16 | 0.6 g | 0.5 g | 2.2 g | 1.1 g |
|  | 34% | 12% | 55% |  |

# seafood seasoning

■□□ **KETO**  **NUT FREE**  **DAIRY FREE**

**PREP TIME:** 2 minutes

**YIELD:** 1 cup (1 tablespoon per serving)

¼ cup smoked paprika

3 tablespoons fine sea salt

3 tablespoons garlic powder

2 tablespoons onion powder

2 tablespoons ground dried oregano

2 tablespoons ground dried thyme

1½ tablespoons fresh ground black pepper

1½ tablespoons cayenne pepper

Place all of the ingredients in a bowl and mix well. Store in an airtight container, preferably away from heat and light. It will keep for 3 months, but it's best used within 1 month.

| NUTRITIONAL INFO (per serving) | | | | |
|---|---|---|---|---|
| calories | fat | protein | carbs | fiber |
| 23 | 0.4 g | 0.8 g | 4 g | 1.5 g |
| | 16% | 14% | 70% | |

# how to preserve herbs

*Freezing and drying herbs are great ways to preserve them for the long winter months. Drying works best for hard, or "woody," herbs, which are suitable for long cooking times—though I have also found them to freeze well. Hard herbs include oregano, rosemary, sage, and thyme. Freezing is best for soft herbs, which are added toward the end of cooking or used raw on the finished dish. Soft herbs include basil, chives, dill, lovage, mint, parsley, and tarragon.*

*I often freeze all my herbs, but no matter what you do, I highly recommend skipping those expensive spice stores and hopping on over to your nearest farmers' market to purchase organic herbs. (Not all booths at farmers' markets are organic; make sure to look for a sign or ask.) It's important to use organic herbs because, as with foods like lettuce, celery, and peppers, you eat the entire plant. It's less important to purchase organic produce when the food is protected by a thick, inedible outer peel—like avocados or bananas.*

*The little time spent freezing and drying herbs is well worth the money saved and the fresh taste in the dead of winter!*

## FREEZE-DRYING HERBS

**STEP 1:** Purchase or harvest organic herbs.

**STEP 2:** Rinse the herbs in water. Gently pat them dry, or do what my mom does and gently spin them dry in a salad spinner (she loves kitchen gadgets, whereas I am a minimalist). Be careful not to crush them.

**STEP 3:** Using your fingers, strip the leaves off the stems.

**STEP 4:** Place the leaves on a rimmed baking sheet in a single layer. Place in the freezer.

**STEP 5:** Once frozen, place the herbs in glass containers or jars, making sure to label and date them. (Freeze-dried herbs often look alike.) Store in a dark pantry. For best flavor, use within 6 months.

## FREEZING HERBS IN OIL

**STEPS 1–3:** Follow steps 1 through 3 for freeze-drying herbs.

**STEP 4:** Place a tablespoon of leaves in each compartment of an ice cube tray, then fill each compartment with a tablespoon of MCT oil or high-quality olive oil. Place the tray in the freezer.

**STEP 5:** Once frozen, place the herb-filled ice cubes in a glass container or gallon-size freezer bag, making sure to label and date it. Store in the freezer for up to 6 months.

## AIR-DRYING HERBS

**STEPS 1–2:** Follow steps 1 and 2 for freeze-drying herbs.

**STEP 3:** Divide the herbs into small bunches, tying the ends together with string.

**STEP 4:** Hang the bunches upside down in a clean area where they won't get dusty. If you're concerned about dust, poke a hole in the bottom of a small paper bag and insert the string through the hole, leaving the top of the bag (now the bottom) open for air circulation. Hang for several days until dry; the exact time will vary depending on the temperature and humidity of the room in which they are hanging.

**STEP 5:** Once the herbs are totally dry, crunch the leaves off the stems.

**STEP 6:** Place the leaves in airtight glass containers, making sure to label and date them. For best flavor, use dried herbs within 6 months.

TIPS: *For a fresh taste of summer in the middle of winter, use basil frozen in cubes of olive oil to make pesto and serve over zucchini noodles (page 284).*

*When substituting dried herbs for fresh, use two-thirds less than the recipe calls for. For example, if a recipe calls for 1 tablespoon fresh thyme leaves, use 1 teaspoon dried.*

# brown butter syrup

**KETO**

**PREP TIME:** 1 minute

**COOK TIME:** 5 minutes

**YIELD:** 1½ cups (2 tablespoons per serving)

½ cup (1 stick) unsalted butter

½ cup powdered erythritol

1 ounce (2 tablespoons) cream cheese (optional)

½ cup unsweetened almond milk

1 teaspoon maple extract or 2 drops of maple oil (optional)

¼ teaspoon fine sea salt

*To make brown butter syrup, I highly recommend using Swerve confectioners'-style sweetener. You can use pure erythritol, such as the brands Zevia or Organic Zero, but as the syrup cools in the refrigerator, the almond milk will separate from the butter, which will solidify into chunks. If you decide to use a different sweetener, add an ounce of cream cheese to help the sauce emulsify.*

1. In a large saucepan, heat the butter over high heat, whisking every few seconds. The butter will foam up to the top of the saucepan and then fall back down. When you see lots of brown flecks, remove from the heat. Watch closely; you do not want black flecks.

2. With the saucepan off the heat, whisk in the erythritol until smooth. If you used a brand of erythritol other than Swerve confectioners'-style sweetener, add the cream cheese (see headnote). Then whisk in the almond milk, maple extract, if using, and salt.

3. Store in a glass jar in the fridge for up to 2 weeks—if it lasts that long! This syrup will thicken in the fridge because the butter hardens as it cools; reheat in a pan on the stovetop or in the microwave.

| NUTRITIONAL INFO (per serving) | | | | |
|---|---|---|---|---|
| calories | fat | protein | carbs | fiber |
| 77 | 8.4 g | 0.2 g | 0.2 g | 0 g |
| | 98% | 1% | 1% | |

breakfast

# keto pancakes and syrup

**KETO**

**PREP TIME:** 7 minutes

**COOK TIME:** About 5 minutes per pancake

**YIELD**: 12 (5-inch) pancakes (3 per serving)

3 large eggs, separated

2 tablespoons vanilla egg white protein (or vanilla whey protein if not dairy-sensitive)

1 teaspoon vanilla extract or other extract, such as almond or maple

1 teaspoon stevia glycerite

Coconut oil, unsalted butter, or ghee, for frying

½ cup Brown Butter Syrup (page 78), for serving

1. Whip the egg whites in a clean, dry, nonreactive metal bowl for a few minutes, until very stiff. Blend in the yolks, protein powder, vanilla extract, and stevia.

2. Heat the oil in a skillet over medium-high heat until a drop of water sizzles when added to the pan. Once it is hot, scoop ¼ cup of the batter into the pan and, using a spoon, form it into a circle. Fry the pancake until golden brown on both sides, about 2 minutes per side. Remove from the heat, place on a plate, and cover with foil to keep warm.

3. Repeat with the rest of the batter, adding a little more oil between pancakes if needed.

4. Top with the syrup and serve.

| NUTRITIONAL INFO (per serving) | | | | |
|---|---|---|---|---|
| calories | fat | protein | carbs | fiber |
| 170 | 15 g | 8.2 g | 0.6 g | 0 |
| | 79% | 19% | 1% | |

# french scrambled eggs

**KETO** **NUT FREE**

**PREP TIME:** 5 minutes, plus 24 hours for the gravlax

**COOK TIME:** 7 minutes

**YIELD:** 2 servings

2 tablespoons coconut oil or unsalted butter

6 large eggs, beaten

1 cherry tomato, finely diced (optional)

2 tablespoons chopped fresh chives

½ teaspoon fine sea salt

½ teaspoon fresh ground black pepper

2 tablespoons crème fraîche or sour cream

4 ounces Gravlax (page 236), chopped into small pieces

*These are not just any scrambled eggs. These are the creamiest scrambled eggs you will ever have! French scrambled eggs are so succulent and luscious, they will change the way you think of scrambled eggs. I love them over a fried and buttered slice of Keto Bread (page 276) with a side of Dairy-Free Hollandaise (page 47).*

1. Melt the oil in a small saucepan over medium-low heat.

2. In a large bowl, combine the eggs, diced tomato, if using, chives, salt, and pepper.

3. Pour the egg mixture into the saucepan and cook for a few minutes, whisking constantly.

4. When the eggs reach the texture you like, remove from the heat and add the crème fraîche, mixing well. Add the gravlax and stir gently. Serve immediately.

| NUTRITIONAL INFO (per serving) | | | | |
|---|---|---|---|---|
| calories | fat | protein | carbs | fiber |
| 476 | 37 g | 32 g | 4.4 g | 0.6 g |
| | 70% | 27% | 3% | |

# dairy-free breakfast pizza

 **KETO**    **NUT FREE**    **DAIRY FREE**

**PREP TIME:** 10 minutes

**COOK TIME:** 25 minutes

**YIELD:** One pizza (6 servings)

Bacon fat or coconut oil spray, for the pan

### FOR THE CRUST

6 large eggs, separated

½ teaspoon cream of tartar

¼ cup unflavored egg white protein (or ½ cup unflavored whey protein if not dairy-sensitive)

2 teaspoons dried Italian spices (optional)

1 tablespoon MCT oil, for brushing

1 cup Pizza Sauce (page 59)

6 cooked bacon slices and/or ½ pound crumbled cooked breakfast sausage

Several handfuls of chopped fresh herbs

3 large eggs

Fine sea salt and fresh ground black pepper

1 cup Dairy-Free Hollandaise made with bacon fat (page 47), for serving

### ADDITIONAL TOPPING SUGGESTIONS

Sliced green bell pepper

Sliced onion

Sliced mushrooms

1. Preheat the oven to 325°F. Grease a 9½-by-13-inch sheet pan or an 8-inch cast-iron skillet with bacon fat.

2. Make the crust: Whip the egg whites and cream of tartar in a clean, dry, nonreactive metal bowl until very stiff (I use a stand mixer and let it go for 5 minutes). Slowly sift the protein powder into the whites while whisking.

3. Place the yolks and dried Italian spices in a small bowl and beat with a fork until combined. Using a spatula, gently fold the beaten yolks into the whites.

4. Spoon the egg mixture into the prepared pan. Smooth it out across the bottom of the pan and work it up the sides to create a lip on the edges. Bake for 18 minutes, or until golden brown on the top.

5. Remove the pizza crust from the oven and brush it with the MCT oil. Top with the sauce, bacon and/or sausage, herbs, and any additional toppings of your choosing.

6. Crack each egg into an individual ramekin, then carefully slip them onto the pizza. Shake on a little salt and pepper.

7. Place the pizza in the oven and bake for 5 to 7 minutes, until the eggs are just set and golden.

8. Drizzle the hollandaise on top and serve.

**BUSY FAMILY TIP:** *One of my recipe testers commented that she likes to cook a huge batch of these pizza crusts and freeze them. She said, "It takes only minutes to pull them out, top them, and pop them in the oven. This is my favorite pizza crust, and it's now a staple in our house."*

| NUTRITIONAL INFO (per serving) | | | | |
|---|---|---|---|---|
| calories | fat | protein | carbs | fiber |
| 571 | 53.5 g | 19.5 g | 5.8 g | 5 g |
|  | 84% | 14% | 4% |  |

# floating islands

**KETO**

**PREP TIME:** 25 minutes

**COOK TIME:** 30 minutes

**YIELD:** 4 servings

4 cups unsweetened vanilla almond milk, divided

1 vanilla bean (about 6 inches long)

6 large eggs, separated

⅔ cup powdered erythritol, divided

¼ teaspoon fine sea salt

¼ cup Brown Butter Syrup (page 78), warmed

### SPECIAL EQUIPMENT

Strainer

**BUSY FAMILY TIP:** *I always have Brown Butter Syrup (page 78) in my fridge, which makes breakfast a little easier. All I have to do is rewarm the syrup in a saucepan on the stovetop (or in the microwave) for about 20 seconds, and it's ready to use on dishes like this.*

*I know that the words* floating islands *probably make you think of dessert, but these are a sweet and tasty way to change up how you "break-your-fast" with eggs.*

1.  Make the custard: In a medium-sized saucepan, bring 2 cups of the almond milk to a boil and remove from the heat.

2.  Split the vanilla bean in half lengthwise and add it to the almond milk. Cover and steep for about 15 minutes. Scrape the seeds from the vanilla bean and return them to the almond milk; discard the pod.

3.  In a small bowl, mix the egg yolks with ⅓ cup of the erythritol and the salt until thick and pale yellow in color.

4.  Pour the almond milk mixture very slowly into the sweetened egg yolks while beating them continuously.

5.  Pour the mixture back into the saucepan and gently cook over low heat, stirring constantly, until it forms a custard thick enough to coat the back of a spoon, 15 to 20 minutes. (If you do this step too quickly or over higher heat, the eggs will scramble.)

6.  Pour the custard through a fine-mesh strainer into a shallow serving dish. Set aside. If you are making extra, refrigerate in an airtight container until ready to use. Can be served warm or chilled.

7.  Make the "islands": Beat the egg whites until stiff peaks form, then very slowly add the remaining ⅓ cup of erythritol while beating.

8.  Place the remaining 2 cups of almond milk in a sauté pan or other large, shallow pan and bring to a low simmer.

9.  Using a large slotted spoon, form 2-by-3-inch egg shapes out of the whites and poach them in the almond milk for 30 seconds on each side. You should end up with 8 "islands." Do not overcook. Put the islands on a clean towel to drain.

10. Assemble: Divide the custard among 4 small serving bowls. Carefully arrange the islands in the custard, 2 per bowl. Drizzle the syrup over the islands. Serve immediately.

### NUTRITIONAL INFO (per serving)

| calories | fat | protein | carbs | fiber |
|----------|--------|---------|-------|-------|
| 181 | 14.2 g | 10.5 g | 1.7 g | 1 g |
| | 71% | 23% | 4% | |

# creamy zucchini hash browns

**KETO** **NUT FREE**

**PREP TIME:** 8 minutes, plus 15 minutes for the zucchini to drain

**COOK TIME:** 10 minutes

**YIELD:** 4 cakes (1 per serving)

4 cups shredded zucchini (about 2 medium zucchini)

2 teaspoons fine sea salt

1 large egg, beaten

¼ cup grated Parmesan cheese (about 1 ounce; substitute nutritional yeast if dairy-sensitive)

2 tablespoons chopped green onion

½ teaspoon cayenne pepper or fresh ground black pepper (optional)

¼ cup coconut oil, bacon fat, or duck fat, for frying

½ recipe Dairy-Free Hollandaise (page 47) or Traditional Hollandaise (page 47), for serving

1. Place the zucchini in a medium-sized bowl and toss with the salt. Let sit for 10 to 15 minutes. Squeeze out any moisture and discard the liquid.

2. Add the egg, Parmesan, green onion, and cayenne, if using. Mix well to combine.

3. Heat the coconut oil in a large skillet over medium-high heat. Using your hands, form the zucchini mixture into 4 cakes about 2½ inches in diameter and ½ inch thick. Place in the hot pan and fry for about 5 minutes per side, or until golden brown. Remove and place on a cooling rack (if you place them on a paper towel, they will get soggy).

4. Serve with hollandaise.

| NUTRITIONAL INFO (per serving) | | | | |
|---|---|---|---|---|
| calories | fat | protein | carbs | fiber |
| 436 | 46 g | 3 g | 2.3 g | 0.4 g |
| | 95% | 3% | 2% | |

# keto bagels

**KETO** **NUT FREE** **DAIRY FREE**

**PREP TIME:** 5 minutes

**COOK TIME:** 20 minutes

**YIELD:** 12 bagels (1 per serving)

½ cup vanilla egg white protein

2 tablespoons coconut flour

1 teaspoon baking powder

¼ teaspoon fine sea salt

½ teaspoon xanthan gum (see Note; optional)

¼ cup coconut oil, melted

10 large eggs

2 teaspoons blueberry extract or unsalted butter extract or a few drops of butter oil (optional)

| NUTRITIONAL INFO (per serving) | | | | |
|---|---|---|---|---|
| calories | fat | protein | carbs | fiber |
| 119 | 8.9 g | 7.8 g | 2 g | 1 g |
| | 67% | 26% | 7% | |

1. Preheat the oven to 325°F. Grease two 6-cavity donut pans.

2. In a medium-sized bowl, mix together the protein powder, coconut flour, baking powder, and salt. If you are using xanthan gum, combine it with the coconut oil in a separate bowl until smooth. Add the coconut oil, eggs, and extract, if using, to the bowl with the dry ingredients and mix to form a dough.

3. Spoon the dough into the prepared cavities of the donut pans. Bake for 20 minutes, or until light golden brown on the top. Store in an airtight container in the refrigerator for up to 1 week or in the freezer for up to 1 month.

**NOTE:** *The xanthan gum gives the bagels a nice chewy texture.*

# bagels and lox

**KETO** **NUT FREE**

**PREP TIME:** 5 minutes, plus 24 hours for the gravlax

**YIELD:** 1 serving

1 tablespoon cream cheese (about ½ ounce)

½ teaspoon finely chopped green onion

1 Keto Bagel (above), cut in half

¼ ounce Gravlax (page 236)

Pinch of finely chopped fresh dill

1 teaspoon capers

1 lemon wedge

In a small bowl, mix together the cream cheese and green onion. Smear the mixture on each half of the bagel. Top with the gravlax, dill, capers, and a squeeze of lemon.

| NUTRITIONAL INFO (per serving) | | | | |
|---|---|---|---|---|
| calories | fat | protein | carbs | fiber |
| 171 | 12.8 g | 9.3 g | 4.7 g | 1 g |
| | 67% | 22% | 11% | |

# breakfast sushi

**KETO** ■■□  **NUT FREE**

**PREP TIME:** 10 minutes

**COOK TIME:** 5 minutes

**YIELD:** 1 serving

Bacon fat, lard, or unsalted butter, for the pan

2 large eggs

¼ teaspoon fine sea salt

2 tablespoons shredded sharp cheddar cheese (about ½ ounce; substitute nutritional yeast if dairy-sensitive)

1 sheet nori

2 slices bacon, cooked until crisp

¼ avocado, sliced

½ yellow tomato, sliced

**FOR THE SPICY MAYO**

2 tablespoons Copycat Baconnaise (page 65) or mayonnaise

1½ teaspoons Sriracha or hot sauce of choice

*At a Japanese restaurant, my husband once overheard the sushi chef tell a waiter that he adds over 3 quarts of sugar to each batch of rice. That's 34 grams of added sugar per cup of rice! We never eat rice anyway because it has such a high glycemic index, but that sure is another reason not to eat restaurant-made sushi!*

1. Grease a medium-sized skillet with the bacon fat and heat over medium heat. In a small bowl, whisk together the eggs and salt. Pour into the hot skillet, then reduce the heat to low. Sprinkle with the cheese and cook without stirring for 3 to 5 minutes, until the eggs are cooked through.

2. Place the nori sheet on a piece of parchment paper. Place the eggs on the nori, cutting the egg to fit the nori sheet and leaving about ¼ inch of the nori exposed on all sides. Place the cooked bacon, avocado slices, and tomato slices along the edge of the nori that is closest to you. Roll up as tightly and gently as you can. Slice the roll into ½-inch-thick circles.

3. In a small bowl, mix the baconnaise and Sriracha. Drizzle over the breakfast sushi rolls or place in a small bowl for dipping, and serve.

| NUTRITIONAL INFO (per serving) | | | | |
|---|---|---|---|---|
| calories | fat | protein | carbs | fiber |
| 717 | 63 g | 28 g | 10.3 g | 5 g |
| | 79% | 16% | 6% | |

# creamy breakfast shake

KETO

**PREP TIME:** 4 minutes

**YIELD**: 2 servings

1 cup unsweetened vanilla almond milk

1 cup crushed ice

½ cup chopped avocado (about ½ avocado)

2 ounces cream cheese (about ¼ cup)

2 tablespoons powdered erythritol or 1 teaspoon stevia glycerite, or more to taste

1 tablespoon lemon juice

1 teaspoon strawberry extract or other flavored extract of choice

¼ teaspoon fine sea salt

## OPTIONAL HEALTHY ADDITIONS

1 tablespoon aloe vera

1 tablespoon l-glutamine powder

1 tablespoon grass-fed powdered gelatin

## SPECIAL EQUIPMENT

Blender

*I do not recommend drinking liquid calories for weight loss. Chewing releases hormones that signal satisfaction, making it much easier to feel full on solid food—even with the same number of calories that are in a shake. But since ketogenic eating is about more than weight loss, if you are looking for a tasty shake that is ketogenic, this is a great option. An equally tasty dairy-free version is the Dairy-Free Key Lime Shake on page 96.*

*You might think that avocado would be too earthy in a shake, but the lemon juice cuts its vegetal flavor, and using avocado adds creaminess along with healthy fats for a yummy, tart, and creamy breakfast.*

Place all of the ingredients in a blender and blend until very smooth. Enjoy!

| NUTRITIONAL INFO (per serving) | | | | |
|---|---|---|---|---|
| calories | fat | protein | carbs | fiber |
| 213 | 18.6 g | 6.4 g | 5.3 g | 3 g |
| | 79% | 12% | 10% | |

# dairy-free key lime shake

 **KETO** | **DAIRY FREE**

**PREP TIME:** 5 minutes, plus 15 minutes to chill

**COOK TIME:** 12 minutes

**YIELD:** 2 servings

½ cup powdered erythritol or 1 teaspoon stevia glycerite

1 tablespoon grated key lime zest (see Note)

¼ cup fresh key lime juice (see Note)

6 large egg yolks

1 teaspoon lime extract or a few drops of lime oil (optional)

¼ teaspoon fine sea salt

¼ cup coconut oil

1 cup unsweetened almond milk (optional, for single serving)

## OPTIONAL HEALTHY ADDITIONS

1 tablespoon aloe vera

1 tablespoon l-glutamine powder

1 tablespoon grass-fed powdered gelatin

## SPECIAL EQUIPMENT

Strainer

1. Combine the erythritol, lime zest, lime juice, egg yolks, lime extract, and salt in a medium-sized heavy saucepan and whisk to blend. Add the coconut oil and whisk constantly over medium heat until the mixture thickens and coats back of spoon thickly (do not boil), about 12 minutes.

2. Pour the mixture through a fine-mesh strainer into a medium-sized bowl. Place the bowl in a larger bowl filled with ice water and whisk occasionally until the curd is completely cool, about 15 minutes. It can be served now or stored in the fridge for up to 5 days.

*To make one serving:* Place half of the mixture in a blender and add 1 cup of almond milk. Blend until smooth. Store the other half of the mixture in the fridge until ready to consume.

NOTE: *If you can't find fresh key limes, you can use regular lime zest and juice instead.*

VARIATION: DAIRY-FREE KEY LIME ICE POPS. *To make ice pops, mix the egg and lime mixture with the almond milk. Pour into 12 ice pop molds and freeze until set, about 4 hours.*

| NUTRITIONAL INFO (per serving) | | | | |
|---|---|---|---|---|
| calories | fat | protein | carbs | fiber |
| 397 | 40.8 g | 8.1 g | 1.8 g | 0 g |
| | 92% | 8% | 2% | |

# ham-n-cheese mini quiches

**■■□ KETO**  **NUT FREE**

**PREP TIME:** 10 minutes

**COOK TIME:** 10 minutes

**YIELD**: 24 mini quiches (2 per serving)

24 large eggs

1 cup cubed ham

½ cup shredded Swiss cheese (about 2 ounces)

½ cup shredded sharp cheddar cheese (about 2 ounces)

¼ cup chopped fresh flat-leaf parsley

2 tablespoons chopped fresh chives

1 teaspoon fine sea salt

1 teaspoon fresh ground black pepper

6 yellow cherry tomatoes, quartered, for garnish (optional)

1. Preheat the oven to 325°F. Grease a 24-well mini-muffin pan.

2. In a large bowl, whisk the eggs with a fork until well combined. Add the ham, cheeses, parsley, chives, salt, and pepper.

3. Pour the egg mixture into the greased muffin cups, filling them about three-quarters full.

4. Bake for about 10 minutes, until the center is firm. If using cherry tomatoes, use a toothpick to secure a tomato quarter to the top of each quiche. Serve warm.

**BUSY FAMILY TIP:** *This is my favorite way to use up leftover holiday ham! And if I have any leftovers from this dish, I let them cool, wrap them tightly in parchment paper, and store them in the fridge for easy breakfasts on the go. They keep in the fridge for up to 1 week and can be frozen for up to 1 month. Reheat in a 325°F oven for 3 minutes or microwave on low for 30 seconds, or until the cheese starts to melt.*

| NUTRITIONAL INFO (per serving) | | | | |
| --- | --- | --- | --- | --- |
| calories | fat | protein | carbs | fiber |
| 253 | 16.1 g | 21.9 g | 4.8 g | 1.1 g |
|  | 57% | 35% | 8% | |

# avocado egg cups

KETO   NUT FREE   DAIRY FREE

**PREP TIME:** 5 minutes
**COOK TIME:** 20 minutes
**YIELD:** 2 servings

1 large Hass avocado, halved and pitted

2 large eggs

Fine sea salt and fresh ground black pepper

**OPTIONAL TOPPINGS**

¼ cup diced yellow tomato

1 tablespoon diced red onion

¼ cup Dairy-Free Nacho Cheese Sauce (page 64)

2 tablespoons chopped fresh cilantro or flat-leaf parsley, or your favorite herb

1.  Preheat the oven to 350°F.

2.  Put the avocado halves cut side up in a small baking dish or medium-sized cast-iron or other oven-safe skillet.

3.  Crack an egg into the center of each avocado half and sprinkle with salt and pepper. Place in the oven for 15 to 20 minutes, until the egg is cooked to your desired doneness. (In my oven, 17 minutes gets me perfect egg yolks, still runny but with solid whites.)

4.  Top with the desired toppings and enjoy while still hot!

**FUN FAMILY TIP:** *I wish I could have an avocado tree at my house, but living in Wisconsin, that isn't possible. Sprouting an avocado pit is as close as I am going to get. This is a great project to teach your children about germination. The process is really easy:*

*1. Fill a small jar with water.*

*2. Lick all the tasty goodness off the pit and clean it completely.*

*3. Insert 4 toothpicks into the pit.*

*4. Suspend the pit over the jar so it touches the water.*

*5. Place in a warm, sunny area and wait about 6 weeks for it to sprout.*

| NUTRITIONAL INFO (per serving) | | | | |
|---|---|---|---|---|
| calories | fat | protein | carbs | fiber |
| 490 | 45.8 g | 10.7 g | 11.6 g | 7.6 g |
| | 84% | 9% | 9% | |

# *strawberry popovers*

## WITH STRAWBERRY "BUTTER"

**KETO**  DAIRY FREE

**PREP TIME:** 10 minutes

**COOK TIME:** 27 minutes

**YIELD:** 12 popovers (2 per serving)

¼ cup vanilla egg white protein (or ½ cup vanilla whey protein if not dairy-sensitive)

1 teaspoon baking powder

¼ teaspoon baking soda

½ cup coconut oil, melted, divided, plus more for greasing the pan

2 cups unsweetened almond milk, warmed (see Notes)

4 large eggs

½ teaspoon fine sea salt

1 teaspoon strawberry extract (see Notes)

1 teaspoon stevia glycerite

**FOR THE STRAWBERRY "BUTTER"**

¼ cup coconut oil, melted

2 tablespoons powdered erythritol or 1 drop of stevia glycerite

1 teaspoon strawberry extract

1 drop of natural pink food coloring (optional)

Sprinkle of fine sea salt

*These popovers are best fresh out of the oven. If you are not planning to serve 12 popovers, I suggest that you bake just the amount you're planning to eat right away and save the remaining batter for later. Leftover batter will keep in an airtight container in the fridge for up to 5 days.*

1. Preheat the oven to 425°F.

2. Grease two 6-well popover pans or one 12-well muffin pan. Place the pan(s) in the hot oven for about 8 minutes.

3. Meanwhile, in a medium-sized bowl, blend together the protein powder, baking powder, and baking soda. Then add ¼ cup of the coconut oil, the warm almond milk, eggs, salt, strawberry extract, and stevia.

4. Carefully remove the hot pan from the oven. Drop 1 teaspoon of coconut oil into each hot well and then pour in the batter, filling each well two-thirds full. Bake for 15 minutes, then reduce the temperature to 325°F and bake for an additional 10 to 12 minutes, until golden brown and a touch crispy on the outside. Do not open the oven door until the popovers are fully baked.

5. Meanwhile, make the strawberry "butter" by mixing all of the ingredients for the butter in a medium-sized bowl until smooth and well combined.

6. Serve the popovers hot with the strawberry "butter."

**NOTES:** *It's very important to warm the almond milk. If it isn't warmed, it will solidify the melted coconut oil.*

*If strawberry isn't your thing, these popovers are equally delicious when made with other fruit-flavored extracts, such as raspberry or cherry.*

**VARIATION: SAVORY POPOVERS.** *To make savory popovers, replace the vanilla egg white protein with unflavored egg white protein and omit the strawberry extract and stevia.*

| NUTRITIONAL INFO (per serving) | | | | |
|---|---|---|---|---|
| calories | fat | protein | carbs | fiber |
| 308 | 30 g | 8.6 g | 1.7 g | 0 g |
| | 88% | 11% | 2% | |

# caramel apple dutch baby

KETO | DAIRY FREE

**PREP TIME:** 5 minutes

**COOK TIME:** 20 minutes

**YIELD:** 2 servings

2 tablespoons unsalted butter or coconut oil

**FOR THE BATTER**

3 large eggs

¾ cup unsweetened almond milk

¼ cup vanilla egg white protein or egg whites (or vanilla whey protein if not dairy-sensitive)

1 teaspoon baking powder

1 teaspoon stevia glycerite or ¼ cup powdered erythritol

2 teaspoons apple extract

¼ teaspoon fine sea salt

**FOR THE CARAMEL APPLE SAUCE (MAKES 1½ CUPS)**

½ cup (1 stick) unsalted butter or coconut oil

½ cup powdered erythritol

½ cup unsweetened almond milk

¼ teaspoon fine sea salt

1 teaspoon apple extract

**SPECIAL EQUIPMENT**

Blender

1. Preheat the oven to 400°F.

2. In a medium-sized cast-iron skillet, melt the 2 tablespoons of butter over medium heat and set aside.

3. In a blender, combine the eggs, almond milk, protein powder, baking powder, stevia, apple extract, and salt. Blend for about 1 minute, until foamy. Pour the batter into the skillet. Bake for about 18 to 20 minutes, until the pancake is puffed and golden brown.

4. Meanwhile, make the sauce: Before you begin, make sure you have everything ready to go—the milk and the butter next to the pan, ready to put in. You'll need to work fast or the erythritol will burn. Heat the butter on high heat in a heavy-bottomed 2- or 3-quart saucepan. As soon as it comes to a boil, watch for specks of brown. Immediately add the erythritol, almond milk, and sea salt to the pan. Whisk until the sauce is smooth and then stir in the apple extract.

5. Let cool in the pan for a couple minutes, then pour into a glass mason jar and let cool to room temperature.

6. Remove the pancake from the oven and cut into two portions. Serve each with 2 tablespoons of the sauce.

7. The remaining sauce will keep in the refrigerator for up to 2 weeks. To reheat, place in a saucepan and heat on low until ready to serve.

| NUTRITIONAL INFO (per serving) | | | | |
|---|---|---|---|---|
| calories | fat | protein | carbs | fiber |
| 698 | 67 g | 23 g | 3.5 g | 0.7 g |
| | 86% | 13% | 2% | |

# mock apple porridge

**KETO** · **NUT FREE** · **DAIRY FREE**

**PREP TIME:** 2 minutes

**COOK TIME:** 5 minutes

**YIELD:** 1 serving

2 large eggs

⅓ cup canned, full-fat coconut milk (or heavy cream if not dairy-sensitive)

2 tablespoons powdered erythritol

1 teaspoon apple extract

¼ teaspoon fine sea salt

2 tablespoons coconut oil (or unsalted butter if not dairy-sensitive)

Sprinkle of ground cinnamon

*Miss the taste of apple cinnamon oatmeal? You must try this creamy breakfast porridge. The flavors remind me of a lazy breakfast in the fall.*

*If you have a hard time getting your kids to eat eggs, this is a great way to work them into their diet, as one of my clients noted: "Our pediatrician has wanted my son to eat eggs for years, and this is the first recipe that has enabled that. He absolutely loved this porridge, as apple is one of his favorite flavors. He said that the taste was like apple pie in a hot cereal."*

1. In a small bowl, whisk together the eggs, cream, erythritol, apple extract, and salt.

2. In a medium-sized saucepan, melt the oil over medium heat. Add the egg mixture and cook, scraping the bottom with a wooden spoon, until the mixture thickens and starts curdling, about 4 minutes. Use a whisk to help separate the curds.

3. Once the curds form and the mixture has thickened, remove from the heat and transfer to a serving bowl. Sprinkle with cinnamon and serve.

| NUTRITIONAL INFO (per serving) | | | | |
|---|---|---|---|---|
| calories | fat | protein | carbs | fiber |
| 528 | 51.9 g | 13.4 g | 2.6 g | 0 g |
| | 88% | 10% | 2% | |

# keto soft-boiled eggs

KETO    NUT FREE

**PREP TIME:** 2 minutes

**COOK TIME:** 7 minutes

**YIELD:** 3 servings

6 large eggs

6 teaspoons unsalted butter (or bacon fat if dairy-sensitive)

½ teaspoon fine sea salt

1 teaspoon chopped fresh herbs, such as chives, for garnish

3 slices Keto Bread (page 276), fried in 2 tablespoons bacon fat and cut into triangles, for serving (optional)

1. Fill a medium-sized saucepan about halfway with water and bring it to a boil.

2. Decrease the temperature so that the water is at a rapid simmer, then gently lower the eggs into the water one at a time.

3. Cook the eggs for 5 to 7 minutes, depending on how runny you prefer the yolks: 5 minutes will give you runny yolks and 7 minutes will give you yolks that are just set.

4. Drain the eggs and rinse under cold water for 30 seconds.

5. Use a knife to take the cap off the tip of each egg and dot the warm yolk with 1 teaspoon of butter. Sprinkle with the salt and chopped herbs and enjoy straight from the shell, preferably with plenty of fried keto bread for dipping. Soft-boiled eggs should be made to order and eaten immediately.

| NUTRITIONAL INFO (per serving) | | | | |
|---|---|---|---|---|
| calories | fat | protein | carbs | fiber |
| 260 | 20.5 g | 17.9 g | 1.4 g | 0 g |
| | 71% | 28% | 2% | |

# breakfast lasagna

KETO

NUT
FREE

**PREP TIME:** 10 minutes

**COOK TIME:** 45 minutes

**YIELD:** 12 servings

## FOR THE EGGS

18 large eggs

Fine sea salt and fresh ground black pepper

## FOR THE GRAVY

1 pound pork sausage, removed from casing and crumbled

16 ounces cream cheese (about 2 cups)

1½ cups beef bone broth (page 42)

Fine sea salt and fresh ground black pepper

1 pound thin-shaved ham

1 cup shredded mozzarella cheese (about 4 ounces)

1 cup grated Parmesan cheese (about 4 ounces)

1. Preheat the oven to 325°F.

2. Grease a very large sauté pan and soft-scramble the eggs over medium-low heat. Season with salt and pepper to taste. Remove from the heat and set aside.

3. Make the gravy: Cook the sausage in large skillet over medium heat for 5 to 6 minutes, until thoroughly heated, stirring frequently. Gradually add the cream cheese and broth; cook until the mixture comes to a soft simmer and thickens, stirring constantly until smooth. Reduce the heat to medium-low and simmer for 2 minutes, stirring constantly. Season to taste with salt and pepper. Set aside.

4. In a 3-quart baking dish, assemble the lasagna: Start with a thin layer of gravy, followed by the first layer of "noodles" (thin-shaved ham), then a layer of soft-scrambled eggs, another layer of gravy, ¼ cup of the mozzarella, and ¼ cup of the Parmesan. Repeat the layers (gravy, "noodles," scrambled eggs, gravy, cheeses).

5. Top with a final layer of "noodles" and a little more cheese. Bake for 25 to 35 minutes, until the cheese is melted.

**BUSY FAMILY TIP:** *This lasagna can be assembled a day or two before baking and kept in the fridge for stress-free entertaining.*

| NUTRITIONAL INFO (per serving) | | | | |
|---|---|---|---|---|
| calories | fat | protein | carbs | fiber |
| 423 | 29.5 g | 34.5 g | 4.9 g | 0 g |
| | 63% | 33% | 5% | |

## TIPS FOR CREATING
# *the perfect omelet*

*The flavorings and fillings for omelets are endlessly variable, but the basic method is the same. The following are helpful tips for getting successful results every time, regardless of the fillings and flavorings you use.*

- Create an omelet station. Have everything ready, including a serving plate, next to the pan. The eggs can easily overcook while you're running to the fridge to get an onion or tomatoes.

- Crack the eggs into a bowl and whisk vigorously with a tablespoon of water. The water creates a creamy, fluffy omelet.

- Add enough butter or coconut oil to coat the pan to prevent sticking. Once the butter begins to foam, add the eggs to the pan. Stir continuously with a heat-proof spatula over low heat.

- Use medium heat, not high. Cook low and slow. Protein (including egg protein) shrinks and gets tough in high heat.

- When the omelet is lightly set, stop stirring. Knowing exactly when to stop stirring is the key to an evenly smooth omelet. If you are like me and prefer a runny omelet, stop stirring earlier.

- If you are adventurous, add chopped chicken livers to the omelet filling!

## HAM-N-"CHEESE" OMELET

**PREP TIME:** 3 minutes

**COOK TIME:** 2 minutes

**YIELD:** 1 serving

2 large eggs

1 tablespoon water

⅛ teaspoon fine sea salt

⅛ teaspoon fresh ground black pepper

1 tablespoon coconut oil or unsalted butter

1 ounce ham, chopped

1 ounce Dairy-Free Nacho Cheese Sauce (page 64)

1 or 2 slices Keto Bread (page 276), fried in 2 tablespoons bacon fat, for serving (optional)

1. Crack the eggs into a small bowl. Add the water, salt, and pepper and whisk with a fork.

2. Preheat an 8-inch skillet over medium-low heat. Melt the coconut oil in the pan, then pour in the egg mixture and swirl it in the pan. For a few seconds, gently stir the egg mixture with a spatula (as if you were going to make scrambled eggs), then swirl the eggs in the pan to make a nice round shape. Reduce the heat to avoid any color or burning.

3. Continue cooking for about 1 minute. The eggs will be set on the bottom but slightly liquid on top.

4. Remove the pan from the heat. Add the ham and "cheese" sauce to the center of the omelet. Fold the omelet and plate it immediately. Alternatively, you can fill the omelet with ham only and serve the cheese sauce on the side for dipping.

5. Serve with fried keto bread, if desired.

| NUTRITIONAL INFO (per serving) | | | | |
|---|---|---|---|---|
| calories | fat | protein | carbs | fiber |
| 552 | 48 g | 25 g | 4.9 g | 0.7 g |
| | 78% | 18% | 4% | |

# SALMON AND CHIVE OMELET

**KETO** ■■■   NUT FREE   DAIRY FREE

**PREP TIME:** 5 minutes, plus 24 hours for the gravlax

**COOK TIME:** 2 minutes

**YIELD:** 1 serving

1 ounce Gravlax (page 236), chopped

2 teaspoons thinly sliced fresh chives

1 teaspoon finely chopped fresh dill

2 large eggs

1 tablespoon water

⅛ teaspoon fine sea salt

⅛ teaspoon fresh ground black pepper

1 tablespoon coconut oil or unsalted butter

1 or 2 slices Keto Bread (page 276), fried in 2 tablespoons bacon fat, for serving (optional)

1. In a small bowl, combine the gravlax, chives, and dill and set aside.

2. Crack the eggs into another small bowl. Add the water, salt, and pepper and whisk with a fork.

3. Preheat an 8-inch skillet over medium-low heat. Melt the coconut oil in the pan, then pour in the egg mixture and swirl it in the pan. For a few seconds, gently stir the egg mixture with a spatula (as if you were going to make scrambled eggs), then swirl the eggs in the pan to make a nice round shape. Reduce the heat to avoid any color or burning.

4. Continue cooking for about 1 minute. The eggs will be set on the bottom but slightly liquid on top.

5. Remove the pan from the heat. Add the gravlax and herb mixture to the center of the omelet. Fold the omelet and plate it immediately. Serve with fried keto bread, if desired.

| NUTRITIONAL INFO (per serving) | | | | |
|---|---|---|---|---|
| calories | fat | protein | carbs | fiber |
| 357 | 27.6 g | 26.1 g | 2 g | 0 g |
| | 70% | 29% | 2% | |

# HERB GOAT CHEESE OMELET

■■■ KETO   NUT FREE

**PREP TIME:** 5 minutes

**COOK TIME:** 2 minutes

**YIELD:** 1 serving

---

1 ounce goat cheese (about 1 tablespoon)

1 tablespoon thinly sliced fresh chives

1½ teaspoons finely chopped fresh flat-leaf parsley

½ teaspoon thinly sliced fresh tarragon

2 large eggs

1 tablespoon water

⅛ teaspoon fine sea salt

⅛ teaspoon fresh ground black pepper

1 tablespoon coconut oil or unsalted butter

1 or 2 slices Keto Bread (page 276), fried in 2 tablespoons bacon fat, for serving (optional)

1. In a small bowl, combine the goat cheese, chives, parsley, and tarragon.

2. Crack the eggs into another small bowl. Add the water, salt, and pepper and whisk with a fork.

3. Preheat an 8-inch skillet over medium-low heat. Melt the coconut oil in the pan, then pour in the egg mixture and swirl it in the pan. For a few seconds, gently stir the egg mixture with a spatula (as if you were going to make scrambled eggs), then swirl the eggs in the pan to make a nice round shape. Reduce the heat to avoid any color or burning.

4. Continue cooking for about 1 minute. The eggs will be set on the bottom but slightly liquid on top.

5. Remove the pan from the heat. Crumble the herb goat cheese over the center of the omelet. Fold the omelet and plate it immediately. Serve with fried keto bread, if desired.

| NUTRITIONAL INFO (per serving) | | | | |
|---|---|---|---|---|
| calories | fat | protein | carbs | fiber |
| 445 | 35.9 g | 28.8 g | 2.2 g | 0 g |
| | 73% | 26% | 2% | |

# MUSHROOM AND ONION OMELET

**■■■ NUT DAIRY**
**KETO FREE FREE**

**PREP TIME:** 5 minutes

**COOK TIME:** 10 minutes

**YIELD:** 1 serving

¼ cup sliced button or cremini mushrooms

2 tablespoons very thinly sliced yellow onion

2 tablespoons coconut oil or unsalted butter, divided

¼ teaspoon plus ⅛ teaspoon fine sea salt

2 large eggs

1 tablespoon water

⅛ teaspoon fresh ground black pepper

1 or 2 slices Keto Bread (page 276), fried in 2 tablespoons bacon fat, for serving (optional)

1. Place the mushrooms, onion, and 1 tablespoon of the coconut oil in a medium-sized sauté pan and fry until the mushrooms are golden brown and the onion is translucent, about 8 minutes. Make sure not to crowd the mushrooms or they won't brown. Add ⅛ teaspoon of the salt. Remove from the heat and set aside.

2. Crack the eggs into a small bowl. Add the water, remaining ¼ teaspoon of salt, and the pepper and whisk with a fork.

3. Preheat an 8-inch skillet over medium-low heat. Melt the remaining tablespoon of coconut oil in the pan, then pour in the egg mixture and swirl it in the pan. For a few seconds, gently stir the egg mixture with a spatula (as if you were going to make scrambled eggs), then swirl the eggs in the pan to make a nice round shape. Reduce the heat to avoid any color or burning.

4. Continue cooking for about 1 minute. The eggs will be set on the bottom but slightly liquid on top.

5. Remove the pan from the heat. Add the mushroom and onion mixture to the center of the omelet. Fold the omelet and plate it immediately. Serve with fried keto bread, if desired.

| NUTRITIONAL INFO (per serving) | | | | |
| --- | --- | --- | --- | --- |
| calories | fat | protein | carbs | fiber |
| 455 | 38.8 g | 24 g | 3.9 g | 0.6 g |
| | 77% | 21% | 3% | |

# MAPLE BACON
## *breakfast patties*

**KETO**   NUT FREE   DAIRY FREE

**PREP TIME:** 10 minutes, plus 30 minutes to freeze the pork and 3 hours to chill the sausages

**COOK TIME:** 10 minutes

**YIELD**: 24 (2-inch) patties (2 per serving)

2¼ pounds boneless pork shoulder, cut into 1-inch cubes

½ pound bacon, diced

⅓ cup pork or beef bone broth (page 42)

2¼ teaspoons finely chopped fresh flat-leaf parsley

2¼ teaspoons finely chopped fresh sage

2 teaspoons finely chopped fresh thyme

1½ teaspoons fine sea salt 1 teaspoon red pepper flakes

1 teaspoon maple extract

½ teaspoon ground nutmeg

½ teaspoon finely grated fresh ginger

½ teaspoon fresh ground black pepper

¼ teaspoon stevia glycerite

1 tablespoon lard or coconut oil, for frying

*Making homemade sausage may seem daunting, but it is a great way to control what goes into your food and is definitely worth your time. Just taking a look at the list of additives included in store-bought products will tell you why it's worthwhile.*

*If you do not have a meat grinder or grinder attachment for your stand mixer, you can purchase ground pork or ask your butcher to grind it for you.*

1. Line a rimmed baking sheet with parchment paper. Spread the pork cubes out on the lined baking sheet and freeze for 30 minutes.

2. Remove the pork from the freezer and, using the coarse disk that came with your meat grinder, grind the pork into a large bowl. Add the rest of the ingredients and mix together with your hands until the seasonings are distributed throughout the meat. To check the seasoning, fry up a small dab of the mixture in a skillet over medium heat; taste it and add more seasoning if desired.

3. Form the sausage mixture into twenty-four 2-inch patties.

4. Refrigerate the sausages for a few hours to allow the flavors to meld. Cook within 3 days.

5. To cook, add 1 tablespoon of lard to a large sauté pan over medium heat. Sauté the patties until their internal temperature reaches 160°F, about 10 minutes.

**BUSY FAMILY TIP:** *Make a double batch and freeze for easy meals.*

| NUTRITIONAL INFO (per serving) | | | | |
|---|---|---|---|---|
| calories | fat | protein | carbs | fiber |
| 334 | 27 g | 21.4 g | 0.7 g | 0 g |
| | 73% | 26% | 1% | |

# chai muffins

 **KETO** NUT FREE DAIRY FREE

**PREP TIME:** 15 minutes

**COOK TIME:** 20 minutes

**YIELD:** 12 muffins (1 per serving)

## FOR THE BATTER

½ cup coconut flour

½ cup powdered erythritol

¼ teaspoon fine sea salt

¼ teaspoon baking soda

5 large eggs

1 teaspoon stevia glycerite

1 vanilla bean (about 6 inches long), split lengthwise and seeds scraped, or 1 teaspoon vanilla extract

¾ cup strong chai tea

½ cup coconut oil (or unsalted butter if not dairy-sensitive), melted

## FOR THE STREUSEL TOPPING (OPTIONAL)

½ cup Chai "Sugar" (page 348)

2 tablespoons coconut oil (or unsalted butter if not dairy-sensitive), softened

## FOR THE CHAI GLAZE (OPTIONAL)

½ cup coconut oil, softened

⅓ cup strong chai tea, cooled

¼ cup powdered erythritol

1 vanilla bean (about 6 inches long), split lengthwise and seeds scraped, or 1 teaspoon vanilla extract

⅛ teaspoon fine sea salt

1. Preheat the oven to 350°F. Grease a standard, 12-well muffin pan and line with muffin cup liners.

2. In a medium-sized bowl, mix together the coconut flour, erythritol, salt, and baking soda. In a separate medium-sized bowl, mix together the eggs, stevia, vanilla, chai tea, and coconut oil. Slowly add the wet ingredients to the dry ingredients and stir until very smooth. Fill the wells of the prepared muffin pan about two-thirds full with batter.

3. If making the streusel topping, combine the chai "sugar" and softened coconut oil with a fork until small crumbs form. Top the batter in each muffin well with 1 rounded tablespoon of the streusel mixture.

4. Bake for 18 to 20 minutes, until a toothpick inserted in the middle of a muffin comes out clean. Remove from the oven and allow to cool before removing the muffins from the pan.

5. If glazing the muffins, place all of the ingredients for the glaze in a blender and process until smooth. Drizzle on top of the muffins.

6. Store the muffins in an airtight container in the fridge for up to 1 week or in the freezer for up to 1 month.

**TIP:** *Ketosis isn't all about weight loss, but if you are using ketosis as a weight-loss tool, I recommend avoiding coconut flour–based baked goods like these muffins.*

| NUTRITIONAL INFO (per serving) | | | | |
|---|---|---|---|---|
| calories | fat | protein | carbs | fiber |
| 218 | 21.6 g | 3.7 g | 3.2 g | 2.1 g |
| | 89% | 7% | 6% | |

# huevos rancheros

KETO NUT FREE

**PREP TIME:** 10 minutes

**COOK TIME:** 18 minutes

**YIELD:** 4 servings

## TOPPING IDEAS

4 slices bacon, cooked and crumbled

½ cup salsa

1 avocado, peeled, pitted, and diced

1 green onion, sliced

½ bell pepper, seeded and diced

1 chili pepper, thinly sliced

3 to 4 tablespoons chopped fresh cilantro

4 large eggs, fried

## FOR THE TORTILLAS

3 large eggs, separated

2 tablespoons unflavored egg white protein (or unflavored whey protein if not dairy-sensitive)

1 teaspoon onion powder

1 teaspoon Taco Seasoning (page 74), optional

1 ounce cream cheese (about 2 tablespoons), very soft (or reserved egg yolks if dairy-sensitive)

2 tablespoons coconut oil, lard, ghee, or unsalted butter, plus more if needed, for frying

¼ pound grass-fed ground beef, browned, or ½ cup of your favorite chili

1. Prepare the toppings of your choice (except the fried eggs, which should be cooked at the last minute).

2. Make the tortillas: Make sure there are no spots of yolk in the egg whites and place the whites in a clean, dry, nonreactive metal bowl and whip with a hand mixer or stand mixer until very stiff. Slowly add the egg white protein, onion powder, and taco seasoning. Then gently stir in the cream cheese.

3. Heat the coconut oil in a small skillet over medium-high heat. Scoop ¼ cup of the tortilla dough into the skillet and flatten with a spoon to form a 5-inch circle that is about ¼ inch thick. Fry the tortillas one at a time until firm and golden brown on both sides, about 2 minutes per side. Remove to paper towels to drain the excess oil. Place on a serving platter and cover to keep warm until ready to serve. Add more oil to the pan between tortillas if needed.

4. When the tortillas are done, fry the eggs, if using, over easy in the skillet in 2 tablespoons of heated oil.

5. Place the tortillas on plates and spread a layer of meat on them. Top each with an egg, if using, and the additional toppings of your choice. My favorite combination is chili, a fried egg, crumbled bacon, avocado, and salsa.

6. Store leftover tortillas in an airtight container in the fridge for up to 1 week or in the freezer for up to 1 month. To reheat, heat a skillet over medium-high heat and warm each side for about 30 seconds.

| NUTRITIONAL INFO (per serving) | | | | |
|---|---|---|---|---|
| calories | fat | protein | carbs | fiber |
| 524 | 39 g | 35 g | 9.5 g | 4.4 g |
| | 67% | 27% | 7% | |

# french toast custard

**KETO** **NUT FREE** **DAIRY FREE**

**PREP TIME:** 5 minutes, plus 1 hour to chill

**COOK TIME:** 5 minutes

**YIELD:** 4 servings

2 cups canned, full-fat coconut milk, divided

1 tablespoon grass-fed powdered gelatin

3 large egg yolks

1 teaspoon stevia glycerite

2 teaspoons ghee (optional)

1 teaspoon ground cinnamon

1 vanilla bean (about 6 inches long), split lengthwise and seeds scraped, or 1 teaspoon vanilla extract

1 teaspoon maple extract

¼ teaspoon fine sea salt

1 slice bacon, cooked and cut into 1-inch pieces

1. Pour ¼ cup of the coconut milk into a small bowl. Sprinkle the gelatin on top and let it sit while you prepare the rest of the ingredients.

2. In a medium-sized saucepan, whisk the remaining 1¾ cups of coconut milk with the egg yolks, stevia, ghee, if using, and cinnamon until well combined. Warm the mixture over medium-low heat for about 5 minutes, but don't let it boil or the yolks will scramble.

3. Remove the egg mixture from the heat and whisk in the gelatin mixture, then add the vanilla, maple extract, and salt.

4. Pour the custard into 4 small serving cups. Place in the refrigerator for 1 hour, or until the custard is set.

5. To serve, garnish with a small piece of bacon. This custard is best at room temperature but can be served cold.

| NUTRITIONAL INFO (per serving) | | | | |
|---|---|---|---|---|
| calories | fat | protein | carbs | fiber |
| 332 | 31 g | 6.9 g | 5.2 g | 0 g |
| | 84% | 8% | 6% | |

appetizers

# herb salmon dip

**KETO** | **NUT FREE**

**PREP TIME:** 5 minutes, plus 1 hour to chill

**YIELD:** 8 servings

6 ounces cream cheese (about ¾ cup), softened

3 tablespoons mayonnaise

1 tablespoon lime juice

½ teaspoon fine sea salt

2 teaspoons chopped fresh dill

⅛ teaspoon fresh ground black pepper

1 recipe homemade canned salmon (page 248) or 1 (7½-ounce) can salmon, drained

2 green onions, thinly sliced

*My mom always serves this at family gatherings, and it is one of my favorite dips. I love it with celery, pickles, fried Keto Bread (page 276), or slices of Caramel Apple Dutch Baby (page 104).*

1. In a medium-sized bowl, combine the cream cheese, mayonnaise, lime juice, salt, dill, and pepper; mix until well combined and smooth. Gently stir in the salmon and green onions.

2. Cover and refrigerate for at least 1 hour. Store in an airtight container in the fridge for up to 5 days.

| NUTRITIONAL INFO (per serving) | | | | |
|---|---|---|---|---|
| calories | fat | protein | carbs | fiber |
| 145 | 12.8 g | 6.9 g | 1 g | 0 g |
| | 79% | 19% | 3% | |

# antipasti platter

**PREP TIME:** 2 minutes

**YIELD:** 6 servings

12 ounces fresh mozzarella cheese, sliced into rounds

2 tablespoons high-quality extra-virgin olive oil or MCT oil

2 tablespoons chopped fresh basil and/ or oregano

Fine sea salt and fresh ground black pepper

24 pitted olives of choice

4 ounces salami, thinly sliced

Arrange the cheese slices on a platter or large cutting board. Drizzle them with the olive oil and sprinkle on the fresh herbs and a pinch of salt and pepper. Add the olives and meats to the platter and serve.

| NUTRITIONAL INFO (per serving) | | | | |
|---|---|---|---|---|
| calories | fat | protein | carbs | fiber |
| 289 | 21.9 g | 18.8 g | 4.1 g | 0.9 g |
| | 68% | 26% | 6% | |

# beef carpaccio

**KETO** **NUT FREE**

**PREP TIME:** 10 minutes, plus 2 hours to chill the tenderloin

**YIELD:** 4 servings

8 ounces beef tenderloin or thinly sliced bresaola (see Note)

4 tablespoons Fat-Burning Salad Dressing (page 57), divided

2 cups arugula

½ cup diced yellow tomatoes

¼ cup capers

2 ounces Parmesan cheese, freshly shaved (about ½ cup)

½ teaspoon fine sea salt

½ teaspoon fresh ground black pepper

1. If using tenderloin: Wrap the tenderloin in parchment paper and place in the freezer for 2 hours. Once semifrozen, unwrap and slice the beef into thin, ⅛-inch pieces. Place the slices on a sheet of parchment paper. Top with another piece of parchment and lightly pound the meat with a meat mallet until paper thin. Repeat until all of the slices of beef are pounded thin.

2. Arrange the slices of tenderloin or bresaola on a serving platter, overlapping slightly. Drizzle all but 1½ teaspoons of the salad dressing over the meat.

3. Toss the arugula, tomatoes, and capers with the remaining salad dressing and arrange on top of the meat. Sprinkle with the Parmesan, salt, and pepper.

**BUSY FAMILY TIP:** *You can save time by asking your butcher to pound the meat for you.*

**NOTE:** *If you don't want to use raw beef for this recipe, use bresaola, which is a cured red meat.*

| NUTRITIONAL INFO (per serving) | | | | |
|---|---|---|---|---|
| calories | fat | protein | carbs | fiber |
| 256 | 17.8 g | 21.7 g | 1.9 g | 0.6 g |
| | 63% | 34% | 3% | |

# curry chicken stuffed endive

 **KETO**  **NUT FREE**  **DAIRY FREE**

**PREP TIME:** 15 minutes, plus 3 hours to chill

**COOK TIME:** 1 hour 45 minutes

**YIELD:** 12 servings

3 tablespoons MCT oil, bacon fat, or lard

2 pounds chicken leg quarters

2 teaspoons fine sea salt, divided

1 teaspoon fresh ground black pepper

¼ cup diced yellow onion

1 head roasted garlic (see page 46)

2 cups chicken bone broth (page 42)

1 cup diced celery

¼ cup chopped green onions, white and green parts

1½ cups mayonnaise

¼ cup chopped dill pickles

3 tablespoons curry powder

3 heads white and/or red endive, leaves removed and cleaned

Sliced or diced red onion, for garnish (optional)

**SPECIAL EQUIPMENT**

Food processor

1. Heat the MCT oil in a deep sauté pan over medium-high heat. Season the chicken with 1 teaspoon of the salt and the pepper. Place the chicken in the hot oil and sauté for about 8 minutes, or until golden brown on all sides.

2. Add the diced onion to the pot and squeeze the roasted garlic from the head into the pot. Cook on medium heat for about 8 minutes, stirring occasionally, until the onion is golden brown.

3. Add the broth, reduce the heat, and simmer, covered, for about 1½ hours, until chicken is almost falling off the bone. Remove the chicken from the pan and let it cool slightly so that you can handle it.

4. Remove the meat from the bones and dice it into small pieces, saving the bones and liquid for making bone broth. Place the chicken pieces, celery, and green onions in a mixing bowl.

5. In the bowl of a food processor, combine the mayonnaise, dill pickles, curry powder, and remaining 1 teaspoon of salt. Process until smooth.

6. Pour the dressing over the chicken and vegetables and toss to evenly coat. Refrigerate for a few hours to allow the flavors to meld.

7. Serve at room temperature in endive leaves, about 2 tablespoons per leaf. Garnish with red onion if desired.

| NUTRITIONAL INFO (per serving) | | | | |
|---|---|---|---|---|
| calories | fat | protein | carbs | fiber |
| 378 | 32.8 g | 15.3 g | 7.2 g | 4.9 g |
| | 78% | 16% | 8% | |

# grilled halloumi
## WITH PROSCIUTTO AND PESTO

**KETO** **NUT FREE**

**PREP TIME:** 5 minutes

**COOK TIME:** 12 minutes

**YIELD:** 6 servings

½ pound Halloumi cheese, cut into ¼-inch-thick slices

1 tablespoon MCT oil or melted unsalted butter

6 slices prosciutto

¼ cup pesto (see page 272)

½ cup chopped yellow tomato

Fresh marjoram or basil leaves, for garnish (optional)

*Halloumi is a slightly rubbery and firm cheese that is delicious but on the salty side. The texture reminds me of a thick feta, but it has a different flavor profile. Halloumi has one unique quality: you can grill or fry it! When heated, Halloumi gets creamy and its saltiness subsides, making it into a robust, savory morsel.*

1. Preheat a grill or panini maker to medium-high heat.

2. Brush each side of the cheese slices with MCT oil or melted butter. Place onto the hot grill or panini maker for 3 minutes on each side, or until golden brown with grill marks. Meanwhile, place the prosciutto onto a serving platter, leaving a little space between each slice.

3. Remove the cheese slices from the grill and divide equally among the prosciutto. Sprinkle evenly with the pesto and yellow tomato. Sprinkle a few fresh marjoram or basil leaves around the platter, if desired. Serve warm.

| NUTRITIONAL INFO (per serving) | | | | |
|---|---|---|---|---|
| calories | fat | protein | carbs | fiber |
| 185 | 15 g | 11.3 g | 1.3 g | 0 g |
| | 73% | 24% | 3% | |

# PAN-FRIED PROSCIUTTO-WRAPPED
## *string cheese*

**KETO** — **NUT FREE**

**PREP TIME:** 10 minutes

**COOK TIME:** 4 minutes

**YIELD:** 8 pieces (2 per serving)

2 tablespoons MCT oil

2 tablespoons unsalted butter

8 pieces string cheese, frozen

8 very thin slices prosciutto

Chopped fresh herbs, such as sage, tarragon, or thyme (optional)

Marinara sauce, homemade (page 60) or store-bought, for dipping (optional)

1. Heat the MCT oil and butter in a sauté pan over medium-high heat. Unwrap the cheese.

2. Wrap one piece of prosciutto around each piece of string cheese, making sure to cover all the cheese and the ends. The prosciutto will stick to the cheese. If desired, roll the prosciutto-covered cheese in chopped herbs for a crispy herb crust.

3. Place each frozen, prosciutto-wrapped cheese stick into the hot oil and fry, turning frequently, until the outsides become slightly crisp and the cheese becomes gooey. This will take only a few minutes.

4. Remove to a platter, let cool slightly, and enjoy with marinara sauce!

| NUTRITIONAL INFO (per serving) | | | | |
|---|---|---|---|---|
| calories | fat | protein | carbs | fiber |
| 334 | 28.4 g | 17.3 g | 2 g | 0 g |
| | 76% | 21% | 3% | |

# celery boats

**PREP TIME:** 15 minutes

**COOK TIME:** 12 minutes

**YIELD:** 8 servings (2 boats per serving)

4 large eggs

¼ cup mayonnaise or Copycat Baconnaise (page 65)

1 tablespoon Dijon mustard (page 49)

1½ teaspoons chopped fresh dill or your favorite herb

1 teaspoon paprika

Fine sea salt and fresh ground black pepper to taste

8 large stalks celery

16 pitted black olives

Fresh dill, for garnish

*I garnished this dish with hibiscus sea salt, which is typically used in Spanish cooking and adds a pretty purple color. But if you can't find hibiscus salt, you can also season it with regular sea salt.*

1. Place the eggs in a saucepan and cover with cold water. Bring the water to a boil, cover, and remove from the heat. Let the eggs stand in the hot water for 10 to 12 minutes. Remove the eggs from the hot water, place in a bowl of ice water to cool, and peel. Slice the eggs into ¼-inch rounds.

2. Pop the yolks of 16 of the slices and reserve the whites to make sails. In a large bowl, combine the rest of the egg slices and yolks, mayonnaise, mustard, dill, paprika, and salt and pepper. Mash well with a fork or wooden spoon.

3. With a vegetable peeler, cut a thin slice down the length of the rounded side of each celery rib so that the celery ribs can lie open side up without rocking. Cut the celery ribs into sixteen 3-inch-long pieces and fill with the egg salad.

4. Place an olive inside each reserved slice of egg white. Place a toothpick through the one side of the egg white, the olive, and the other side of the egg white, so it holds its shape.

5. Stick the toothpick with the egg white sail into the edge of a celery boat. Garnish with sea salt and dill.

| NUTRITIONAL INFO (per serving) | | | | |
|---|---|---|---|---|
| calories | fat | protein | carbs | fiber |
| 192 | 17.2 g | 7 g | 3.2 g | 1.5 g |
|  | 81% | 15% | 7% |  |

# ham salad

**KETO**  **NUT FREE**  **DAIRY FREE**

**PREP TIME:** 15 minutes

**COOK TIME:** 12 minutes

**YIELD:** 12 servings

2 large eggs

3 cups ground fully cooked ham

2 tablespoons finely chopped celery

1 tablespoon plus 1 teaspoon finely diced dill pickles, plus more for garnish (optional)

2 teaspoons diced green onions

1 cup mayonnaise

1 tablespoon preferred homemade mustard (pages 48 to 50)

⅓ small cucumber (about 1½ inches), for serving

1 tablespoon diced red onion, for garnish (optional)

1. Place the eggs in a saucepan and cover with cold water. Bring the water to a boil, cover, and remove from the heat. Let the eggs stand in the hot water for 10 to 12 minutes. Remove the eggs from the hot water and place in a bowl of ice water to cool. Peel and chop the eggs.

2. In a large bowl, combine the chopped eggs, ham, celery, pickles, and green onions. Combine the mayonnaise and mustard in a separate bowl, then pour over the ham mixture. Stir to coat. Refrigerate until serving time.

3. To serve, cut the cucumber piece into ⅛-inch slices. Place 1½ tablespoons of the ham salad on each cucumber slice. Garnish with diced pickles and red onion, if desired.

| NUTRITIONAL INFO (per serving) | | | | |
|---|---|---|---|---|
| calories | fat | protein | carbs | fiber |
| 189 | 17.1 g | 6.7 g | 1.8 g | 0.5 g |
| | 81% | 14% | 4% | |

# *mini frico cups*

**KETO** ■■□  **NUT FREE**

**PREP TIME:** 15 minutes

**COOK TIME:** 10 minutes

**YIELD:** 12 frico cups (1 per serving)

2 cups grated Parmesan cheese (about 8 ounces)

### FOR THE FILLING

1 cup chopped arugula

4 slices bacon, cooked and crumbled into tiny pieces

1 cup quartered yellow tomatoes

2 tablespoons mayonnaise

¼ cup roughly chopped fresh flat-leaf parsley

2 ounces blue cheese, crumbled (about ½ cup), for garnish

*Frico is an Italian dish that basically consists of crispy fried cheese. What's not to love about that? Preparing these appetizers may seem daunting at first, but once you get the hang of it, they are very simple to prepare. Make sure you have the filling ready to go just before serving; if you fill the frico cups too early before serving, they can get a bit soft and lose their crispiness.*

1. Preheat the oven to 375°F. Line a rimmed baking sheet with parchment paper.

2. Drop 1 large tablespoon of the Parmesan cheese into a 2½-inch jar cover or cookie cutter and use your fingers to spread the cheese to fill the cover, forming a circle. Then flip the cheese out onto the prepared baking sheet. Repeat until you have 6 circles of cheese, keeping them about 2 inches apart on the baking sheet.

3. Bake the cheese rounds for 5 minutes, or until lightly browned and bubbly. Once you remove them from the oven, they start to harden, so you must work fast. Use a spatula or knife to transfer the rounds to a mini-muffin pan and gently press to form a cup. If the rounds become too cool and brittle to mold, place them back in the hot oven for 30 seconds so they become flexible again.

4. Let the cheese cups cool in the mini-muffin pan for 5 minutes and remove. Repeat the entire process with the rest of the cheese, for a total of 12 cheese cups.

5. Place the arugula, bacon, yellow tomatoes, and mayo in a small bowl and stir well to combine. Fill each frico cup with 2 tablespoons of the arugula mixture. Garnish with the parsley and blue cheese and serve.

| NUTRITIONAL INFO (per serving) | | | | |
|---|---|---|---|---|
| calories | fat | protein | carbs | fiber |
| 131 | 10.1 g | 9.1 g | 1.4 g | 0 g |
| | 69% | 28% | 4% | |

# blt bites

**KETO** **NUT FREE** **DAIRY FREE**

**PREP TIME:** 10 minutes

**COOK TIME:** 30 minutes

**YIELD:** 16 bites (2 per serving)

2 tablespoons coconut oil, for greasing the pan

12 slices bacon

1 cup arugula

6 tablespoons homemade ranch dressing, regular or dairy-free (pages 54 to 55), or mayonnaise, plus more for garnish (optional)

¼ cup chopped cherry tomatoes

2 tablespoons chopped chives

1. Preheat the oven to 375°F. Turn a mini-muffin pan upside down and place on a rimmed baking sheet (to catch the grease). Grease the bottom part of the upside-down muffin pan, which is facing up.

2. Cut 8 bacon slices in half crosswise, creating 16 half-sections. Cut the other 4 slices crosswise into 4 even sections each, creating 16 smaller quarter-sections. To make 1 bacon cup, you will need 1 quarter-section of bacon and 1 half-section of bacon.

3. Place one of the quarter-section pieces of bacon on top of an upside-down muffin cup. Take one of longer slices and wrap it around the sides of the muffin cup, with as much overlap as possible between the 2 pieces because the bacon will shrink. Secure the ends with a toothpick. Repeat until you have 16 bacon cups secured.

4. Bake for 27 to 30 minutes, or until browned but not overly crisp (if they're too crisp, they will be impossible to remove from the muffin pan). Remove from the oven and allow to cool for a few minutes, then gently remove from the muffin pan. Let cool completely.

5. Meanwhile, chop the arugula and stir in the ranch dressing. Once cool, fill each cup with the dressed arugula, a few pieces of chopped cherry tomatoes, and a sprinkle of chives. If desired, drizzle extra dressing on top.

| NUTRITIONAL INFO (per serving) | | | | |
|---|---|---|---|---|
| calories | fat | protein | carbs | fiber |
| 274 | 25 g | 10 g | 3 g | 0 g |
| | 82% | 14% | 4% | |

# nirvana meatballs

**KETO** **NUT FREE**

**PREP TIME:** 8 minutes

**COOK TIME:** 15 minutes

**YIELD:** 8 servings

½ pound ground pork

½ pound ground chicken (preferably dark meat)

2 ounces cream cheese (about ¼ cup), softened

2 large eggs

2 tablespoons finely chopped celery

1 to 3 tablespoons crumbled blue cheese (¼ to ¾ ounce), according to taste

1 teaspoon fine sea salt

½ teaspoon fresh ground black pepper

## FOR THE SAUCE

½ cup melted unsalted butter or coconut oil

½ cup hot sauce of choice, such as Buffalo wing sauce

## FOR SERVING

½ cup homemade ranch dressing, regular or dairy-free (pages 54 to 55)

Celery sticks

Blue cheese chunks

1. Preheat the oven to 350°F. Line a rimmed baking sheet with parchment paper.

2. In a medium-sized bowl, combine the ground pork, ground chicken, cream cheese, eggs, celery, blue cheese, salt, and pepper. The mixture will be sticky. Form into 1-inch balls.

3. Place the meatballs on the prepared baking sheet and bake for 15 minutes. Once the meatballs are done, remove from the oven and place in a serving bowl.

4. Combine the butter and hot sauce in a small bowl. Pour the sauce over the meatballs and stir gently to coat.

5. Serve with the ranch dressing, celery sticks, and blue cheese.

TIP: *Before forming the mixture into balls, test the seasoning by making a small patty and cooking it. The mixture should taste amazing! If it doesn't, it likely needs more salt.*

| NUTRITIONAL INFO (per serving) | | | | |
|---|---|---|---|---|
| calories | fat | protein | carbs | fiber |
| 282 | 22.3 g | 19.2 g | 1 g | 0 g |
| | 71% | 27% | 1% | |

# easy greek meze

KETO    NUT FREE

**PREP TIME:** 8 minutes

**YIELD:** 16 meze bites (2 per person)

1 (6-inch) cucumber, cut into 16 ¼-inch-thick slices

¼ teaspoon fine sea salt

¼ teaspoon fresh ground black pepper

4 slices salami, quartered

4 ounces feta cheese, cut into 16 small cubes

8 grape or cherry tomatoes, halved

16 pitted Kalamata olives

2 tablespoons Greek Salad Dressing (page 58)

1. Set the cucumber slices on a large serving platter and season with the salt and pepper. Place a salami quarter on top of the cucumber, then top with a small cube of feta, a tomato half, and an olive. Insert a toothpick through the stack to secure.

2. Drizzle with the dressing and serve.

| NUTRITIONAL INFO (per serving) | | | | |
|---|---|---|---|---|
| calories | fat | protein | carbs | fiber |
| 120 | 8.3 g | 4.9 g | 7.1 g | 1.6 g |
| | 62% | 16% | 23% | |

# spring rolls

 KETO   NUT FREE   DAIRY FREE

**PREP TIME:** 15 minutes, plus 10 minutes to marinate filling

**COOK TIME:** 10 minutes

**YIELD:** 8 spring rolls (2 per serving)

## FOR THE WRAPS

3 quarts water

1 tablespoon fine sea salt

1 head green or purple cabbage

Cilantro stems, scallions, or chives to tie up wraps (optional)

## FOR THE FILLING

½ pound ground pork or chicken

¼ cup finely chopped green onions

2 tablespoons snipped fresh flat-leaf parsley

2 cloves garlic, minced

1 tablespoon MCT oil or dark sesame oil

2 teaspoons lime juice

1 teaspoon grated fresh ginger

½ teaspoon fine sea salt

¼ teaspoon grated lime zest

¼ teaspoon fresh ground black pepper

1 tablespoon coconut oil, for frying

## FOR THE DIPPING SAUCE

¼ cup beef bone broth (page 42; see Note)

3 tablespoons coconut oil (no substitutes, it will thicken the cooled sauce)

2 tablespoons lime juice

2 tablespoons powdered erythritol or 1 drop of stevia glycerite

1 tablespoon almond butter

1 tablespoon coconut aminos or wheat-free tamari sauce

1 teaspoon fish sauce

1 teaspoon grated fresh ginger

½ clove garlic, minced

1. Prepare the wraps: Fill a 4- to 5-quart pot with the 3 quarts water and 1 tablespoon salt and bring to a boil.

2. Meanwhile, make an ice water bath in a large bowl.

3. Remove 8 outer leaves from the cabbage. Make a cut through each individual leaf at the base where it attaches to the core. Trim some of the woody stem area from the leaf. Set the rest of the head of cabbage aside to use for the filling.

4. Place the 8 cabbage leaves in the boiling water; blanch for 30 seconds to 1 minute, until just wilted. Cool quickly by dunking the cabbage leaves into the ice water for 1 minute. Remove the leaves from the water and lay flat on a cloth towel to dry.

5. Make the filling: Finely chop about 2 cups of cabbage from the remainder of the head.

6. In a large bowl, combine the chopped cabbage with the filling ingredients (except the coconut oil) and marinate for at least 10 minutes (or up to overnight) in the refrigerator.

7. Heat a wok or large sauté pan over high heat. When hot, swirl in a tablespoon of coconut oil. Stir-fry the ground pork filling until browned. Transfer the browned filling from the wok to a bowl and set aside.

8. Assemble the rolls: Take a blanched cabbage leaf and lay it flat, with the base end toward you. Place ¼ cup of the filling in the center of the leaf. Fold the base end over the filling and fold both sides in and over the filling so that it seals the open edges. Continue to roll to the end of the leaf, wrapping tightly. Tie with a stem of cilantro, green onion, or chive, if desired. Repeat with the remaining leaves and filling.

9. Make the dipping sauce: In a small saucepan, combine all of the sauce ingredients and heat over medium heat, whisking continuously, until very smooth. Remove the sauce from the heat, pour into a serving dish, and allow to cool completely before serving.

**NOTE:** *Homemade bone broth creates a thicker dipping sauce. Store-bought beef broth or stock will work, but the sauce won't be as thick.*

| NUTRITIONAL INFO (per serving) | | | | |
| --- | --- | --- | --- | --- |
| calories | fat | protein | carbs | fiber |
| 288 | 22 g | 19 g | 3.5 g | 0.6 g |
|  | 69% | 26% | 5% |  |

# bacon-wrapped cheese curds

**KETO**    **NUT FREE**

**PREP TIME:** 10 minutes

**COOK TIME:** 8 minutes

**YIELD:** 4 servings

---

2 tablespoons MCT oil

2 tablespoons unsalted butter

2 ounces bacon

4 ounces cheese curds, frozen

2 tablespoons chopped fresh herbs, such as cilantro or flat-leaf parsley (optional)

¼ cup BBQ Mustard (page 50) or Keto Ketchup (page 62), for serving

1. Heat the MCT oil and butter in a sauté pan over medium-high heat.

2. Wrap a piece of bacon around each frozen cheese curd, being careful to completely cover the cheese. Secure the bacon with a toothpick. If desired, roll the bacon-wrapped cheese curds in chopped herbs for a crispy herb crust.

3. Working in batches to avoid overcrowding the pan, place the wrapped cheese curds in the hot oil, turning frequently, until the outsides become slightly crisp and the cheese becomes gooey. This will take only a few minutes per batch.

4. Remove to a platter, let cool slightly, and enjoy with mustard or ketchup.

**BUSY FAMILY TIP:** *You can freeze the bacon-wrapped cheese curds until you're ready to fry them.*

**VARIATION: PROSCIUTTO-WRAPPED CHEESE CURDS.** *Replace the bacon with 2 ounces of very thinly sliced prosciutto. Cut the prosciutto slices in half and wrap around the cheese curds. The prosciutto is sticky enough to attach to the cheese without toothpicks. Continue with the recipe as described above.*

| NUTRITIONAL INFO (per serving) | | | | |
|---|---|---|---|---|
| calories | fat | protein | carbs | fiber |
| 317 | 27.5 g | 10.9 g | 7.6 g | 0.6 g |
| | 78% | 13% | 9% | |

# *nacho cheese crisps*

KETO ■■□    NUT FREE

**PREP TIME:** 10 minutes

**COOK TIME:** 30 minutes

**YIELD:** 6 servings

½ cup shredded extra-sharp cheddar cheese (about 2 ounces), frozen

3 large egg whites

⅛ teaspoon cream of tartar

2 teaspoons Taco Seasoning (page 74)

### SPECIAL EQUIPMENT

Food processor

1. Preheat the oven to 300°F. Line a baking sheet with parchment paper.

2. Put the frozen shredded cheese in a food processor and chop it into tiny pieces.

3. In a mixing bowl, whip the egg whites with the cream of tartar until very stiff peaks form. Sprinkle the chopped frozen cheese on top of the whites. Then, with a rubber spatula, very carefully fold the cheese into the egg whites, being sure not to disturb the fluffy whites while still thoroughly spreading the cheese throughout.

4. Carefully place the mixture into a large sealable plastic bag, then cut a ½-inch hole in one corner of the bag. Gently squeeze the mixture onto the prepared baking sheet in strips about 2½ inches long and ½ inch wide. Lightly sprinkle the top of each puff with the taco seasoning.

5. Bake for 20 to 30 minutes. The longer you can bake them, the crispier they will be, but don't let them get too brown. For even crispier puffs, turn off the oven and leave them in the oven for at least 30 more minutes.

6. Store in a tightly sealed, airtight container for up to 7 days. Best eaten fresh.

| NUTRITIONAL INFO (per serving) | | | | |
|---|---|---|---|---|
| calories | fat | protein | carbs | fiber |
| 57 | 3.5 g | 4.6 g | 1.8 g | 0.7 g |
| | 55% | 32% | 13% | |

# beef and lamb

# bbq meatloaf

**PREP TIME:** 10 minutes, plus 15 minutes to rest

**COOK TIME:** 1 hour 25 minutes

**YIELD:** 8 servings

1 tablespoon unsalted butter or MCT oil

1 medium yellow onion, chopped

1 teaspoon fine sea salt

2 large eggs

2 pounds grass-fed ground beef

½ pound ground liver (or ½ pound more ground beef)

1 cup finely chopped button or portobello mushrooms

¼ cup tomato sauce, homemade (page 59) or store-bought

2 teaspoons liquid smoke

½ cup nutritional yeast (or shredded extra-sharp cheese if not dairy-sensitive)

8 slices bacon

1 recipe Keto Ketchup (page 62), Keto BBQ Sauce (page 63), or Tomato Sauce (page 59), for serving

*One recipe tester who loved this dish—she said, "I don't know if it's the smokiness, the tang from the cheese, or the delicious bacon flavor, but this is my new favorite meatloaf recipe"—made an interesting variation that's worth trying if you like extra-crispy bacon. Here's what she did: "While the finished meatloaf was resting, I removed the bacon slices and placed them on a foil-lined pan to bake for an additional 10 minutes. Then I crumbled the crispy bacon on top of the meatloaf slices."*

1. Preheat the oven to 400°F.

2. Melt the butter in a heavy skillet over medium-low heat. Add the onion and salt and gently cook for about 20 to 25 minutes, until the onions are golden. Remove to a bowl to cool.

3. In a large bowl, combine the eggs, ground beef, ground liver, mushrooms, tomato sauce, liquid smoke, and nutritional yeast. When the onion mixture has cooled so that it's not hot to the touch, add it to the bowl and work everything together with your hands.

4. Place the mixture into a 9-by-5-inch loaf pan (or you could make individual servings in a 12-cup muffin pan). Cover the meatloaf with the bacon slices, tucking the bacon ends underneath the meatloaf so that they don't curl up during cooking.

5. Bake for 1 hour, until the juices run clear. Let the meatloaf rest for 15 minutes. Serve with ketchup, barbecue sauce, or tomato sauce.

**BUSY FAMILY TIP:** *Leftover meatloaf makes a great sandwich! I recommend placing one slice of meatloaf and ¼ cup arugula or 1 to 2 red leaf lettuce leaves between two slices of Keto Bread (page 276) that have been fried in bacon fat. It's especially delicious served with Keto BBQ Sauce (page 63).*

| NUTRITIONAL INFO (per serving) | | | | |
|---|---|---|---|---|
| calories | fat | protein | carbs | fiber |
| 569 | 36.8 g | 48.9 g | 8.4 g | 2.2 g |
|  | 58% | 34% | 6% |  |

# asian meatballs

**KETO** ■■□  **NUT FREE**  **DAIRY FREE**

**PREP TIME:** 12 minutes

**COOK TIME:** 25 minutes

**YIELD:** 8 servings

2 pounds grass-fed ground beef

2 large eggs, beaten

¾ cup finely chopped button mushrooms

4 tablespoons finely chopped green onions

2 tablespoons coconut aminos or wheat-free tamari sauce

2 teaspoons grated fresh ginger

1 clove garlic, crushed into a paste

**FOR THE SAUCE**

¼ cup beef bone broth (page 42)

¼ cup coconut oil

¼ cup coconut aminos

⅓ cup powdered erythritol

2 tablespoons chopped green onions

2 teaspoons grated fresh ginger

1 clove garlic, minced

¼ teaspoon guar gum (optional; include if using store-bought broth)

Black sesame seeds, for garnish (optional)

*When making the mouthwatering glaze for these meatballs, I highly suggest you use homemade bone broth. Store-bought broth will work but the glaze will not be thick, though adding a small amount of guar gum can help thicken it somewhat.*

*These meatballs may be served as an appetizer with toothpicks or as a main dish served over Zucchini "Pasta" (page 284), Slow Cooker Cabbage "Pasta" (page 282), or sautéed bok choy, as shown in the photo.*

1. Preheat the oven to 400°F.

2. In a large bowl, mix together the ground beef, eggs, mushrooms, green onions, coconut aminos, ginger, and garlic. Mix until well combined. Shape into 1½-inch meatballs and place on a rimmed baking sheet.

3. Bake for 20 minutes, or until browned.

4. Meanwhile, make the sauce: In a small saucepan, combine the broth, coconut oil, coconut aminos, erythritol, green onions, ginger, and garlic. Heat over medium-high heat until bubbling, stirring well to combine. Remove from the heat. If you used store-bought stock, sift in the guar gum and let it sit for 5 minutes to thicken. Add a pinch more guar gum if you would like a thicker glaze.

5. Remove from the meatballs from the oven, place on a serving tray, and serve with the sauce. Garnish with black sesame seeds if desired.

| NUTRITIONAL INFO (per serving) | | | | |
|---|---|---|---|---|
| calories | fat | protein | carbs | fiber |
| 403 | 28 g | 33.2 g | 3.1 g | 0 g |
| | 63% | 33% | 3% | |

# steak

## WITH BROWN BUTTER BÉARNAISE

**KETO** **NUT FREE**

**PREP TIME:** 5 minutes, plus 40 minutes to rest before cooking and 5 minutes to rest after

**COOK TIME:** 10 minutes

**YIELD:** 4 servings

2 T-bone or rib-eye steaks, 1½ to 2 inches thick (about 2 pounds total)

1 tablespoon fine sea salt (or to taste)

2 teaspoons fresh ground black pepper (or to taste)

Melted coconut oil or lard, for greasing the grill

¼ cup Brown Butter Béarnaise (page 66) or Herb-Infused Compound "Butter" (page 44), for serving

**SPECIAL EQUIPMENT**

Grill

1. Season the steaks generously with salt and pepper. Let the seasoned steak rest for at least 40 minutes at room temp.

2. Preheat a grill to high heat. If you are using charcoal, after the briquettes are heated, move them to one side of the grill so you have both direct and indirect heat.

3. Brush the grill grates with melted coconut oil or lard. Place the steaks on the hot grill and do not move them for about 2 to 3 minutes. Use tongs to flip the steaks and grill for 2 to 3 more minutes.

4. If you're using a gas grill, turn the heat down to medium-low and close the grill lid if you have one. If you're using charcoal, move the steaks to the side of the grill without charcoal to finish cooking with indirect heat and close the grill lid. Cook for an additional 3 minutes for rare, 4 minutes for medium-rare, 5 minutes for medium, 6 to 7 minutes for medium-well, and 8 to 10 minutes for well done, using the following temperatures as a guide to your desired doneness:

   *Rare:* 120°F to 125°F

   *Medium-rare:* 130°F to 135°

   *Medium:* 140°F to 145°F

   *Medium-well:* 150°F to 155°F

   *Well done:* 160°F+

5. Use tongs to remove the steaks from the grill and cover to keep warm. Let them rest for at least 5 minutes before cutting into them. Serve with the béarnaise sauce or compound "butter."

**TIPS:** *You can let the seasoned steaks rest for up to 4 days in the fridge, wrapped loosely in parchment paper, before grilling. Just make sure to let them come to room temp before cooking.*

*Beef is a tasty way to increase your zinc levels—ounce for ounce, it has more zinc than any food but oysters. Zinc is crucial for the synthesis of thyroid hormones, and a zinc deficiency can result in hypothyroidism. Low levels of zinc often cause extreme cravings for salty foods and sweets after a meal; you'll also see white spots on your fingernails. If you know you have hypothyroidism, you may have noticed that hair loss is one symptom. Hair loss due to hypothyroidism may not improve, even with medication, without zinc supplements. Just be careful not to increase your zinc intake too fast, or you may experience some nausea.*

| NUTRITIONAL INFO (per serving) | | | | |
|---|---|---|---|---|
| calories | fat | protein | carbs | fiber |
| 761 | 59.6 g | 52.4 g | 0.3 g | 0 g |
| | 71% | 28% | 0% | |

# meaty spaghetti

■□□  NUT
KETO  FREE

**PREP TIME:** 15 minutes

**COOK TIME:** 1 hour 50 minutes

**YIELD:** 8 servings

1 tablespoon coconut oil

4 ounces bacon or pancetta, diced

½ cup chopped yellow onion

¾ cup diced celery

1 tablespoon minced garlic

1 teaspoon fine sea salt

½ teaspoon fresh ground black pepper

2 bay leaves

¼ cup fresh flat-leaf parsley

3 tablespoons fresh thyme

3 tablespoons fresh oregano

½ teaspoon ground cinnamon

½ teaspoon ground nutmeg

1 pound grass-fed ground beef

½ pound pork sausage, casings removed, or ground pork

½ pound finely chopped beef liver

2 cups tomato sauce, homemade (page 59) or store-bought

4 cups crushed tomatoes and their juice

1 cup beef or chicken bone broth (page 42)

½ teaspoon stevia glycerite (optional, for a little sweetness)

¼ cup heavy cream (if not dairy-sensitive)

2 tablespoons unsalted butter (if not dairy-sensitive)

2 medium zucchini, cut into thin "noodles," for serving

1 cup grated Parmesan cheese (about 4 ounces), for serving (if not dairy-sensitive)

| NUTRITIONAL INFO (per serving) | | | | |
|---|---|---|---|---|
| calories | fat | protein | carbs | fiber |
| 468 | 30 g | 33.6 g | 15.2 g | 4.1 g |
| | 58% | 29% | 13% | |

1. In a large pot, heat the coconut oil over medium-high heat. Add the bacon and cook for 4 to 5 minutes, stirring frequently, until the bacon is browned and the fat is rendered.

2. Add the onion and celery. Cook for 4 to 5 minutes, stirring frequently, until soft.

3. Add the garlic, salt, pepper, bay leaves, parsley, thyme, oregano, cinnamon, and nutmeg. Cook for 30 seconds, stirring constantly.

4. Turn the heat to low, then add the beef, sausage, and liver. Cook for about 7 minutes, or until the meat is no longer pink, stirring frequently.

5. Add the tomato sauce and cook for 1 to 2 minutes, stirring constantly.

6. Add the tomatoes and their juice, broth, and stevia, if using, and bring to a boil.

7. Reduce the heat to medium-low and simmer, stirring occasionally to keep the sauce from sticking to the bottom of the pan, until the sauce is thickened and flavorful, about 1½ hours.

8. If not dairy-sensitive, add the cream and butter, stir well, and simmer for 2 minutes.

9. Remove from the heat and cover to keep warm until ready to serve. Before serving, discard the bay leaves and adjust the seasoning to taste.

10. Serve over the zucchini noodles topped with grated Parmesan cheese.

## SLOW COOKER
# beefy asian noodles

**■□□ KETO**  **NUT FREE**  **DAIRY FREE**

**PREP TIME: 10** minutes

**COOK TIME:** 6 to 8 hours

**YIELD:** 6 servings

1 (2-inch) piece fresh ginger, peeled and grated

½ small head green cabbage, cored and cut into thin strips

1 medium zucchini, cut into ½-inch cubes

½ cup diced yellow onion

1 pound grass-fed ground beef

2 tablespoons coconut oil

1 teaspoon dark sesame oil

¼ cup coconut aminos or wheat-free tamari sauce

¼ cup chicken bone broth (page 42)

2 tablespoons tomato sauce, homemade (page 59) or store-bought

1 teaspoon to 1 tablespoon hot sauce (to taste)

1 tablespoon powdered erythritol or 1 drop of stevia glycerite

1 (16-ounce) package kelp noodles or 2 (7-ounce) packages Miracle Noodles

Chopped green onion, for garnish (optional)

**SPECIAL EQUIPMENT**

Slow cooker

1. Grease the cooking pot of a 4-quart slow cooker.

2. Place the grated ginger, cabbage, zucchini, onion, ground beef, coconut oil, and sesame oil in the slow cooker. With a wooden spoon, crumble the beef into small, bite-sized chunks.

3. In a small bowl, combine the coconut aminos, broth, tomato sauce, hot sauce, and erythritol. Add the sauce and the kelp noodles, if using, to the slow cooker and cook on medium heat for 6 to 8 hours, until the beef and veggies are cooked through.

4. If using Miracle Noodles, drain, rinse, and add them just before serving. Stir the noodles through the beef and veggies to heat through.

5. Garnish with green onion, if desired, and serve.

| NUTRITIONAL INFO (per serving) | | | | |
|---|---|---|---|---|
| calories | fat | protein | carbs | fiber |
| 286 | 18.1 g | 23.4 g | 6.9 g | 2.3 g |
| | 57% | 33% | 10% | |

# chimichurri flank steak

**KETO** NUT FREE DAIRY FREE

**PREP TIME:** 15 minutes, plus 2 hours to marinate and 45 minutes to rest

**COOK TIME:** 8 minutes

**YIELD:** 6 servings

1½ pounds flank steak

**FOR THE MARINADE**

¼ cup MCT oil

2 cloves garlic, minced

2 tablespoons fine sea salt

1 tablespoon fresh ground black pepper

1 teaspoon ground dried oregano

1 teaspoon ground dried thyme

MCT oil, for greasing the grill

¾ cup Fat-Burning Chimichurri Sauce (page 70), for serving

6 lime wedges, for serving

**SPECIAL EQUIPMENT**

Grill

1. Place two layers of plastic wrap on a large surface and place the flank steak on it. Cover the steak with additional plastic wrap. Using a mallet, pound the flank steak until it is ¼ inch thick. You may want to flip the meat to pound everything evenly.

2. Mix the marinade ingredients together in a large, deep bowl. Place the flattened flank steak in the bowl, turning it to coat, and let marinate for 2 hours or overnight in the fridge.

3. About 45 minutes before you're ready to cook the flank steak, remove it from the marinade, season it with the salt and pepper, and allow it to come to room temperature.

4. Preheat a grill to medium-high heat. Brush the grill rack with oil. Grill the steaks to desired doneness, 3 to 4 minutes per side for medium-rare, turning the steaks a quarter turn after 1½ minutes to form crisscross grill marks, if desired. Transfer the steak to a cutting board and let rest for 5 to 8 minutes.

5. Thinly slice the steaks across the grain. Transfer to a platter and serve with the chimichurri sauce and lime wedges to add a little acidity and balance the flavors.

| NUTRITIONAL INFO (per serving) | | | | |
|---|---|---|---|---|
| calories | fat | protein | carbs | fiber |
| 391 | 27.5 g | 31.7 g | 2.8 g | 0.6 g |
| | 63% | 32% | 3% | |

# teriyaki steak roll-ups
## WITH SAUTÉED MUSHROOMS

**KETO** | NUT FREE | DAIRY FREE

**PREP TIME:** 15 minutes, plus 2 hours to marinate and 45 minutes to rest

**COOK TIME:** 45 minutes

**YIELD:** 6 servings

2 pounds flank steak

2 tablespoons coconut oil, for frying

**FOR THE MARINADE**

½ cup coconut aminos or wheat-free tamari sauce

3 tablespoons MCT oil

1 tablespoon grated fresh ginger

2 cloves garlic, minced

½ teaspoon stevia glycerite

**FOR THE FILLING**

¼ cup coconut oil

2 cups thinly sliced green onions, plus more for garnish

3 tablespoons grated fresh ginger

Fine sea salt

**FOR THE TERIYAKI SAUCE**

1 cup coconut aminos or wheat-free tamari sauce

½ cup MCT oil

½ cup vegetable glycerin or powdered erythritol

1 teaspoon grated fresh ginger

½ teaspoon stevia glycerite

1 teaspoon fish sauce

⅛ to ¼ teaspoon guar gum (optional)

2 teaspoons chopped green onions

**FOR THE MUSHROOMS**

6 tablespoons coconut oil

1 pound button mushrooms, sliced

1 clove garlic, thinly sliced

2 tablespoons teriyaki sauce, from recipe above

¼ teaspoon fine sea salt

¼ teaspoon fresh ground black pepper

*Vegetable glycerin, which is often used as a sweetener in foods marketed to diabetics, is an important ingredient in this recipe. It tastes sweet but it is not metabolized as sugar in the body and does not cause a rise in blood sugar. It also has attracts moisture—just as the glycerin in a body lotion helps your skin stay soft, vegetable glycerin helps give foods a great mouthfeel. You can find it online and in most health food stores.*

1. Place two layers of plastic wrap on a large surface and place the flank steak on it. Cover the steak with additional plastic wrap. Using a mallet, pound the flank steak until it is ¼ inch thick. You may want to flip the meat to pound everything evenly.

2. If your steak isn't in a rectangle or square shape, use a knife to cut out the odd edges so it is.

3. Mix the marinade ingredients together in a large, deep bowl. Place the flattened flank steak in the bowl, turning it to coat, and let marinate for 2 hours or overnight in the fridge.

4. About 45 minutes before you're ready to cook the flank steak, remove it from the marinade and allow it to come to room temperature.

5. While the steak comes to room temperature, make the filling: Heat the ¼ cup coconut oil in a small saucepan over medium-high heat. While the oil heats, combine the green onions and ginger in a medium-sized bowl and season well with salt. When the oil is hot, fry the green onions and ginger for a minute, then remove from the heat.

6. Lay the steak out so the grain of the meat runs left to right, not up and down. This is important because the steak will be more tender if you slice across the grain. Spread the green onion and ginger mixture on the steak, leaving a 1-inch border at the top edge.

7. Starting at the edge closest to you, tightly roll the steak in a jelly-roll fashion. Tie the rolled steak tightly with twine, spacing the ties 1½ inches apart.

8. Preheat the oven to 425°F.

9. Heat the 2 tablespoons of coconut oil in a large sauté pan over medium-high heat. Sear the tied flank steak in the hot pan. This is just to sear the outside, not cook the steak. Sear for a minute on each side.

10. Remove from the sauté pan and place on a rack in a roasting pan, seam side down. (If you don't have a rack, you can lay the steak on celery sticks. Elevating the steak helps it cook evenly.)

BUSY FAMILY TIP: *You can save time by asking the butcher to pound out the meat for you.*

11. Roast the steak for 20 minutes, or until the interior temperature is 130°F in the center of the steak. After you remove the steak from the oven, let it rest for 10 minutes before slicing.

12. While the steak is roasting and then resting, make the teriyaki sauce and mushrooms. To make the sauce: Place the coconut aminos, MCT oil, vegetable glycerin, ginger, stevia, and fish sauce in a small saucepan and bring to a boil. Reduce the heat and, if you desire a thicker sauce, sift in the guar gum and allow to sit for 5 minutes to thicken. If you desire an even thicker sauce, add ⅛ teaspoon more guar gum. Stir in the green onion.

13. To make the mushrooms: Heat the 6 tablespoons coconut oil in a large saucepan over medium heat. Add the mushrooms, garlic, teriyaki sauce, salt, and pepper and cook, stirring often, in the hot oil until mushrooms are lightly browned, about 5 minutes. Reduce the heat to low and simmer until the mushrooms are tender, about 8 minutes.

14. To serve, cut the roll-up into ½-inch-thick slices and serve with a drizzle of the sauce on top, plus extra on the side for dipping. Serve the mushrooms on the side or under the roll-ups.

| NUTRITIONAL INFO (per serving) | | | | |
|---|---|---|---|---|
| calories | fat | protein | carbs | fiber |
| 821 | 66 g | 45.9 g | 8 g | 1.6 g |
| | 72% | 22% | 4% | |

# swedish meatballs

**KETO**  **NUT FREE**

**PREP TIME:** 8 minutes

**COOK TIME:** 1 hour

**YIELD:** 8 servings as a main dish, 16 as an appetizer

1½ pounds grass-fed ground beef

¼ pound ground pork

1 large egg

¼ cup tomato sauce, homemade (page 59) or store-bought

¼ cup minced yellow onion

1 tablespoon coconut aminos or wheat-free tamari sauce

1 tablespoon dry mustard

1 clove garlic, minced

2 teaspoons fine sea salt

1 teaspoon fresh ground black pepper

1 teaspoon liquid smoke

**FOR THE SAUCE**

½ cup (1 stick) unsalted butter

2 ounces cream cheese (about ¼ cup), softened

⅓ cup beef bone broth (page 42)

½ cup grated Parmesan cheese (about 2 ounces)

⅛ teaspoon ground nutmeg

*These amazing meatballs may be served as an appetizer with toothpicks or as a main dish over Zucchini "Pasta" (page 284) or Slow Cooker Cabbage "Pasta" (page 282).*

1. Preheat the oven 325°F.

2. In a large bowl, combine the ground beef, ground pork, egg, tomato sauce, onion, coconut aminos, mustard, garlic, salt, pepper, and liquid smoke. Mix until well combined.

3. Shape into 1½-inch meatballs and place on a rimmed baking sheet. Bake the meatballs for 45 to 60 minutes, until cooked through and browned.

4. Meanwhile, make the sauce: Place the butter in a saucepan and heat until the butter sizzles and brown flecks appear, stirring constantly to keep the butter from burning. Reduce the heat to low. Stir in the cream cheese, broth, Parmesan, and nutmeg. Simmer for at least 15 minutes. The flavors open up if you simmer longer.

5. When the meatballs are done, remove them from the oven, place them on a serving tray, and serve with the sauce.

| NUTRITIONAL INFO (per serving) | | | | |
|---|---|---|---|---|
| calories | fat | protein | carbs | fiber |
| 426 | 32.1 g | 31.3 g | 2.1 g | 0 g |
| | 68% | 29% | 2% | |

# reubens

**KETO** **NUT FREE** **DAIRY FREE**

**PREP TIME:** 10 minutes

**COOK TIME:** 5 minutes

**YIELD:** 6 sandwiches

### FOR THE THOUSAND ISLAND DRESSING

¾ cup Copycat Baconnaise (page 65) or mayonnaise

¼ cup chopped dill pickles

¼ cup tomato sauce, homemade (page 59) or store-bought

2 tablespoons powdered erythritol or 1 drop stevia glycerite

⅛ teaspoon fine sea salt

⅛ teaspoon fish sauce

1 pound corned beef

2 tablespoons bacon fat

1 loaf Keto Bread (page 276), cut into 12 slices

2 cups fermented sauerkraut

1. Make the dressing by combining all of the ingredients in a jar.

2. Slice the corned beef against the grain into ¼-inch-thick slices. Set aside.

3. Heat the bacon fat in a large skillet over medium heat. Fry the bread slices until golden brown.

4. Assemble the sandwiches by layering corned beef, sauerkraut, and a smear of Thousand Island dressing between two slices of fried bread.

| NUTRITIONAL INFO (per serving) | | | | |
|---|---|---|---|---|
| calories | fat | protein | carbs | fiber |
| 291 | 23.6 g | 10.6 g | 9.1 g | 1.6 g |
| | 73% | 15% | 13% | |

## SLOW COOKER

# bbq short ribs

■■□ KETO   NUT FREE   DAIRY FREE

**PREP TIME:** 10 minutes

**COOK TIME:** 8 hours

**YIELD:** 8 servings

3 slices bacon, finely diced

2 tablespoons diced yellow onion

1 cup tomato sauce, homemade (page 59) or store-bought

¼ cup coconut aminos or wheat-free tamari sauce

⅓ cup powdered erythritol

¼ cup coconut vinegar

1 head roasted garlic (see page 46) or 3 cloves raw garlic, smashed with the side of a knife

2 teaspoons liquid smoke

8 grass-fed beef short ribs (4 pounds)

**SPECIAL EQUIPMENT**

Slow cooker    Blender

*I absolutely love this recipe. I often make extras, pull the meat off the bone, and use it to make a sandwich with fried Keto Bread (page 276). It's also great addition to a nacho platter.*

1. In a sauté pan, sauté the bacon and onion until the bacon is crisp. Add the tomato sauce, coconut aminos, erythritol, vinegar, garlic, and liquid smoke and stir until smooth. Place this mixture into a blender and blend until you have a very smooth sauce.

2. Place the sauce into a 4- to 6-quart slow cooker. Add the short ribs, arranging them in a single layer on top of the sauce.

3. Cook, covered, on low for 7 to 8 hours, until the meat is tender and easily pulls away from the bone.

4. Transfer the short ribs to plates. Spoon the sauce over the short ribs to serve.

| NUTRITIONAL INFO (per serving) | | | | |
|---|---|---|---|---|
| calories | fat | protein | carbs | fiber |
| 749 | 68.6 g | 28.4 g | 1.8 g | 0.5 g |
| | 82% | 15% | 1% | |

## PHILLY "CHEESE" STEAK

*stuffed portobellos*

■■□ KETO  NUT FREE  DAIRY FREE

**PREP TIME:** 15 minutes

**COOK TIME:** 40 minutes

**YIELD:** 8 servings

2 pounds strip loin

8 large portobello mushrooms, cleaned and stems removed

3 tablespoons MCT oil, melted duck fat, or lard, divided

Fine sea salt and fresh ground black pepper

**FOR THE ONIONS AND PEPPERS**

2 tablespoons lard, duck fat, or coconut oil (or unsalted butter if not dairy-sensitive)

1 cup diced yellow onion

1 red bell pepper, seeded and diced

1 yellow bell pepper, seeded and diced

1 green bell pepper, seeded and diced

1 teaspoon fine sea salt

¼ teaspoon fresh ground black pepper

1 cup Dairy-Free Nacho Cheese Sauce (page 64)

1. To make the steak very easy to slice, place it in freezer for 30 minutes. Meanwhile, preheat the oven to 450°F.

2. Make the onions and peppers: Heat the 2 tablespoons lard in a large sauté pan over medium heat. Add the onion and cook slowly until the onion is golden brown and caramelized, about 30 minutes, stirring occasionally (you may need to turn the heat to low).

3. Meanwhile, prepare the portobellos: Place the portobello caps on a rimmed baking sheet gill side up and brush with 1 tablespoon of the MCT oil. Roast the caps for 12 minutes, until light golden brown and fork-tender. Remove them from the oven and season with salt and pepper.

4. Preheat a griddle or grill pan over high heat. Remove the steak from freezer and slice it very thin. Brush the steak slices with the remaining 2 tablespoons of MCT oil and season with salt and pepper. Cook for 45 to 60 seconds per side.

5. When the onions have cooked 30 minutes and are fully caramelized, increase the heat to medium and add the bell peppers. Season the peppers and onion with the salt and pepper and sauté for 10 minutes, until the peppers are softened.

6. Assemble the stuffed mushrooms: Place several slices of the meat in each baked portobello mushroom cap and top with the "cheese" sauce and sautéed peppers and onion.

| NUTRITIONAL INFO (per serving) | | | | |
|---|---|---|---|---|
| calories | fat | protein | carbs | fiber |
| 651 | 57 g | 31 g | 5 g | 1.3 g |
|  | 79% | 19% | 3% |  |

# taco salad

## IN A CRISPY CHEESE BOWL

**KETO** ■□□  **NUT FREE**

**PREP TIME:** 15 minutes

**COOK TIME:** 35 minutes

**YIELD:** 6 servings

### FOR THE CHEESE BOWLS

2 cups grated Parmesan cheese (about 8 ounces)

### FOR THE TACO SALAD

¾ pound grass-fed ground beef

2 tablespoons diced yellow onion

1 cup chopped yellow, red, and/or green bell pepper

1 tablespoon Taco Seasoning (page 74)

1 cup salsa

¼ cup chopped fresh cilantro

4 cups chopped red leaf lettuce

2 cups diced yellow tomatoes

1 cup shredded sharp cheddar cheese (about 4 ounces)

¼ cup chopped green onions

¼ cup sliced black olives

Small handful of fresh cilantro leaves, for garnish (optional)

6 tablespoons sour cream, for garnish (optional)

1. Preheat the oven to 375° F. Line a rimmed baking sheet with parchment paper.

2. Make the cheese bowls: Spread ⅓ cup of the Parmesan on the parchment in a 6-inch circle. Work in batches of 2 at a time so you can form the bowls before the cheese hardens.

3. Place the baking sheet in the oven and allow the cheese to brown for 9 to 10 minutes. Wearing protective gloves, remove the pan from the oven, grab onto the parchment, and flip each Parmesan circle over an upside down 5-inch bowl. With your hands protected by gloves and working quickly because the cheese hardens as it cools, gently press on the circle to shape the pliable cheese around the bowl. Peel off the parchment paper and let the Parmesan bowls cool about 5 minutes before removing them from the bowl. If the Parmesan hardens before you can form the bowl, place it back in the oven for 1 minute to soften the cheese and try again.

4. Repeat the process of browning the cheese and forming the bowls twice more, for a total of 6 bowls.

5. Make the salad: In a large skillet, cook the beef, yellow onion, and bell pepper with the taco seasoning over medium heat until beef is browned, stirring to crumble the meat. Add the salsa and cilantro, then turn the heat to low simmer to keep warm.

6. To serve, place about ⅔ cup of the lettuce in each cheese bowl and top with meat mixture. Sprinkle each serving with diced tomatoes, cheese, green onions, and black olives. Garnish with cilantro and sour cream, if desired.

| NUTRITIONAL INFO (per serving) | | | | |
|---|---|---|---|---|
| calories | fat | protein | carbs | fiber |
| 363 | 24.3 g | 29.5 g | 9.6 g | 2.3 g |
| | 60% | 31% | 9% | |

# braised lamb shanks

## AND MUSHROOMS

■□□ KETO  NUT FREE  DAIRY FREE

**PREP TIME:** 10 minutes

**COOK TIME:** 3½ hours

**YIELD:** 8 servings

2 tablespoons bacon fat, lard, or MCT oil, divided

4 (1-pound) lamb or beef shanks

2½ teaspoons fine sea salt, divided

½ cup sliced red onion

4 cups button or cremini mushrooms

2 heads roasted garlic (see page 46) or 4 cloves raw garlic, minced

1 medium yellow tomato, chopped

5 cups beef bone broth (page 42), divided (plus more if needed)

2 tablespoons finely chopped fresh rosemary

10 to 12 fresh thyme sprigs, tied together in a bundle

¼ cup Herb-Infused Compound "Butter" (page 44), for serving

1. Preheat the oven to 400°F.

2. Coat the bottom of a large Dutch oven generously with 1 tablespoon of the bacon fat and heat over high heat. Season the lamb liberally with 2 teaspoons of the salt and sear in the hot fat. Brown well on all sides. Remove the shanks from the pot to a sheet tray.

3. Add the remaining tablespoon of bacon fat to the Dutch oven and add the onion and mushrooms, then squeeze the roasted garlic from the heads into the pot. Season with the remaining ½ teaspoon of salt, or to taste. Sauté the onion and mushrooms until they are very brown, about 12 to 15 minutes.

4. Add the chopped tomato, 2 cups of the broth, rosemary, and the thyme bundle to the pot. Cook over medium heat, stirring frequently, until the liquid has reduced by about half, about 30 minutes.

5. Add the lamb shanks back to the pot and pour in the remaining 3 cups of broth. The shanks should be submersed; if they are not, add more broth. Cover and put in the preheated oven. Cook for 2½ hours, turning the shanks over about halfway through the cooking time. Check the shanks every 45 minutes or so. If the liquid has reduced too much, add more broth. After 2½ hours, remove the lid to allow the shank to brown for about 15 minutes. When the lamb shanks are done, the meat should be extremely tender.

6. Transfer to serving bowls, smother with the compound "butter," and serve.

| NUTRITIONAL INFO (per serving) | | | | |
|---|---|---|---|---|
| calories | fat | protein | carbs | fiber |
| 465 | 25.9 g | 51.1 g | 6.8 g | 2.2 g |
| | 50% | 44% | 6% | |

# lamb tikka masala

**KETO** | **NUT FREE** | **DAIRY FREE**

**PREP TIME:** 15 minutes, plus 2 hours to marinate

**COOK TIME:** 1 hour

**YIELD:** 8 servings

## FOR THE MARINADE

1 cup canned, full-fat coconut milk

1 head roasted garlic (see page 46), pureed, or 3 cloves raw garlic, minced

1 tablespoon grated fresh ginger

½ teaspoon cayenne pepper

½ teaspoon ground cumin

½ teaspoon ground coriander

1 teaspoon fine sea salt

2 pounds boneless lamb leg sirloin, cubed

## FOR THE MASALA SAUCE

3 tablespoons coconut oil

1 medium yellow onion, finely diced (about 1¼ cups)

1 head roasted garlic (see page 46), pureed, or 3 cloves raw garlic, minced

2 teaspoons grated fresh ginger

1 tablespoon tomato paste

1 tablespoon garam masala (see Note)

¼ teaspoon cayenne pepper

2 large tomatoes (preferably yellow), chopped (reserve juices)

1 teaspoon stevia glycerite

½ teaspoon fine sea salt

⅔ cup canned, full-fat coconut milk

½ cup chopped fresh cilantro

Keto Naan (page 278), for serving (optional)

*This tasty dish is one of the favorites of my recipe testers. I often serve it over Slow Cooker Cabbage "Pasta" (page 282), but my favorite way to eat it is on a bed of Miracle Rice without utensils, scooping it up with Keto Naan (page 278), as shown in the photo.*

1. Make the marinade: In large bowl, whisk together the coconut milk, garlic, ginger, cayenne, cumin, coriander, and salt. Add the cubed lamb to the bowl and toss to coat in the marinade. Cover and refrigerate for 2 hours or overnight.

2. Make the masala sauce: Heat the oil in large sauté pan over medium heat. Add the onion and cook, stirring frequently, until golden, about 8 minutes. Add the garlic, ginger, tomato paste, garam masala, and cayenne and cook, stirring frequently, until fragrant, about 5 minutes. Add the tomatoes with their juices, stevia, and salt and bring to a boil.

3. Reduce the heat to low, cover, and simmer for 15 minutes. Stir in the coconut milk, return to a simmer, and let simmer, uncovered, for 30 minutes. Then remove from heat and keep warm.

4. While the sauce simmers, cook the lamb: Preheat a broiler or grill to high heat. If broiling, place the oven rack in the upper-middle position (about 6 inches from heat). Place the lamb cubes onto skewers about ¼ inch apart. Grill or broil until slightly charred on the outside, flipping halfway through cooking, about 2 minutes per side.

5. Once cooked, remove the lamb from the heat and allow to rest for 5 minutes. Stir the chunks into warm sauce. Stir in the cilantro, taste, and add more salt if desired. Serve with naan, if desired.

**NOTE:** *To make your own garam masala, combine 2 teaspoons ground coriander, ½ teaspoon fresh ground black pepper, ¼ teaspoon ground cardamom, and ¼ teaspoon ground cinnamon.*

**VARIATION: CHICKEN TIKKA MASALA.** *To make this dish with chicken, simply substitute the lamb with 2 pounds boneless chicken thighs cut into 1-inch cubes.*

| NUTRITIONAL INFO (per serving) | | | | |
|---|---|---|---|---|
| calories | fat | protein | carbs | fiber |
| 489 | 37.8 g | 29.7 g | 6.8 g | 1.2 g |
| | 70% | 24% | 6% | |

# zucchini tot hot dish

**KETO** **NUT FREE**

**PREP TIME:** 10 minutes, plus 30 minutes for the tots

**COOK TIME:** 30 minutes

**YIELD:** 8 servings

1 pound grass-fed ground beef

¼ cup chopped yellow onion

1 teaspoon fine sea salt

¼ teaspoon fresh ground black pepper

1 recipe Zucchini Tots (page 300)

8 ounces cream cheese (about 1 cup), softened

½ cup beef bone broth (page 42; see Note)

1½ cups shredded cheddar cheese (about 6 ounces)

1. Preheat the oven to 400°F.

2. In a large skillet over medium-high heat, brown the ground beef with the onion for 5 to 7 minutes, until the beef is fully cooked. Season with the salt and pepper.

3. Spread the beef mixture evenly over the bottom of a 2-quart casserole dish. Arrange the zucchini tots evenly over the beef layer.

4. In a small bowl, stir together the cream cheese and broth until smooth. Pour over the tater tot and beef layers. Sprinkle the cheddar cheese evenly over the top.

5. Bake for 20 to 25 minutes, until the cheese is bubbly and slightly brown.

**NOTE:** *If using store-bought broth, use only ¼ cup—since it isn't as thick as homemade bone broth, any more will make the sauce too thin.*

| NUTRITIONAL INFO (per serving) | | | | |
|---|---|---|---|---|
| calories | fat | protein | carbs | fiber |
| 457 | 35 g | 30.5 g | 4.8 g | 1.2 g |
| | 69% | 27% | 4% | |

# pork

# easy mortadella ravioli

KETO

**PREP TIME: 8** minutes

**COOK TIME:** 6 minutes

**YIELD:** 4 servings

12 thin slices mortadella or good-quality bologna

12 ounces goat cheese

12 fresh basil leaves

1½ cups marinara sauce, homemade (page 60) or store-bought

1 tablespoon unsalted butter or coconut oil

1. Lay the slices of the mortadella on a clean, dry work area. Spoon 1 ounce (about 2 tablespoons) of goat cheese in the center of each slice and lay a basil leaf on top of the cheese.

2. Fold each mortadella over the cheese to form a square packet. Secure the edges with toothpicks, creating mortadella ravioli.

3. Warm the marinara sauce in a saucepan over medium-low heat.

4. While the sauce is warming, fry the ravioli: Heat the butter in a large sauté pan over medium-high heat. Fry each mortadella ravioli until the meat is slightly charred on both sides and the cheese is melted, about 6 minutes. Remove from the heat and discard the toothpicks.

5. Pour the warmed marinara sauce on a serving platter. Lay the fried ravioli on top and serve.

**BUSY FAMILY TIP:** *The mortadella ravioli can be refrigerated for up to 2 days before cooking. Allow the ravioli to come to room temperature before cooking.*

| NUTRITIONAL INFO (per serving) | | | | |
|---|---|---|---|---|
| calories | fat | protein | carbs | fiber |
| 677 | 55.6 g | 34.7 g | 9.1 g | 0.8 g |
|  | 74% | 21% | 5% | |

# smoked pork chops
## WITH APPLE GLAZE

**KETO** ■■□  **NUT FREE**  **DAIRY FREE**

**PREP TIME:** 7 minutes, plus 4 hours to brine the chops and soak the wood chips and blocks

**COOK TIME:** 2 hours

**YIELD:** 4 servings

### FOR THE BRINE

6 bags apple tea

4 cups boiling water

½ cup fine sea salt

½ cup powdered erythritol (optional)

4 center cut, bone-in pork chops, about 1½ inches thick

### FOR THE RUB

2 tablespoons smoked paprika

1 tablespoon powdered erythritol

2 teaspoons onion powder

2 teaspoons fine sea salt

½ teaspoon ground dried thyme

MCT oil

### FOR THE APPLE GLAZE

1 apple tea bag

¼ cup boiling water

¼ cup (½ stick) unsalted butter, coconut oil, or bacon fat, softened

¼ cup powdered erythritol

1 teaspoon apple extract

Pinch of fine sea salt (omit if using bacon fat)

### SPECIAL EQUIPMENT

Smoker with thermometer | 4 cups wood chips (preferably apple wood) | 5 or 6 wood blocks

*If you're like me and grew up on chewy, dry pork chops, this recipe will totally change the way you look at pork chops. First, brining the chops makes a big difference, adding a ton of moisture and an amazing flavor. Second, smoking the chops—particularly with apple wood chips—gives these tender bites a delicious depth of flavor.*

1. Make the brine: In a medium-sized saucepan, steep the 6 apple tea bags in the 4 cups of boiling water for 3 minutes. Squeeze out any liquid in the bags and discard. Add the salt and erythritol, if using, to the tea. Stir until all of the salt is dissolved. Pour the brine into a large shallow lasagna pan or casserole dish and allow it to cool to room temperature.

2. Place the pork chops in the dish and submerge them in the cooled brine. Place into the fridge and let the chops brine for at least 4 hours, or overnight if you desire.

3. While the chops are brining, soak the wood chips and blocks in water for 1 hour.

4. Once the chops are done brining, take them out of the fridge and rinse well under cold water. Dry well and set aside.

5. Make the rub: In a small bowl, stir together the paprika, erythritol, onion powder, salt, and thyme until well combined.

6. Brush the chops with a little MCT oil, then generously season both sides with the rub mixture, rubbing it all over the meat.

7. Let the chops rest at room temperature while you prepare your smoker. Before firing up your smoker, read the manufacturer's directions. There are wood, electric, propane, and charcoal smokers, and each type works differently. Start the smoker and if it came with a water bowl, add water to it. Add the soaked wood chips and blocks. When the temperature reaches 225°F you can start smoking the chops.

8. Place the pork chops on a rack or right on the smoker grate for maximum smoke exposure, leaving about 1 inch between the chops so the smoke can penetrate the sides of the meat.

9. Smoke the chops until their internal temperature reaches 145°F, which is the safe temperature the USDA suggests for pork. Smoking time will vary depending on the thickness of the chops. If you are using 1½-inch-thick chops, it will take about 2 hours to reach 145°F.

TIP: *Smoke until the chops reach 150°F to tenderize the chops a bit more. But if your chops are lean, make sure to remove them at 145°F so they don't dry out. Spend the money on a good digital meat thermometer, such as the Maverick ET-732 or my husband's favorite kitchen gadget, the remarkable Thermapen. He loves how fast it reads internal temperature.*

10. While the meat smokes, prepare the glaze: Steep the apple tea bag in ¼ cup of boiling water for 3 minutes. Squeeze water from bag and discard the bag. Add the butter, erythritol, apple extract, and salt (omit the salt if you used bacon fat instead of butter). Place in a blender and puree until smooth. As the fat cools a bit the mixture will become a nice paste to smear on top of the chop.

11. Remove the chops from the smoker and serve with the apple glaze.

| NUTRITIONAL INFO (per serving) | | | | |
|---|---|---|---|---|
| calories | fat | protein | carbs | fiber |
| 418 | 36.6 g | 19 g | 3 g | 1.4 g |
|  | 79% | 18% | 3% |  |

# kielbasa and braised cabbage

**KETO** **NUT FREE** **DAIRY FREE**

**PREP TIME:** 5 minutes

**COOK TIME:** 35 minutes

**YIELD:** 6 servings

6 slices bacon, chopped into small pieces

1 head roasted garlic (see page 46) or 3 cloves raw garlic, minced

¼ cup beef bone broth (page 42)

¼ cup chopped yellow onion

1 teaspoon stevia glycerite

¼ teaspoon red pepper flakes

¼ teaspoon fine sea salt

1 tablespoon caraway seeds

1 small head cabbage, sliced into thin, noodlelike strips

1 pound Polish kielbasa, cut into 2- to 3-inch lengths

½ cup preferred homemade mustard (pages 48 to 50), for serving

1. In a large skillet, fry the chopped bacon over medium-high heat until browned. Remove the bacon from the pan and place on paper towels to drain. Leave the bacon drippings in the pan.

2. Squeeze the roasted garlic from the head into the pan with the bacon drippings. Then add the broth, onion, stevia, red pepper flakes, salt, and caraway seeds and stir to combine. Add the cabbage and gently stir. Cover and cook over medium heat for 10 to 15 minutes, until the cabbage is fork-tender.

3. Add the kielbasa to the pan and cook, covered, for an additional 10 to 15 minutes, until the kielbasa is cooked through. Sprinkle the bacon pieces over the top. Serve with the mustard.

**BUSY FAMILY TIP:** *If you would like to make this meal even easier, simply open a jar of fermented sauerkraut, which is what I did when I took the photo at right. All you have to do is warm the sauerkraut and kielbasa, and dinner is ready in an instant!*

| NUTRITIONAL INFO (per serving) | | | | |
|---|---|---|---|---|
| calories | fat | protein | carbs | fiber |
| 351 | 26.1 g | 17.1 g | 12.2 g | 4.2 g |
| | 67% | 19% | 14% | |

# asian lettuce wraps

■□□ KETO  NUT FREE  DAIRY FREE

**PREP TIME:** 12 minutes

**COOK TIME:** 15 minutes

**YIELD:** 4 servings

## FOR THE BACON VINAIGRETTE

4 ounces bacon (about 4 slices), cut crosswise into ½-inch-wide strips

2 cups sliced button mushrooms

3 tablespoons coconut vinegar

¼ cup beef or chicken bone broth (page 42)

2 tablespoons MCT oil

½ teaspoon stevia glycerite (optional; for sweet flavor)

Fine sea salt and fresh ground black pepper

2 tablespoons chopped fresh flat-leaf parsley

## FOR THE PORK FILLING

1 pound ground pork

¼ cup diced yellow onion

2 cloves garlic, minced

1 tablespoon coconut aminos or wheat-free tamari sauce

¼ teaspoon fish sauce (optional; for umami)

2 teaspoons minced fresh ginger

1 tablespoon coconut vinegar

1 bunch green onions, chopped

2 teaspoons dark sesame oil

## FIXINGS

1 head Boston lettuce, leaves separated

½ bunch fresh mint

½ bunch fresh basil

½ bunch fresh cilantro

1 medium cucumber, thinly sliced

1 cup fried sliced shallots, green onions, or onions (optional; see Note)

1. Make the vinaigrette: Cook the bacon pieces in a medium-sized skillet over medium heat, stirring often, until the bacon starts to crisp. Add the mushrooms and cook, tossing occasionally, until tender, 5 to 6 minutes.

2. Add the vinegar and broth and simmer until reduced by half, about 1 minute. Stir in the MCT oil and stevia, if using. Season to taste with salt and pepper. Finally, stir in the parsley. Remove from the heat and set aside.

3. Make the filling: In a medium-sized skillet over medium-high heat, brown the ground pork, stirring often to break up the meat. Remove the meat from the pan, leaving the drippings in the pan. Cook the onion in the same pan over medium heat, stirring frequently. Add the garlic, coconut aminos, fish sauce, if using, ginger, and vinegar to the onions and stir. Stir in the green onions, sesame oil, and cooked pork and continue cooking until the onions are soft, about 2 minutes.

4. Rinse the whole lettuce leaves and pat dry, being careful not tear them. Arrange the lettuce leaves around the outer edge of a large serving platter and pile the pork filling in the center. To eat, each person spoons a portion of the meat into a lettuce leaf and fills it with desired herbs, cucumber slices, and fried shallots, if using. The lettuce is wrapped around the meat like a burrito. Serve with the vinaigrette for dipping.

**NOTE:** *To make the fried shallots, place ¼ cup coconut or MCT oil and 1 cup of sliced shallots in a small saucepan. Place the saucepan over medium heat. Cook gently, stirring occasionally, for about 15 minutes (turn down the heat if they seem to be coloring too quickly), until they become dark golden brown but not black. Transfer the shallots to a colander or sieve and let drain before serving.*

**BUSY FAMILY TIP:** *The vinaigrette can be made 1 day ahead and stored in the refrigerator until you're ready to eat. Reheat before serving.*

| NUTRITIONAL INFO (per serving) | | | | |
|---|---|---|---|---|
| calories | fat | protein | carbs | fiber |
| 468 | 25.9 g | 44.5 g | 14.2 g | 3.9 g |
| | 50% | 38% | 12% | |

# pork belly in aromatic spices

**PREP TIME:** 8 minutes, plus 3 days to cure the pork belly

**COOK TIME:** 7 hours

**YIELD:** 24 servings (one 2-inch slice per serving)

¼ cup cumin seeds

¼ cup fennel seeds

¼ cup coriander seeds

4 teaspoons black peppercorns

4 cinnamon sticks

3 star anise

1 tablespoon plus 1 teaspoon white peppercorns

4 teaspoons whole cloves

1 cup fine sea salt

⅔ cup powdered erythritol

½ pork belly (6 pounds)

2 quarts chicken or beef bone broth (page 42)

3 cups kimchi (preferably sugar-free), for serving (optional)

---

**SPECIAL EQUIPMENT**

Food processor

*This recipe makes a lot of pork belly, but it's great to slice up, freeze, and use later for easy dinners. After a busy day, it's nice to be able to take one serving out of the freezer, fry it until crispy on all sides, and serve it with kimchi.*

1. In a small food processor or coffee grinder, grind the cumin seeds, fennel seeds, coriander seeds, black peppercorns, cinnamon sticks, star anise, white peppercorns, and whole cloves. Place the ground mixture in a medium-sized bowl and stir in the salt and erythritol.

2. Rub the pork belly with the spice cure, place it in a large, nonreactive metal bowl, cover tightly with foil, and refrigerate for 3 days.

3. Preheat the oven to 200°F.

4. Remove the pork belly from the refrigerator, rinse it, and place it in a casserole dish that just fits the pork belly, so it is nice and snug in the dish.

5. Cover the pork belly with the broth. Tightly cover the dish with a lid or aluminum foil and place it in the oven. Cook for 7 hours, then remove the belly from the oven and discard the liquid. Cut the belly into 2-inch slices.

6. When you are ready to eat, heat a cast-iron skillet over medium-high heat. Place each slice of pork belly that you want to serve on the pan and sear the fat side of the belly until crispy. Serve with kimchi, if desired.

| NUTRITIONAL INFO (per serving) | | | | |
|---|---|---|---|---|
| calories | fat | protein | carbs | fiber |
| 350 | 28.8 g | 18.3 g | 5.3 g | 2.6 g |
| | 74% | 21% | 6% | |

# stromboli

**KETO**  NUT FREE

**PREP TIME:** 10 minutes

**COOK TIME:** 25 minutes

**YIELD:** 6 servings

## FOR THE DOUGH

¼ cup (½ stick) unsalted butter

1¼ cups shredded mozzarella cheese (about 5 ounces)

1 teaspoon garlic powder

1 teaspoon red pepper flakes

¼ cup finely ground pork rinds or store-bought "pork dust"

2 tablespoons coconut flour

1 large egg, beaten

## FOR THE FILLING

¾ cup shredded mozzarella cheese (about 3 ounces)

12 slices salami

¼ cup Pizza Sauce (page 59) or Yellow Marinara Sauce (page 60), for serving

*I don't usually use coconut flour or almond flour because the fiber content can throw people out of ketosis, but this recipe uses just a tiny amount of coconut flour, and it is just too amazing not to include! Everyone has a different tolerance for fiber and carbs, so make sure this amount of coconut flour falls within your tolerance. Testing your ketones will tell you if you're in ketosis, so you can be your own best advocate (see page 13).*

1. Preheat the oven to 400°F.

2. In a small saucepan, melt the butter and set aside. In a large saucepan over medium heat, combine the mozzarella with the garlic powder and red pepper flakes. Heat until the cheese is melted and you can stir it with a fork. Alternatively, you can microwave the butter and cheese in heat-proof bowls.

3. Add the ground pork rinds, coconut flour, egg, and melted butter to the melted cheese and mix until a smooth dough forms.

4. Grease a sheet of parchment paper and roll out the dough on the paper to form a 14-by-8-inch rectangle. Cut ½-inch-wide, 2-inch-long strips into the long sides of the rectangle, keeping a solid rectangle of dough in the center. These strips of dough will be folded over the filling.

5. Place the shredded mozzarella and salami slices in the middle of the dough, leaving a ½-inch border all around the solid portion of the dough, and fold the strips over the filling so the flaps overlap. Pinch the dough on the ends to seal.

6. Place the filled stromboli on a baking sheet and place in the oven. Bake for 14 to 18 minutes, until light golden brown. Slice and serve with sauce on the side.

| NUTRITIONAL INFO (per serving) | | | | |
|---|---|---|---|---|
| calories | fat | protein | carbs | fiber |
| 355 | 27.9 g | 21.6 g | 4.8 g | 1.2 g |
|  | 71% | 24% | 5% |  |

# *mini lettuce wraps*

**KETO**  **NUT FREE**

**PREP TIME:** 5 minutes

**YIELD:** 3 servings

6 Boston lettuce leaves

3 tablespoons mayonnaise, divided

2 tablespoons preferred homemade mustard (pages 48 to 50), divided (optional)

4 to 6 ounces sliced ham

½ avocado, sliced

2 ounces Swiss cheese, sliced (omit if dairy-sensitive)

6 fresh chives (optional; for securing sandwiches)

**ADDITIONAL FIXINGS (OPTIONAL)**

6 tomato slices

2 tablespoons chopped red onion

2 tablespoons chopped cucumber

1. Lay the lettuce leaves flat on a large plate. Spread 1½ teaspoons mayo and 1 teaspoon mustard, if using, on each leaf. Lay equal amounts of the meat, avocado, and cheese on each leaf. Add additional fixings of your choosing, if desired. (My favorites are listed in the ingredients list, but you can use anything you like!)

2. Tuck the sides of the leaf slightly over the filling, then roll the long edge up like a burrito. Secure with chives if desired.

| NUTRITIONAL INFO (per serving) | | | | |
|---|---|---|---|---|
| calories | fat | protein | carbs | fiber |
| 339 | 27.3 g | 14.5 g | 10.5 g | 4.6 g |
|  | 72% | 17% | 12% |  |

# armadillo eggs

**KETO** **NUT FREE**

**PREP TIME:** 10 minutes

**COOK TIME:** 20 minutes

**YIELD:** 6 servings (2 eggs per serving)

8 ounces cream cheese (about 1 cup), softened

½ cup shredded cheddar cheese (about 2 ounces)

1 clove garlic, minced

1 tablespoon chopped fresh cilantro

½ teaspoon ground cumin

½ teaspoon fine sea salt

12 small jalapeño peppers

2 pounds chorizo sausage

12 slices thin-cut bacon

1. Preheat the oven to 375°F.

2. In a medium-sized bowl, combine the cream cheese, cheddar, garlic, cilantro, cumin, and salt. Place the mixture into a large sealable plastic bag and cut off one of the bottom corners.

3. Cut the tops off the jalapeños. Using a very small spoon (like an iced tea spoon) or a small knife, scrape out the ribs and seeds.

4. Stuff each jalapeño with a few tablespoons of the cheese mixture by squeezing the mixture into the opening of the jalapeño.

5. Flatten about 2½ ounces (3 tablespoons) of chorizo sausage in the palm of your hand, and place a stuffed jalapeño in the center. Fold the sausage up and around the jalapeño, forming an egg shape.

6. Wrap with a thin slice of bacon. Secure with a toothpick.

7. Place on a rimmed baking sheet and bake for 20 minutes, or until the sausage is cooked through and the bacon is crispy.

| NUTRITIONAL INFO (per serving) | | | | |
|---|---|---|---|---|
| calories | fat | protein | carbs | fiber |
| 764 | 66.7 g | 36.6 g | 2.4 g | 1 g |
| | 79% | 19% | 1% | |

poultry

# lasagna roll-ups

**PREP TIME:** 10 minutes

**COOK TIME:** 25 minutes

**YIELD:** 4 servings

¾ pound ⅛-inch-sliced roast turkey or chicken breast (about 16 slices)

**FOR THE FILLING**

1 cup ricotta cheese (about 7½ ounces)

1 large egg

⅓ cup grated Parmesan cheese (about 1⅓ ounces)

1½ cups shredded mozzarella cheese (about 6 ounces)

3 medium tomatoes, sliced very thin

Handful of fresh basil leaves

2 cups marinara sauce, homemade (page 60) or store-bought

**VARIATION: DAIRY-FREE LASAGNA ROLL-UPS.** *To make it dairy-free, simply replace the ricotta, mozzarella, and Parmesan with 2 cups of pureed avocado (from about 3 large avocados) and ⅓ cup of nutritional yeast. The creamy texture of the avocado, cheeselike flavor of the nutritional yeast, and classic Italian flavors of the basil and marinara make for an amazing dairy-free lasagna!*

*The main recipe for this fabulous ketogenic lasagna uses cheese, but I've also included a variation that's dairy-free. I often recommend that my nutrition clients avoid dairy in the beginning of their journey to give them a chance to heal if they are dairy-sensitive, so I like to offer them a recipe for a tasty Italian meal that is ketogenic yet dairy-free. In the dairy-free variation, avocado provides the creaminess instead of ricotta. I've received many positive comments about my Protein Noodle Lasagna (from my cookbook The Art of Healthy Eating), so I decided to start with that idea of using thinly shaved organic roast turkey or chicken as the "noodles."*

*Serve with my keto bread smothered in butter or MCT oil and garlic to make garlic bread (see page 276)!*

1. Preheat the oven to 325°F.

2. Align the turkey slices in a single layer on a large sheet of parchment or wax paper with the short ends facing you.

3. Make the filling: In a large mixing bowl, whisk together the ricotta cheese and egg until well blended. Stir in the Parmesan cheese, then mix in the mozzarella cheese.

4. Place ¼ cup of the cheese mixture over each slice of turkey breast and spread it into an even layer.

5. Place 3 tomato slices over the cheese mixture on each slice of turkey, then top with 3 or 4 fresh basil leaves.

6. Starting at the short end of a turkey slice, tightly roll up the "noodle" and place the roll-up seam side down in a pie pan or 8-inch square baking dish. Repeat with the rest of the "noodles."

7. Top each roll-up with 2 to 3 tablespoons of the marinara sauce.

8. Place in the oven and bake for 20 to 25 minutes, until the cheese is melted.

| NUTRITIONAL INFO (per serving) | | | | |
|---|---|---|---|---|
| calories | fat | protein | carbs | fiber |
| 467 | 25.7 g | 50 g | 9.3 g | 2.6 g |
| | 50% | 43% | 8% | |

# buffalo chicken stuffed avocados

**KETO** ■■□

**NUT FREE**

**PREP TIME:** 8 minutes

**COOK TIME:** 2 hours

**YIELD:** 12 servings

## FOR THE CHICKEN

3 tablespoons bacon fat, lard, or ghee

6 chicken leg quarters (about 3 pounds)

2 teaspoons fine sea salt

1 teaspoon fresh ground black pepper

¼ cup diced yellow onion

1 head roasted garlic (see page 46)

½ cup Buffalo wing–style hot sauce

2 cups chicken bone broth (page 42)

6 large avocados, halved and pitted, peel on

6 tablespoons blue cheese crumbles (about 1½ ounces; omit if dairy-sensitive)

12 tablespoons homemade ranch dressing, regular or dairy-free (pages 54 to 55)

1. Make the chicken: Heat the fat in a deep sauté pan over medium-high heat. Season the chicken with the salt and pepper. Place chicken in the hot fat and sauté for about 8 minutes, or until golden brown on all sides. Add the diced onion and squeeze the roasted garlic from the head into the pan. Cook over medium heat for about 8 minutes, stirring occasionally, until the onion is golden brown.

2. Add the hot sauce and broth, reduce the heat, and simmer for about 1½ hours, or until the chicken is almost falling off the bone. Remove the legs from the pan and allow them to cool until you can handle them. Shred the meat off the bone and set aside.

3. Preheat the oven to 375°F.

4. Place the avocado halves in a baking dish and carefully fill each with the shredded chicken. Add extra hot sauce if desired. Top each avocado with ½ tablespoon of blue cheese crumbles. Place in the oven for 10 to 12 minutes, or until the cheese is melted.

5. Remove from the oven and drizzle each avocado half with 1 tablespoon of ranch dressing. Serve warm.

| NUTRITIONAL INFO (per serving) | | | | |
|---|---|---|---|---|
| calories | fat | protein | carbs | fiber |
| 475 | 40 g | 23 g | 8 g | 6.5 g |
| | 76% | 19% | 7% | |

# zesty chicken pizza

**KETO** · **NUT FREE**

**PREP TIME:** 10 minutes, plus 8 minutes to make the pizza dough

**COOK TIME:** 2 hours

**YIELD:** One 12-inch pizza (6 servings)

### FOR THE CHICKEN

3 tablespoons bacon fat, lard, or ghee

6 chicken leg quarters (about 3 pounds)

2 teaspoons fine sea salt

1 teaspoon fresh ground black pepper

¼ cup diced yellow onion

1 head roasted garlic (see page 46)

½ cup Buffalo wing–style hot sauce

2 cups chicken bone broth (page 42)

1 recipe dough from Deep Dish BBQ Chicken Pizza (page 212)

### FOR THE PIZZA SAUCE

½ cup tomato sauce, homemade (page 59) or store-bought

¼ cup Buffalo wing–style hot sauce

### TOPPINGS

6 tablespoons blue cheese crumbles (about 1½ ounces; omit if dairy-sensitive)

1 stalk celery, diced

Homemade ranch dressing, regular or dairy-free (pages 54 to 55), for serving

1. Make the chicken: Heat the fat in a deep sauté pan over medium-high heat. Season the chicken with the salt and pepper. Place chicken in the hot fat and sauté for about 8 minutes, or until golden brown on all sides. Add the diced onion and squeeze the roasted garlic from the head into the pan. Cook on medium heat for about 8 minutes, stirring occasionally, until the onion is golden brown.

2. Add the hot sauce and broth, reduce the heat, and simmer for about 1½ hours, or until chicken is almost falling off the bone. Remove the legs from the pan and allow them to cool until you can handle them. Shred the meat off the bone and set aside.

3. While the chicken simmers, make the pizza dough (see page 212). Preheat the oven to 325°F. Grease a lasagna pan or 12-inch cast-iron skillet well and form the dough to fit the pan. Prebake the crust for 8 minutes.

4. Make the sauce: In a small bowl, combine the tomato sauce and hot sauce. Set aside.

5. Remove the pizza crust from the oven and spread the pizza sauce, shredded chicken, blue cheese, and celery pieces evenly over the crust. Place back in the oven and bake for 10 minutes, or until the cheese is melted. Serve with the ranch dressing.

| NUTRITIONAL INFO (per serving) | | | | |
|---|---|---|---|---|
| calories | fat | protein | carbs | fiber |
| 610 | 41.2 g | 55.2 g | 6 g | 0.5 g |
| | 61% | 36% | 4% | |

# DEEP DISH
## *bbq chicken pizza*

■■□ NUT
**KETO** **FREE**

**PREP TIME:** 10 minutes

**COOK TIME:** 30 minutes

**YIELD:** One 12-inch pizza (6 servings)

### FOR THE DEEP DISH PIZZA CRUST

6 large eggs, separated

½ teaspoon cream of tartar

½ cup unflavored egg white protein (or unflavored whey protein if not dairy-sensitive)

3 ounces cream cheese (about 6 tablespoons), softened (or the 6 reserved yolks if dairy-sensitive)

### FOR THE TOPPINGS AND SAUCE

3 slices bacon, diced

2 tablespoons diced yellow onion

2 boneless, skinless chicken thighs, cut into ½-inch cubes

1 cup tomato sauce, homemade (page 59) or store-bought

¼ cup coconut aminos or wheat-free tamari sauce

⅓ cup powdered erythritol or ½ teaspoon stevia glycerite

¼ cup coconut vinegar

1 head roasted garlic (see page 46) or 3 cloves raw garlic, smashed with the side of a knife

2 teaspoons liquid smoke

1 cup shredded provolone or sharp cheddar cheese (about 4 ounces; omit if dairy-sensitive)

### SPECIAL EQUIPMENT

Blender

1. Preheat the oven to 325°F. Grease a lasagna pan or 12-inch cast-iron skillet.

2. Whip the egg whites and cream of tartar until very stiff (I use a stand mixer and let it go for 5 minutes). Slowly sift in the protein powder while the mixer is on low speed. Using a spatula, gently fold the softened cream cheese into the whites.

3. Spoon the dough mixture into the prepared pan and prebake the crust for 18 minutes.

4. Meanwhile, make the sauce and toppings: In a sauté pan, sauté the diced bacon and onion until the bacon is crisp. Add the chicken pieces to sear and cook all the way through, about 5 minutes. Remove the cooked chicken from pan and set aside.

5. Leave the bacon, onion, and drippings in the pan. Add the tomato sauce, coconut aminos, erythritol, vinegar, garlic, and liquid smoke and stir until smooth. Place this mixture into a blender and blend until you have a very smooth sauce.

6. Remove the crust from the oven and increase the oven temperature to 400°F. Top the crust with the sauce, chicken, and shredded provolone and return to the oven. Bake until the cheese melts and starts to brown, about 5 minutes.

**FUN FAMILY TIP:** *For a fun family food event, make this recipe into individual pizzas so kids can build their own. Mini projects help kids get into cooking at an early age, and they love customizing their toppings—my son Micah loves olives on his pizza, for instance, whereas my younger son Kai prefers lots of sauce and sausage. To make mini pizzas, divide the dough into 4 even portions and form it into four greased 4-inch cake pans or 4-inch cast-iron skillets. Prebake the crusts for 10 minutes. Remove from the oven and have your kids top each crust with whatever sauce and toppings they desire. Then bake the topped pizzas until the toppings are hot and melted.*

| NUTRITIONAL INFO (per serving) | | | | |
|---|---|---|---|---|
| calories | fat | protein | carbs | fiber |
| 617 | 42 g | 51.8 g | 5.2 g | 0 g |
| | 61% | 34% | 3% | |

# chicken enchiladas

**KETO** · **NUT FREE**

**PREP TIME:** 10 minutes, plus 20 minutes to rest

**COOK TIME:** 45 minutes

**YIELD:** 8 servings

4 boneless, skinless chicken thighs

1 teaspoon fine sea salt

½ teaspoon ground cumin

½ teaspoon chili powder, plus more for garnish

¼ cup coconut oil

1 cup diced yellow onion

4 cups Enchilada Sauce (page 72), divided

16 large slices roast chicken breast (from the deli counter)

3 cups shredded sharp cheddar cheese (about 12 ounces), divided

**FOR GARNISH**

Sour cream

Diced yellow tomatoes

Fresh cilantro leaves

1. Preheat the oven to 350°F.

2. Season both sides of the chicken thighs with the salt, cumin, and chili powder. Heat the oil in a large skillet over medium heat and cook the chicken on both sides until done in the middle and the juices run clear, about 5 minutes per side. Set it aside on a plate to cool and then shred it with a fork.

3. Place the diced onion in the same skillet you used to cook the chicken and cook, while stirring, for 4 to 5 minutes, until caramelized and very golden brown. Remove the onion from the skillet and set aside.

4. Pour 2 cups of the enchilada sauce into a 9-by-13-inch casserole dish.

5. To assemble the enchiladas, lay a slice of chicken breast on a plate. Sprinkle 2 heaping tablespoons of the shredded cheese down the middle, followed by 3 tablespoons of shredded chicken, then top the chicken with 1 tablespoon of the caramelized onions. Roll it up tightly and place it seam side down in the casserole dish. Repeat with the rest of the chicken breast "tortillas."

6. Pour the remaining 2 cups of sauce over the enchiladas, then sprinkle on the remaining 1 cup of cheddar cheese and dust with a little chili powder. Place the dish in the oven and bake for 30 minutes, or until hot and bubbly.

7. Remove from the oven and let rest for 15 to 20 minutes before serving.

8. Serve with a dollop of sour cream, diced yellow tomatoes, and cilantro.

| NUTRITIONAL INFO (per serving) | | | | |
| --- | --- | --- | --- | --- |
| calories | fat | protein | carbs | fiber |
| 602 | 39.6 g | 47.3 g | 14 g | 4.6 g |
| | 59% | 31% | 9% | |

# herb and ricotta rotolo

■□□ **KETO**   **NUT FREE**

**PREP TIME:** 15 minutes, plus 10 minutes to rest

**COOK TIME:** 30 minutes

**YIELD:** 12 servings

**FOR THE FILLING**

12 ounces ricotta cheese (about 1½ cups)

1 cup grated Parmesan cheese (about 4 ounces)

½ cup fresh oregano, finely chopped

½ cup fresh flat-leaf parsley, finely chopped

1 large egg

1 head roasted garlic (see page 46) or 3 cloves raw garlic, minced

½ teaspoon fine sea salt

¼ teaspoon freshly grated nutmeg or ⅛ teaspoon ground nutmeg

⅛ teaspoon fresh ground black pepper

24 slices roast turkey or chicken breast (from the deli counter), cut into 6-inch-long, 1½-inch-wide strips

2 cups tomato sauce, homemade (page 59) or store-bought, divided

½ cup shredded mozzarella cheese (about 2 ounces)

Grated Parmesan cheese, for serving (optional)

*Rotolo, which is literally translated as "scroll" or "coil," is not widely known outside of Italy. The authentic way of making rotolo is quite technical and time-consuming. It involves spreading a very large sheet of fresh pasta with a filling, forming it into a roulade, wrapping the roulade in a tea towel and poaching it, then slicing it to serve with a sauce. But my keto recipe isn't fussy at all! Here's to easy meals!*

1. Preheat the oven to 300°F.

2. Place all of the filling ingredients in a large bowl and mix to combine.

3. Lay out a slice of the deli meat with the shorter end facing you. Place ⅓ packed cup of filling onto the slice of meat. Roll it up starting with the short end closest to you. Place the roll seam side down. Continue with the remaining deli meat and filling.

4. Place 1 cup of the tomato sauce in the bottom of a 12-inch cast-iron or other ovenproof skillet or sauté pan. Place the rolls into the pan on their ends, snuggled tightly together with the filling facing up. Drizzle the remaining 1 cup of tomato sauce over the rotolo. Place in the oven and bake for 20 minutes, or until the cheese is melted completely.

5. Remove from the oven and sprinkle the mozzarella over the top. Return to the oven for 10 minutes, or until the cheese is golden. Let stand for 10 minutes before serving. Serve with Parmesan cheese, if desired.

| NUTRITIONAL INFO (per serving) | | | | |
|---|---|---|---|---|
| calories | fat | protein | carbs | fiber |
| 386 | 14.2 g | 60.5 g | 5.3 g | 1.7 g |
| | 33% | 63% | 5% | |

# BROWN BUTTER
## *chicken and "pasta"*

**KETO**  **NUT FREE**

**PREP TIME:** 6 minutes

**COOK TIME:** 30 minutes

**YIELD:** 4 servings

6 bone-in chicken thighs with skin

½ teaspoon fine sea salt

½ teaspoon fresh ground black pepper

8 tablespoons unsalted butter, divided

4 cups shredded purple or green cabbage (about 1 medium head)

1 head roasted garlic (see page 46) or 3 cloves raw garlic, minced

2 tablespoons chopped fresh thyme, tarragon, sage, or your favorite herb

*I am a huge fan of the television show* Top Chef. *In one episode the contestants were challenged to make a holiday meal entirely in one pot. They could cook something, empty the pot, and reuse it, but everything had to be cooked in that one vessel. Here is my one-pot entry!*

1. Season the chicken thighs with the salt and pepper. Melt 2 tablespoons of the butter in a large pan over medium heat. Once the butter is hot, sear the chicken for 10 minutes, or until golden brown on both sides and cooked through. Remove from the pan and set aside.

2. Place the cabbage in the pan and cook over medium heat, stirring frequently, for 15 minutes, or until cooked. Remove from the pan and set on a serving dish.

3. Place the remaining 6 tablespoons of butter in the pan and heat on high until the butter starts to froth and get golden brown, stirring often. Remove from the heat and squeeze the roasted garlic from the head into the browned butter and stir to incorporate.

4. Arrange the chicken thighs on the cabbage "pasta" and pour the garlicky brown butter over chicken. Sprinkle with thyme or your favorite herb.

| NUTRITIONAL INFO (per serving) | | | | |
|---|---|---|---|---|
| calories | fat | protein | carbs | fiber |
| 459 | 37.6 g | 24.7 g | 5.9 g | 2.4 g |
| | 74% | 22% | 5% | |

# duck confit

KETO    NUT FREE    DAIRY FREE

**PREP TIME:** 8 minutes, plus up to 2 days to cure

**COOK TIME:** 3 hours

**YIELD:** 4 servings

3 tablespoons fine sea salt

2 heads roasted garlic (see page 46) or 4 cloves raw garlic, smashed

½ cup diced shallot or yellow onion

6 sprigs fresh thyme

⅛ teaspoon ground nutmeg

⅛ teaspoon ground cloves

4 duck legs with thighs

4 duck wings, trimmed

½ teaspoon fresh ground black pepper

4 cups duck fat

¼ cup coconut oil or duck fat, for reheating

Sliced endive, for garnish (optional)

1. Sprinkle 1 tablespoon of salt in the bottom of a dish large enough to lay the duck in a single layer. Evenly spread 1 head of roasted garlic, half of the diced shallot, and half of the thyme, nutmeg, and cloves in the dish on top of the salt. Place the duck, skin side up, over the salt and spice mixture, then spread the remaining salt, garlic, shallot, thyme, nutmeg, and cloves on the duck. Top with a touch of pepper. Cover and refrigerate for 1 to 2 days.

2. Preheat the oven to 225°F.

3. Place the 4 cups of the duck fat in a medium-sized saucepan and melt over medium heat. Wipe the salt and seasonings off the duck. Place the duck pieces close together in a single layer in a baking dish with high sides. Pour the melted fat over the duck so that all the pieces are covered in fat.

4. Place the dish in the oven and bake slowly until the duck is fork-tender, about 2½ to 3 hours. Remove from the oven. Cool and store the duck in the fat to preserve it. This will keep in the refrigerator for several weeks.

5. When ready to serve, heat the ¼ cup of coconut oil or duck fat in a cast-iron skillet over high heat. Once the oil is hot, place the duck in the skillet skin side down and fry until golden brown, about 5 minutes. Remove from the heat and place on a serving platter.

6. Garnish with sliced endive, if desired.

**BUSY FAMILY TIP:** *Make a double batch and store in airtight containers in the freezer for up to 3 months for easy dinners.*

| NUTRITIONAL INFO (per serving) | | | | |
|---|---|---|---|---|
| calories | fat | protein | carbs | fiber |
| 675 | 57.8 g | 29 g | 5.5 g | 0.7 g |
|  | 77% | 17% | 3% |  |

# gumbo

**KETO** | **NUT FREE** | **DAIRY FREE**

**PREP TIME:** 10 minutes

**COOK TIME:** 2 hours 20 minutes

**YIELD:** 12 servings

6 boneless chicken thighs with skin

1 teaspoon fine sea salt

1 teaspoon fresh ground black pepper

¼ cup coconut oil, duck fat, or lard, for frying

5 tablespoons bacon fat or duck fat (or unsalted butter if not dairy-sensitive)

⅓ cup chopped yellow onion

2 heads roasted garlic (see page 46) or 6 cloves raw garlic, minced

1 green bell pepper, seeded and chopped

3 stalks celery, chopped

2 tablespoons coconut aminos

2 tablespoons coconut vinegar

1 teaspoon stevia glycerite

1 cup flat-leaf parsley, chopped fine

4 cups beef bone broth (page 42; see Note)

1 (14½-ounce) can stewed tomatoes with juice

2 cups frozen sliced okra

1 pound smoked sausage, cut into ¼-inch-thick slices

½ pound medium shrimp, peeled and deveined

4 green onions, white and green parts, sliced

1. Season the chicken thighs with the salt and pepper. Heat the oil in a large sauté pan over medium-high heat. Cook the chicken for about 8 minutes, until browned on all sides, and remove from the pan.

2. Turn the heat to low and melt the bacon fat in the pan. Add the onion, garlic, bell pepper, and celery and cook for 10 minutes. Add the coconut aminos, vinegar, stevia, and parsley. Season with salt and pepper to taste. Cook, while stirring frequently, for 10 minutes.

3. Add the broth, whisking constantly. Return the chicken to the pan and bring to a boil, then reduce the heat, cover, and simmer for 45 minutes. Add the tomatoes and okra. Cover and simmer for 1 hour.

4. About 10 minutes before the mixture is done simmering, place the sausage and the shrimp in a sauté pan or skillet over medium-high heat. Cook for about 6 minutes, until the shrimp are pink and no longer translucent, flipping halfway through. Remove from the heat.

5. Remove the chicken thighs from the pan. The chicken should be very tender. Remove the meat from the bones and save the bones to make chicken bone broth (I store bones in the freezer). Place the chicken meat and skin back into the pot.

6. Just before serving, add the green onions, cooked sausage, and shrimp.

**NOTE:** *If using store-bought beef broth, which is thinner than homemade bone broth, add 1 teaspoon of guar gum at the same time as the broth as a natural thickener.*

| NUTRITIONAL INFO (per serving) | | | | |
|---|---|---|---|---|
| calories | fat | protein | carbs | fiber |
| 330 | 25.3 g | 20.1 g | 5.7 g | 1.7 g |
| | 69% | 24% | 7% | |

# bbq chicken and "faux" tatoes

**KETO** NUT FREE DAIRY FREE

**PREP TIME:** 8 minutes

**COOK TIME:** 2 hours

**YIELD:** 6 servings

3 tablespoons bacon fat, lard, or ghee

3 pounds chicken legs

2 teaspoons fine sea salt

1 teaspoon fresh ground black pepper

¼ cup diced yellow onion

1 head roasted garlic (see page 46)

2 tablespoons tomato paste

2 teaspoons liquid smoke

½ teaspoon stevia glycerite

1 cup chicken bone broth (page 42; see Note)

¼ cup canned, full-fat coconut milk

1 medium zucchini, cut into ½-inch cubes

Chopped fresh cilantro, for garnish (optional)

1. Heat the fat in a deep sauté pan over medium-high heat. Season the chicken with the salt and pepper. Place the chicken in the hot fat and sauté for about 8 minutes, or until golden brown on all sides. Remove from the pan.

2. Add the diced onion to the pan. Squeeze the roasted garlic from the head into the pan. Cook on medium heat for about 8 minutes, stirring occasionally, until the onion is golden brown. Add the tomato paste, liquid smoke, and stevia. Cook for 5 more minutes, stirring often.

3. Return the seared chicken to the pan and add the broth and coconut milk. Bring to a gentle boil, reduce heat, and simmer for about 1½ hours, or until the chicken is almost falling off the bone. Season to taste with salt and pepper.

4. Add the zucchini chunks to the pan and cook until the zucchini is soft, about 15 minutes. Sprinkle with cilantro if desired before serving.

**NOTE:** *If using store-bought chicken broth, which is thinner than homemade bone broth, add 1 teaspoon of guar gum at the same time as the broth as a natural thickener.*

**BUSY FAMILY TIP:** *This can be made up to 4 days ahead and stored in the refrigerator until you're ready to serve. The flavors get deeper as it rests.*

| NUTRITIONAL INFO (per serving) | | | | |
|---|---|---|---|---|
| calories | fat | protein | carbs | fiber |
| 519 | 25.9 g | 67.5 g | 4 g | 1 g |
| | 45% | 52% | 3% | |

# chicken à la king

**■■□ NUT**
**KETO FREE**

**PREP TIME:** 15 minutes

**COOK TIME:** 35 minutes

**YIELD:** 6 servings

---

6 bone-in chicken thighs with skin

1 teaspoon fine sea salt

1 teaspoon fresh ground black pepper

2 tablespoons bacon fat, duck fat, or coconut oil, divided, for frying

**FOR THE SAUCE**

5 tablespoons unsalted butter

2 cups ½-inch-diced bell peppers (mix of red, green, orange, and/or yellow)

½ cup diced yellow onion

¼ pound button mushrooms, trimmed and quartered

1 cup chicken bone broth (page 42), plus more if needed

4 ounces cream cheese (about ½ cup), softened

3 large egg yolks

1 tablespoon lemon juice

½ teaspoon smoked paprika

1 medium zucchini

Chopped fresh flat-leaf parsley, for garnish

---

**SPECIAL EQUIPMENT**

Spiral slicer
(see Note, page 284)

1. Season the chicken thighs with the salt and pepper. Heat the bacon fat in a large sauté pan over medium-high heat. Cook the chicken for about 8 minutes, until browned on all sides. Lower the heat to medium-low and cook until chicken is done and no longer pink inside, 15 to 20 minutes. Remove from the heat.

2. While the chicken cooks, make the sauce: Heat the butter in a 4-quart saucepan over high heat, whisking occasionally, until it starts to foam and brown specks appear. Lower the heat to medium and add the peppers, onion, and mushrooms and cook, stirring occasionally, until softened, about 6 to 8 minutes.

3. In a bowl, whisk together the broth and cream cheese, then add to the saucepan. (Do not skip whisking first or you will have small bits of cream cheese in the liquid.)

4. In a small bowl, whisk together the yolks, lemon juice, and paprika. Whisk in ½ cup of the sauce from the saucepan, then slowly pour the yolk mixture into the saucepan, stirring constantly. Cook over very low heat (higher heat will cause the sauce to curdle) until the sauce is slightly thickened, about 2 minutes. Remove from the heat and set aside.

5. Remove the skin and chicken meat from the bones and cut the meat and skin into bite-sized pieces. (Save the bones for bone broth; I store bones in the freezer until I'm ready to make broth.) Add the chicken chunks and skin to the sauce, then cook over low heat (do not simmer or the sauce will curdle), stirring occasionally, until the chicken is heated through. Add more broth to thin if desired. Season to taste with salt and pepper.

6. Meanwhile, slice the zucchini into thin "noodles" using a spiral slicer.

7. Spoon the chicken à la king over the zucchini noodles. Garnish with parsley.

| NUTRITIONAL INFO (per serving) | | | | |
|---|---|---|---|---|
| calories | fat | protein | carbs | fiber |
| 358 | 28.1 g | 21.1 g | 6.1 g | 1.5 g |
| | 71% | 24% | 7% | |

# creamy chicken casserole

■■□ KETO   NUT FREE

**PREP TIME:** 7 minutes
**COOK TIME:** 40 minutes
**YIELD:** 8 servings

8 slices bacon

1 medium zucchini, cut into ½-inch cubes

2 large eggs

## FOR THE DRESSING

½ cup Copycat Baconnaise (page 65) or mayonnaise

¼ cup chicken bone broth (page 42)

1 tablespoon snipped chives

1½ teaspoons finely chopped fresh dill

1½ teaspoons finely chopped fresh flat-leaf parsley

½ teaspoon onion powder

½ teaspoon garlic powder

Fine sea salt and fresh ground black pepper to taste

2 cups chopped cooked chicken thigh meat (about ¾ pound)

½ avocado, diced

1 tomato, seeded and diced

½ cup cubed cheddar cheese (about 2 ounces; omit if dairy-sensitive)

## FOR GARNISH (OPTIONAL)

2 tablespoons chopped scallions

2 tablespoons seeded and chopped jalapeño peppers

1. Fry the bacon in a large, oven-safe skillet until crisp. Remove the bacon from the pan, leaving the drippings. Crumble the bacon and set aside.

2. Add the cubed zucchini to the pan and fry for 5 minutes, or until the zucchini is tender and has absorbed the bacon drippings. Remove the zucchini from the pan and allow it to cool.

3. Preheat the oven to 350°F.

4. Place the eggs in a saucepan and cover with cold water. Bring the water to a boil, cover, and remove from the heat. Let the eggs stand in the hot water for 10 to 12 minutes. Remove from the hot water, cool in ice water or under cold running water, then peel and slice.

5. In a large bowl, combine all dressing ingredients and mix well. Add the hard-boiled eggs, chicken, avocado, tomato, cheese (if not dairy-sensitive), bacon crumbles, and cooled zucchini cubes. Toss to combine well.

6. Transfer the mixture to an 8-inch-square baking dish. Place in the oven and bake for 20 minutes. Garnish with the scallions and jalapeños, if desired, before serving.

**VARIATION: CREAMY CHICKEN SALAD.**
*To serve this dish as a salad, place the mixture in the refrigerator to chill completely and allow the flavors to blend, then serve over a bed of lettuce, garnished with scallions and jalapeños, if you wish.*

| NUTRITIONAL INFO (per serving) | | | | |
|---|---|---|---|---|
| calories | fat | protein | carbs | fiber |
| 283 | 25.9 g | 10.5 g | 2.9 g | 1.4 g |
| | 82% | 15% | 4% | |

# fish and
# seafood

# grilled halibut
## WITH SMOKY AVOCADO CREAM

KETO · NUT FREE · DAIRY FREE

**PREP TIME:** 10 minutes

**COOK TIME:** 10 minutes

**YIELD:** 4 servings

### FOR THE AVOCADO CREAM

1 avocado, peeled, halved, and pitted

1 tablespoon plus 1 teaspoon lime juice

¼ cup fish bone broth (page 42) or water, plus more if needed

¼ cup mayonnaise

3 tablespoons coarsely chopped green onions

¼ teaspoon smoked paprika

¼ teaspoon fine sea salt

⅛ teaspoon fresh ground black pepper

4 (8-ounce) halibut steaks

Fine sea salt and fresh ground black pepper

MCT oil, for brushing the fish

Chopped fresh cilantro, for garnish (optional)

2 lime slices, cut into half-moons, for garnish (optional)

### SPECIAL EQUIPMENT

Grill

Blender

*I enjoy serving this preparation of halibut on a bed of BLT Coleslaw (page 289), using purple cabbage to give the dish a beautiful array of colors. But any bright, crunchy, summery side will do. For an added touch of color, sprinkle with some hibiscus sea salt.*

1. Preheat a grill to medium-high heat.

2. While the grill is heating up, make the avocado cream: Place the avocado, lime juice, broth, mayonnaise, green onions, paprika, salt, and pepper in a blender. Puree until very smooth, adding more broth if the sauce is too thick. Set aside for serving.

3. Season the halibut generously with salt and pepper. Brush both sides of the fish with generous amount of MCT oil. Grill for 4 to 5 minutes per side, or until the fish barely flakes. Remove from the heat.

4. Serve with generous amount of avocado cream. Garnish with fresh cilantro and a lime slice if desired.

| NUTRITIONAL INFO (per serving) | | | | |
|---|---|---|---|---|
| calories | fat | protein | carbs | fiber |
| 525 | 28.8 g | 60 g | 4.9 g | 3.6 g |
| | 49% | 46% | 4% | |

# shrimp po' boys

KETO ■■□ · NUT FREE · DAIRY FREE

**PREP TIME:** 10 minutes

**COOK TIME:** 10 minutes

**YIELD:** 2 sandwiches (1 per serving)

**FOR THE DRESSING**

¼ cup mayonnaise or Copycat Baconnaise (page 65)

2 tablespoons Dijon mustard (page 49)

1 teaspoon dill pickle juice

½ teaspoon garlic powder

2 teaspoons Seafood Seasoning (page 75)

½ teaspoon fresh ground black pepper

½ pound medium shrimp, peeled and deveined

2 teaspoons Seafood Seasoning (page 75)

2 tablespoons coconut oil, divided

2 cloves garlic, minced

2 (6-inch) Keto Hot Dog Buns (page 276)

½ medium red onion, sliced thin

1 tomato, sliced thin

**ADDITIONAL TOPPINGS (OPTIONAL)**

Capers

Sliced avocado

Fresh herbs

Diced cabbage

*This New Orleans–inspired sandwich is pretty filling, but if you're looking for a great side to serve with it, try my Creamy Coleslaw (page 288).*

1. Make the dressing: In a bowl, whisk together the mayonnaise, mustard, pickle juice, garlic powder, seafood seasoning, and pepper. Cover and refrigerate until ready to serve.

2. In a large bowl, toss the shrimp with the 2 teaspoons seafood seasoning to coat. Heat a skillet over medium-high heat. Add 1 tablespoon of the oil and the minced garlic and sauté for 5 minutes. Add the shrimp and sauté for 3 minutes on each side, or until they turn opaque and pink. Remove from the heat and set aside.

3. Split the buns lengthwise. Add the remaining tablespoon of coconut oil to the pan and lightly fry the inside of the buns.

4. Divide the dressing between the two sandwiches, coating both sides of the toasted buns. Top with the shrimp, red onion slices, and tomato slices, as well as any additional toppings of your choice.

| NUTRITIONAL INFO (per serving) | | | | |
|---|---|---|---|---|
| calories | fat | protein | carbs | fiber |
| 516 | 34 g | 39 g | 14 g | 3.8 g |
| | 60% | 30% | 11% | |

# gravlax

**PREP TIME:** 5 minutes, plus 24 hours to cure

**YIELD:** About 32 ounces (4 ounces per serving)

1 cup fine sea salt

¼ cup powdered erythritol (optional)

1 tablespoon crushed black peppercorns

1 teaspoon grated fresh ginger

2 cloves garlic, minced

2 (1-pound) fresh salmon fillets, pin bones removed

*My dad is famous for his fish preparations, so I asked him to share his recipe secrets with me. His first instruction—given with a straight face—was, "Catch a bunch of salmon or trout." I love how he's still teaching me to live off the land (and water!) for the freshest and best food possible. When curing fish, as in this recipe, it is particularly important to use very fresh fish that has not been previously frozen. The flavor and texture will change for the worse if you use frozen fish or fish that is not super fresh.*

*Most store-bought gravlax includes sugar in its curing mixture, which lends a sweet undertone. To mimic this traditional flavor, I include a touch of erythritol in my curing mixture. You can leave it out if you prefer, but the gravlax will not have the familiar, traditional flavor profile.*

1. Combine the salt, erythritol, if using, peppercorns, ginger, and garlic in a medium-sized bowl.

2. Place the salmon on a large sheet of parchment paper and spread the spice mixture evenly all over the fish. Fold the parchment tightly around the fish. Secure with tape.

3. Place the wrapped salmon in a lasagna dish or other dish with deep sides (in case some liquid leaks). Place a heavy book or a brick on the fillets. Refrigerate for about 12 hours.

4. Flip the fish over and refrigerate another 12 hours with the weight on top. Remove from the fridge, rinse well, and store in an airtight container in the fridge for up to 2 weeks.

| NUTRITIONAL INFO (per serving) | | | | |
|---|---|---|---|---|
| calories | fat | protein | carbs | fiber |
| 247 | 13.4 g | 31 g | 0.4 g | 0 g |
| | 49% | 50% | 1% | |

# gravlax sushi

**KETO** **NUT FREE** **DAIRY FREE**

**PREP TIME:** 10 minutes, plus 24 hours for the gravlax and 2 hours to chill

**YIELD:** 2 servings

2 slices Gravlax (page 236) (about 1 ounce)

1 ounce cream cheese (about 2 tablespoons), softened

1 avocado, halved, pitted, and sliced

2 thin red pepper strips

2 thin cucumber strips

**FOR SERVING (OPTIONAL)**

Coconut aminos

Wasabi

Pickled ginger (see Note)

1. On a piece of parchment paper, lay the salmon slices, slightly overlapping, to form a 6-by-4-inch rectangle.

2. Spread the cream cheese over the salmon. Place the avocado slices, peppers, and cucumbers along the long side of salmon rectangle. Starting from the edge with the sliced vegetables, roll up salmon like a jellyroll to form a log. Wrap tightly in plastic wrap.

3. Refrigerate for 2 hours, or until firm enough to slice. Slice into 12 sushi pieces. Serve with coconut aminos, wasabi, and pickled ginger, if desired.

**NOTE:** *When using pickled ginger, stay away from pink ginger. Ginger is naturally an ivory color, and the pink color is created with food dye.*

| NUTRITIONAL INFO (per serving) | | | | |
|---|---|---|---|---|
| calories | fat | protein | carbs | fiber |
| 226 | 18.6 g | 10.7 g | 4.8 g | 2.4 g |
| | 74% | 19% | 8% | |

# seafood salad

■■□
KETO  NUT FREE  DAIRY FREE

**PREP TIME:** 10 minutes, plus at least 2 hours to chill

**COOK TIME:** 30 minutes

**YIELD:** 8 servings

6 eggs

### FOR THE SEAFOOD

2 tablespoons bacon fat, lard, or MCT oil

¼ cup diced yellow onion

1 head roasted garlic (see page 46) or 3 cloves raw garlic, minced

1 pound large shrimp, peeled and deveined

1 pound bay scallops, rinsed and patted dry

1 (6-ounce) can crabmeat, drained and flaked

1 (12-ounce) can tuna or salmon, drained and flaked

½ pound squid bodies, cut into ¼-inch circles, rinsed and patted dry

1 tablespoon Seafood Seasoning (page 75)

Fine sea salt and fresh ground black pepper

1 cup mayonnaise or Copycat Baconnaise (page 65)

2 tablespoons preferred homemade mustard (pages 48 to 50)

1 teaspoon ground dried oregano

½ teaspoon ground turmeric

⅛ teaspoon stevia glycerite

1 large green bell pepper, seeded and chopped

2 stalks celery, chopped

3 tablespoons finely diced red onion

Torn leaf lettuce, for serving (optional)

½ teaspoon smoked paprika, for garnish

1. Place the eggs in a saucepan and cover with cold water. Bring the water to a boil, cover, and remove from the heat. Let the eggs stand in the hot water for 10 to 12 minutes. Remove from the hot water, cool in ice water or under cold running water, then peel and chop 5 of the eggs and set aside. Reserve the remaining egg for garnish.

2. Heat the bacon fat over medium heat in a large skillet. Add the onion and garlic and cook, stirring constantly, until translucent, about 7 minutes. Add the shrimp, scallops, crabmeat, and tuna. Cook until the shrimp are pink and the scallops are opaque, 8 to 10 minutes. Add the squid during the last 1½ minutes of cooking. (Squid cooks very quickly and can easily turn rubbery if overcooked.) Add the seafood seasoning and season to taste with salt and pepper. Remove from the heat.

3. In a large bowl, whisk together the mayonnaise, mustard, oregano, turmeric, and stevia. Mix in the bell pepper, celery, red onion, and chopped eggs. Add the seafood mixture and toss until evenly combined. Cover and refrigerate for 2 to 3 hours or overnight to let the flavors blend.

4. When ready to serve, slice the remaining hard-boiled egg. Arrange the seafood salad on a platter or a bed of lettuce leaves, if desired. Garnish with the egg slices and paprika.

| NUTRITIONAL INFO (per serving) | | | | |
| --- | --- | --- | --- | --- |
| calories | fat | protein | carbs | fiber |
| 503 | 31.9 g | 42.6 g | 9.7 g | 1.3 g |
| | 57% | 34% | 8% | |

# grandpa joe's barramundi

**PREP TIME:** 6 minutes

**COOK TIME:** 14 minutes

**YIELD:** 4 servings

2 (1-pound) barramundi fillets, ¾ inch thick

2 tablespoons MCT oil

1 teaspoon fine sea salt

⅓ cup (⅔ stick) unsalted butter, softened

⅓ cup grated Parmesan cheese (about 1⅓ ounces)

⅓ cup mayonnaise

2 tablespoons chopped fresh dill

2 tablespoons chopped green onions

*I've named this recipe in honor of Grandpa Joe, who made this dish for me years ago with trout, halibut, and walleye that he had caught (I don't think he has ever purchased fish from the store). I've used barramundi here because it is a spectacular fish. The meat is light, flaky, and succulent, and because barramundi dine on plankton rather than mercury-filled smaller fish, it has extremely low levels of the toxin, making it a particularly good choice for pregnant women. If you aren't a fan of the flavor of salmon in other dishes but want its nutritional benefits, barramundi has comparable levels of omega-3 and makes an excellent substitute.*

*If you are using a different kind of fish here, make sure the fillets are the same thickness and size to keep the cooking time the same.*

1. Place the oven rack in the top position, about 4 inches below the broiler. Preheat the broiler to high.

2. Rub the fillets with the MCT oil and season with the salt.

3. Place the fillets in a broiler pan and broil for 10 minutes (or 8 minutes if the fillets are less than ¾ inch thick).

4. Meanwhile, make the coating: In a small bowl, combine the softened butter, Parmesan, mayo, dill, and green onions.

5. Remove the fillets from the oven. Spread the fillets with a ½- to ¾-inch-thick coating.

6. Place back in the oven and broil for another 3 to 4 minutes, until the coating browns.

| NUTRITIONAL INFO (per serving) | | | | |
|---|---|---|---|---|
| calories | fat | protein | carbs | fiber |
| 580 | 44 g | 43.9 g | 1.5 g | 0 g |
| | 68% | 30% | 1% | |

# *grilled whole mackerel*

## WITH HOMEMADE TARTAR SAUCE

**KETO**  **NUT FREE**  **DAIRY FREE**

**PREP TIME:** 7 minutes

**COOK TIME:** 30 minutes

**YIELD:** 2 servings

2 whole mackerels (6 ounces each), scaled, gutted, and cleaned

¾ teaspoon fine sea salt

½ teaspoon fresh ground black pepper

2 lemon or lime wedges

¼ cup Tartar Sauce (page 52), for serving

**SPECIAL EQUIPMENT**

Grill

*There are many types of mackerel, and they range in size from very large to quite small. I used Boston mackerel, which is a medium-sized fish.*

1. Preheat a grill to medium heat.

2. Make 3 deep cuts on each side of the fish. Season the fillets with the salt and pepper.

3. Place the fish skin side down on the grill and grill for 15 minutes, then flip them over and grill for another 15 minutes. Remove from the grill. Squeeze lemon over each fish and serve with tartar sauce.

**VARIATION: PAN-FRIED WHOLE MACKEREL.** *To pan-fry the fish, prepare the fish as described above. Preheat a large sauté pan over medium-high with 1 tablespoon of butter or lard. Place the fish in the pan and fry for 12 to 15 minutes, until the flesh is flaky. Flip the fish over and cook for an additional 2 to 3 minutes. Remove from the pan and serve with a squeeze of lemon and tartar sauce.*

| NUTRITIONAL INFO (per serving) | | | | |
|---|---|---|---|---|
| calories | fat | protein | carbs | fiber |
| 509 | 37.6 g | 42.7 g | 1.5 g | 0 g |
| | 66% | 34% | 1% | |

# grilled trout
## WITH LEMON-THYME GLAZE

**KETO** **NUT FREE** **DAIRY FREE**

**PREP TIME:** 10 minutes

**COOK TIME:** 1 hour 10 minutes

**YIELD:** 6 servings

### FOR THE GLAZE

2 lemons

4 tablespoons unsalted butter or coconut oil, divided

½ cup thinly sliced yellow onion

1 large yellow tomato or 3 plum tomatoes, cored and quartered

3 sprigs fresh thyme

4 cups fish, chicken, or beef bone broth (page 42; see Note)

Fine sea salt and freshly ground black pepper

### FOR THE TROUT

2 whole trout (about 1 pound each), scaled, gutted, and cleaned

2 tablespoons MCT oil

Grated zest of 2 lemons

Fine sea salt and freshly ground black pepper

### SPECIAL EQUIPMENT

Grill

*This recipe may look difficult at first, but it's actually quite straightforward. I asked a friend who is an avid fisherman to test this recipe, and it is now in his weekly meal rotation!*

1. Make the glaze: Using a Microplane or box grater, grate the zest from 1 lemon. Cut the other lemon into thin rounds.

2. Melt 2 tablespoons of the butter in a 4-quart saucepan over medium-high heat. Add the onion and cook until soft, about 10 minutes. Add the tomato, thyme, and lemon slices and cook for another 10 minutes. Add the broth and bring to a boil. Reduce the heat to medium-low and simmer for 30 minutes, or until the liquid has reduced by about half.

3. Strain the liquid, discarding the solids, and return the strained liquid to the saucepan. Simmer the liquid for an additional 20 minutes, until it reduces even more. Remove the glaze from the heat and stir in the remaining 2 tablespoons of the butter, the lemon zest, and salt and pepper to taste.

4. Prepare the trout: Preheat a grill or cast-iron grill pan over medium-high heat. Brush the trout with the MCT oil and season inside with the zest and a sprinkling of salt and pepper. Grill on each side for about 7 to 8 minutes, until slightly charred and cooked through.

5. Drizzle the glaze over the trout and serve.

**NOTE:** *If using store-bought broth, which is thinner than homemade bone broth, add 1 teaspoon of guar gum at the same time as the broth as a natural thickener.*

| NUTRITIONAL INFO (per serving) | | | | |
|---|---|---|---|---|
| calories | fat | protein | carbs | fiber |
| 369 | 21 g | 41.6 g | 3.8 g | 1.1 g |
| | 51% | 45% | 4% | |

# canned salmon

**■■□ KETO**    **NUT FREE**    **DAIRY FREE**

**PREP TIME:** 5 minutes

**COOK TIME:** 1 hour 40 minutes

**YIELD:** 8 ounces (4 ounces per serving)

1 (8-ounce) wild-caught, bone-in salmon fillet

Juice of 1 lime or lemon

¾ teaspoon fine sea salt

1 tablespoon fresh herbs, such as dill

**SPECIAL EQUIPMENT**

Pressure canner

2 pint-sized canning jars with lids and rings

*My father taught me how to can salmon, and his instructions for this recipe begins just as all his fish recipes do: Catch a bunch of fresh salmon or trout. There are a few more steps after that, but not many. Canning fish is not as difficult as you might think.*

1. In a medium-sized bowl, combine the salmon fillet with the lime juice and salt. Add your favorite herbs, if desired.

2. Pack the salmon in sterilized pint jars, leaving ½ inch of space at the top of the jars. Put the lids on loosely and seal the rings just until the lid touches the jar. If you put the lids on too tightly, they won't seal well.

3. Pressure cook at 10 pounds for 100 minutes. If it falls below 10 pounds, start over. When it is safe to open the canner, carefully release the pressure and remove the lid of the pressure canner. The canning lids are secure when you push on the top of the lid and it stays down. If the lid pops up, it's not secure yet and the jars need more time in the canner.

4. This salmon will keep for 12 months in your pantry. As my father says, "Enjoy the catching, cooking, and eating."

| NUTRITIONAL INFO (per serving) | | | | |
|---|---|---|---|---|
| calories | fat | protein | carbs | fiber |
| 162 | 7.2 g | 21 g | 3.6 g | 1 g |
| | 40% | 52% | 9% | |

BROILED

sesame-orange salmon

**KETO**    **NUT FREE**    **DAIRY FREE**

**PREP TIME:** 10 minutes, plus 30 minutes to marinate

**COOK TIME:** 12 minutes

**YIELD:** 6 servings

### FOR THE MARINADE

¼ cup MCT oil

2 tablespoons dark sesame oil

2 tablespoons coconut vinegar

2 tablespoons powdered erythritol or 2 to 3 drops of stevia glycerite

2 tablespoons coconut aminos or wheat-free tamari sauce

2 cloves garlic, grated

1 tablespoon grated fresh ginger

1½ pounds salmon fillets, cut into 6 portions

### FOR THE GLAZE

¼ cup coconut oil, melted

2 tablespoons powdered erythritol

1 teaspoon dark sesame oil

1 teaspoon coconut aminos or wheat-free tamari sauce

½ teaspoon grated fresh ginger

1 teaspoon orange flavor or 2 to 3 drops of food-grade orange oil

Fine sea salt and fresh ground black pepper

Fresh thyme sprigs or 2 teaspoons chopped fresh herbs, such as marjoram or dill, for garnish (optional)

Sprinkle of hibiscus salt, for garnish (optional)

1 recipe Slow Cooker Cabbage "Pasta" (page 282), for serving (optional)

1. Make the marinade: In a large shallow bowl or baking dish, such as a lasagna pan, combine the MCT oil, sesame oil, vinegar, erythritol, coconut aminos, garlic, and ginger. Place the salmon in the dish and turn to coat in the marinade. Refrigerate and marinate for 30 minutes.

2. Meanwhile, make the glaze: In a small bowl, combine the melted coconut oil, erythritol, sesame oil, coconut aminos, ginger, and orange flavor and whisk until well combined. Set aside.

3. Place the oven rack in the top position, about 4 inches below the broiler. Preheat the broiler to high.

4. Remove the salmon from the marinade. (Discard the marinade.) Sprinkle with a little bit of salt and pepper, then place on a broiler pan or rimmed baking sheet, skin side down.

5. Broil for about 10 to 12 minutes, depending on the salmon's thickness, until the fish is opaque and flakes easily with a fork.

6. Drizzle the glaze over the salmon, then garnish with your favorite herb and a sprinkle of hibiscus salt, if desired. Serve on top of cabbage "pasta," if desired.

| NUTRITIONAL INFO (per serving) | | | | |
|---|---|---|---|---|
| calories | fat | protein | carbs | fiber |
| 531 | 42.8 g | 25.6 g | 11.5 g | 4.5 g |
| | 73% | 19% | 9% | |

# shrimp scampi
## WITH CABBAGE NOODLES

KETO  NUT FREE  DAIRY FREE

**PREP TIME:** 15 minutes

**COOK TIME:** 25 minutes

**YIELD:** 4 servings

4 slices bacon, chopped

1 pound large shrimp, peeled and deveined

1 small head cabbage, sliced into noodlelike strips, or 2 (7-ounce) packages Miracle Noodles, rinsed and drained

½ cup MCT oil

¼ cup diced yellow onion

5 to 6 cloves garlic, chopped

½ cup fish or chicken bone broth (page 42)

3 tablespoons chopped fresh flat-leaf parsley

1 cup diced yellow tomato

Juice of ½ lemon

½ teaspoon fine sea salt

Fresh ground black pepper to taste

Chopped fresh flat-leaf parsley, for garnish (optional)

Red pepper flakes, for garnish (optional)

Several slices Keto Bread (page 276), fried in bacon fat, for serving (optional)

1. Fry the bacon in a very large sauté pan over medium-high heat until crisp, then remove the bacon from the pan, leaving the drippings. Pat the shrimp dry and sauté them in the bacon fat. Cook the shrimp until they are opaque and pink, about 6 minutes, flipping halfway through cooking. Remove from the pan and set aside with the bacon crumbles.

2. To the sauté pan, add the cabbage strips, MCT oil, onion, garlic, broth, parsley, tomato, lemon juice, salt, and pepper. Sauté over medium heat until tender, about 15 minutes. (If using Miracle Noodles, place in the pan after about 10 minutes, when the onion and tomato are fully softened. Gently warm the noodles through over low heat, about 1 minute.)

3. Add the shrimp and bacon crumbles to the pan and toss everything to coat. Garnish with fresh parsley and/or red pepper flakes and serve with fried keto bread to sop up the tasty sauce, if desired.

**VARIATION: CHICKEN SCAMPI.**
*To make with chicken instead of shrimp, replace the shrimp with 1 pound boneless, skinless chicken thighs, cut into 1-inch pieces, and increase the cooking time in the bacon fat to allow the chicken to cook through.*

| NUTRITIONAL INFO (per serving) | | | | |
|---|---|---|---|---|
| calories | fat | protein | carbs | fiber |
| 514 | 37.3 g | 30.3 g | 15.3 g | 4.9 g |
|  | 65% | 23% | 12% |  |

# vegetarian
# dishes

# fried parmesan tomatoes

**KETO** | **NUT FREE**

**PREP TIME:** 7 minutes

**COOK TIME:** 6 minutes

**YIELD:** 4 servings

4 tablespoons coconut oil

2 large eggs

½ cup grated Parmesan cheese (about 2 ounces)

1 large yellow or green tomato, cut into ½-inch-thick slices

1. In a sauté pan over medium-high heat, heat the coconut oil.

2. Beat the eggs in a shallow dish.

3. Place the grated Parmesan in a separate shallow dish.

4. Dip each slice of tomato into the egg to coat, then into the Parmesan. You may need to use your hands to push the Parmesan onto the tomato.

5. Place the cheese-coated tomato slices in the hot oil, working in batches if needed so as not to overcrowd the pan. Fry until the cheese is golden brown on each side of the tomato.

| NUTRITIONAL INFO (per serving) | | | | |
|---|---|---|---|---|
| calories | fat | protein | carbs | fiber |
| 209 | 19 g | 7 g | 2.3 g | 0 g |
| | 82% | 13% | 4% | |

# creamy "mac"-n-cheese

**KETO**    **NUT FREE**

**PREP TIME:** 5 minutes

**COOK TIME:** 25 minutes

**YIELD:** 6 servings

¼ cup unsalted butter or coconut oil

4 cups very thinly sliced cabbage (about 1 small head) or 2 (7-ounce) packages Miracle Noodles, rinsed and drained

**FOR THE CHEESE SAUCE**

¼ cup (½ stick) unsalted butter

1½ ounces cream cheese (about 3 tablespoons)

¼ cup vegetable broth (page 42)

1 cup shredded sharp cheddar cheese (about 4 ounces)

¼ cup grated Parmesan cheese (about 1 ounce)

Fine sea salt and fresh ground black pepper

½ cup diced tomato or halved cherry tomatoes, for garnish (optional)

1. Place the butter and sliced cabbage into a sauté pan and sauté over medium heat until the cabbage is very tender, about 15 minutes, stirring often so it doesn't burn. Remove from the heat and set aside. (If using Miracle Noodles, place them in a sauté pan with the butter to warm for a minute, then set aside.)

2. Make the cheese sauce: In a saucepan, melt the butter over medium heat. Stir in the cream cheese and broth. Cook, stirring constantly, for 2 minutes, or until thickened. Reduce the heat to low, add the cheddar and Parmesan cheeses, and cook, stirring frequently, until the cheese is melted. Add salt and pepper to taste.

3. Remove the cheese sauce from the heat, pour over the cabbage pasta, and stir to combine. Garnish with yellow tomatoes, if desired.

**VARIATION: BACON "MAC"-N-CHEESE.**
*If you're not a vegetarian, try adding bacon for extra deliciousness. Omit the butter used to cook the cabbage and place 4 slices of bacon, chopped fine, in a large sauté pan. Fry the bacon over medium heat until crisp. Remove the bacon crumbles but leave the drippings in the pan, and cook the cabbage in the bacon drippings. Add the cooked bacon to the dish before serving.*

| NUTRITIONAL INFO (per serving) | | | | |
|---|---|---|---|---|
| calories | fat | protein | carbs | fiber |
| 241 | 23.3 g | 7.5 g | 1.8 g | 0 g |
| | 87% | 12% | 3% | |

# yellow tomato and burrata salad

## WITH "HONEY" DRESSING

**KETO**   **NUT FREE**

**PREP TIME:** 5 minutes

**COOK TIME:** 3 minutes

**YIELD:** 2 servings

1 yellow tomato, quartered

2 cups arugula

1 (4-ounce) round Burrata cheese

¼ cup "Honey" Dressing (page 53)

1. Preheat a broiler or grill to high heat.

2. If broiling, place the oven rack in the upper-middle position (about 6 inches from the heat). Place the tomato quarters on a rimmed baking sheet and broil for 2 to 3 minutes, until coloring or char appears.

3. If grilling, place the tomato quarters on the grill and cook for 2 to 3 minutes, until grill marks appear.

4. Layer the arugula, grilled tomatoes, and Burrata on a large plate. Drizzle with the dressing.

**VARIATION: PROSCIUTTO, TOMATO, AND BURRATA SALAD.** *If you're not a vegetarian, place 2 slices of prosciutto on a large plate and top with the remaining ingredients.*

| NUTRITIONAL INFO (per serving) | | | | |
|---|---|---|---|---|
| calories | fat | protein | carbs | fiber |
| 281 | 24.1 g | 12 g | 4 g | 1.1 g |
| | 77% | 17% | 6% | |

## TOASTED OPEN-FACE
# brie and tomato sandwich

**KETO** **NUT FREE**

**PREP TIME:** 5 minutes

**COOK TIME:** 7 minutes

**YIELD:** 6 open-face sandwiches (1 per serving)

1 pint cherry tomatoes

2 tablespoons MCT oil

Fine sea salt and fresh ground black pepper

6 (½-inch-thick) slices Keto Bread (page 276)

3 tablespoons unsalted butter, softened, or MCT oil

½ pound brie, sliced thin

### NUTRITIONAL INFO (per serving)

| calories | fat | protein | carbs | fiber |
|----------|-----|---------|-------|-------|
| 310 | 27 g | 13.5 g | 2.7 g | 0.7 g |
| | 78% | 17% | 3% | |

1. Place the oven rack in the top position, about 4 inches below the broiler. Preheat the broiler to high. Line a rimmed baking sheet with parchment paper.

2. Put the cherry tomatoes on the prepared baking sheet, drizzle them with the MCT oil, and season them with salt and pepper. Broil them until they burst, about 5 minutes (check often). Remove from the oven and set aside.

3. Grease the bread on both sides with the butter and top each slice with several slices of brie. Place the prepared bread on a rimmed baking sheet and place on the middle rack in the oven to broil for about 2 minutes, until the cheese is bubbling and slightly browned.

4. Remove from the oven and top with the burst tomatoes. Serve immediately.

**BUSY FAMILY TIP:** *To save time, instead of broiling the tomatoes, you can simply top the sandwiches with chopped fresh tomatoes seasoned with salt and pepper.*

# yellow tomato soup
## AND GRILLED CHEESE

■■□ KETO  NUT FREE

**PREP TIME:** 10 minutes

**COOK TIME:** 45 minutes

**YIELD:** 4 servings

### FOR THE SOUP

1 tablespoon unsalted butter

¼ cup diced red onion

1 head roasted garlic (see page 46) or 3 cloves raw garlic, minced

4 ounces cream cheese (about ½ cup), softened (see Note)

1 cup vegetable broth (page 42)

4 cups diced yellow tomatoes with the juices

2 teaspoons dried basil

¼ teaspoon stevia glycerite (or to taste)

1 teaspoon fine sea salt

¼ teaspoon fresh ground black pepper

### FOR THE GRILLED CHEESE SANDWICHES

4 slices sharp cheddar cheese

4 slices Swiss cheese

8 fresh basil leaves

8 slices Keto Bread (page 276)

4 tablespoons unsalted butter, divided, plus more if needed

### SPECIAL EQUIPMENT

Blender

*You are welcome to make this soup with red tomatoes, but it will change the nutritional profile. For more on why I prefer to use yellow tomatoes, see page 38.*

1. Make the soup: Heat the butter in a medium-sized saucepan over medium heat. Add the onion and squeeze the roasted garlic into the pan. Cook, stirring frequently, for 4 to 5 minutes, or until the onion is soft. Add the cream cheese and broth and heat the mixture until the cheese melts and the mixture is simmering, about 7 minutes.

2. Stir in the tomatoes (including their juices), basil, stevia, salt, and pepper. Continue to simmer the mixture for 20 minutes while stirring constantly. Do not boil.

3. Remove the soup from the heat and let it cool a bit, then use an immersion blender to puree until smooth. Alternatively, transfer the slightly cooled soup to a blender and puree until smooth. Return the soup to the heat and keep warm over low heat while you make the grilled cheese sandwiches.

4. First, assemble four sandwiches by putting 1 slice each of cheddar and Swiss cheese and 2 basil leaves between 2 slices of bread.

5. To make the sandwiches in a skillet: Heat 2 tablespoons of the butter in the largest skillet you have over medium heat. Place as many sandwiches as you can comfortably fit in the skillet and fry one side for about 3 to 5 minutes, until golden brown. Flip, add the remaining 2 tablespoons of butter to the pan, and cook for another 3 to 5 minutes, until the cheese melts and the bread is golden brown. Add more butter to the pan and repeat to cook the remaining sandwiches.

   To make the sandwiches with a panini maker: Heat the panini maker to medium-high. Smear ½ tablespoon of butter onto each outer face of the sandwiches. Place the sandwiches in the hot panini maker and press down on the handle to fry until golden brown on both sides, about 3 minutes.

6. Serve the grilled cheese sandwiches with the yellow tomato soup.

| NUTRITIONAL INFO (per serving) | | | | |
|---|---|---|---|---|
| calories | fat | protein | carbs | fiber |
| 463 | 37 g | 26.3 g | 8 g | 1.2 g |
| | 72% | 23% | 7% | |

**NOTE:** *Make sure that the cream cheese is softened, or you will end up with chunks of cream cheese in the soup.*

# deep dish alfredo pizza
## WITH MUSHROOMS

**KETO** · **NUT FREE**

**PREP TIME:** 10 minutes

**COOK TIME:** 1 hour 10 minutes

**YIELD:** One 9-by-13-inch pizza (6 servings)

### FOR THE DEEP DISH CRUST

8 ounces cream cheese (about 1 cup), room temperature

2 large eggs

1 clove roasted garlic (see page 46)

¼ cup grated Parmesan cheese (about 1 ounce)

### FOR THE MUSHROOMS

¼ cup unsalted butter or coconut oil

3 cups button mushrooms, cleaned and sliced

¾ teaspoon fine sea salt

¾ teaspoon fresh ground black pepper

### FOR THE SAUCE

½ cup (1 stick) unsalted butter

1 head roasted garlic (see page 46) or 2 cloves raw garlic, minced

2 ounces cream cheese (about ¼ cup)

⅓ cup vegetable broth (page 42)

½ cup grated Parmesan cheese (about 2 ounces)

### TOPPINGS AND SEASONING

1 cup diced yellow tomatoes

1 cup shredded mozzarella cheese (about 4 ounces)

Fine sea salt and fresh ground black pepper

### SPECIAL EQUIPMENT

Handheld mixer

| NUTRITIONAL INFO (per serving) | | | | |
|---|---|---|---|---|
| calories | fat | protein | carbs | fiber |
| 506 | 47 g | 17.4 g | 5 g | 0.5 g |
| | 84% | 14% | 4% | |

*I grew up in Medford, Wisconsin, the home of the first frozen pizza: Tombstone Pizza! It started in a bar located across the street from a graveyard. My dad worked at the bar making pizzas for his friend who owned it. When the pizzas started to get popular, my dad's friend asked him if he wanted to be a part of the business. He politely said no since my grandpa owned a plumbing business and my dad always knew he was destined to be a plumber, which he is to this day, but he also makes some awesome pizzas!*

*This recipe is inspired by one of my dad's recipes, but naturally I made the crust ketogenic. This deep dish crust is denser and has a creamier mouthfeel than the deep dish crust on page 212, which is airier and lighter. Either crust will work for the toppings in any of the pizza recipes, but follow the cooking times indicated with each recipe.*

1. Preheat the oven to 375°F. Lightly grease a 9-by-13-inch baking dish. (Make sure to use a dish with sides, because the dough has the consistency of batter.)

2. In a large bowl, mix the cream cheese, eggs, garlic, and Parmesan cheese with a handheld mixer until combined. Spread into the greased pan. Prebake for 15 to 20 minutes, until golden brown. Allow the crust to cool for 10 minutes.

3. While the crust is baking, prepare the mushrooms: Heat the ¼ cup butter in a large sauté pan over medium heat. Sauté the mushrooms until soft and golden brown, working in batches if needed so as not to overcrowd the pan. (Otherwise, they will not brown.) Season the mushrooms with the salt and pepper. Remove from the heat.

4. Make the sauce: Place the ½ cup butter in a saucepan with the garlic and cook until light golden brown, stirring constantly so the butter doesn't burn. Turn the heat to low and smash up the garlic in the butter. Stir in the cream cheese, broth, and Parmesan. Simmer for at least 15 minutes (the flavors open up if you simmer longer).

5. Ladle the sauce to cover the bottom of the pizza crust. Evenly top with the sautéed mushrooms, diced tomatoes, and mozzarella. Season with salt and pepper to taste.

6. Bake the pizza for about 25 minutes, until the crust is crisp and golden. Remove from the oven, slice, and serve.

TIP: *If you prefer a nonvegetarian pizza, try adding leftover cooked chicken to this recipe.*

# pizza margherita

■■□ **KETO**    **NUT FREE**

**PREP TIME:** 10 minutes, plus 15 minutes to drain the zucchini

**COOK TIME:** 15 minutes

**YIELD:** One 12-inch pizza (6 servings)

## FOR THE ZUCCHINI CRUST

3 cups shredded zucchini (about 1½ medium zucchini)

1 teaspoon fine sea salt

1½ cups grated Parmesan cheese (about 6 ounces)

1 tablespoon dried oregano

1 teaspoon dried basil

1 large egg, beaten

## TOPPINGS

1 cup Tomato Sauce (page 59), Yellow Marinara Sauce (page 60), or Pizza Sauce (page 59)

1 yellow tomato, cut into ⅛-inch-thick slices

1 (4-ounce) ball fresh mozzarella cheese, cut into ⅛-inch-thick slices

¼ cup fresh basil leaves

## SPECIAL EQUIPMENT

Pizza stone

VARIATION: VEGETARIAN PIZZA.
*Pizza margherita is a tried-and-true base for any style of vegetarian pizza. Simply add your favorite vegetarian toppings, such as sliced olives, chopped bell peppers, or sliced onions.*

*Thin-crust pizzas like this one must be crispy; if not, the sauce and toppings quickly turn a thin crust into a mushy mess. And to create a crispy crust, you must use a preheated cast-iron pizza pan or ceramic pizza stone. Here are my helpful tips for using them:*

*1) Place the pan or stone in the oven before you turn it on. If you place a cold pizza pan or stone in a very hot oven, it could crack.*

*2) Use parchment paper with ceramic pizza stones! If you already use a ceramic pizza stone and have noticed that whenever you use it the kitchen fills with smoke, it is likely because you haven't used parchment paper. If you do not line the ceramic stone with parchment, the oils from the pizza will seep into the porous stone, and whenever you heat the stone, the oils in it will start to burn, leading to a smoke-filled kitchen.*

1. Place a cast-iron pizza pan or pizza stone in the oven and preheat the oven to 525°F. (Preheating the pizza pan/stone helps create a crispier crust.)

2. Make the crust: In a large bowl, combine the shredded zucchini and salt. Toss together and set aside for 10 to 15 minutes. Squeeze as much excess moisture out of the zucchini as you can, discarding the water. Place the zucchini back in the bowl. (Do not skip this step or the pizza crust will be soggy.)

3. To the zucchini, add the Parmesan cheese, oregano, basil, and egg. Mix with your hands to incorporate all of the ingredients.

4. Place a piece of parchment paper that is at least 15 inches long on a large cookie sheet without edges, so you can slide the parchment onto the pizza stone easily.

5. Place the dough onto the parchment paper. Using your hands, spread the dough to form a circle 12 inches in diameter and ¼ inch thick. Pinch the edges to form a crust. Slide the crust on the parchment paper onto the hot pizza stone in the oven. Bake for 8 to 10 minutes, until the crust starts to brown.

6. Remove the crust and stone from the oven. Top the pizza crust with the sauce, tomato slices, cheese slices, and basil. Return to the oven and bake for an additional 4 minutes, until the cheese is melted and golden.

## NUTRITIONAL INFO (per serving)

| calories | fat | protein | carbs | fiber |
|----------|--------|---------|-------|-------|
| 199 | 12.8 g | 17 g | 5 g | 1.6 g |
| | 58% | 34% | 10% | |

**BUSY FAMILY TIP:** *On a rainy day, make five pizza crusts, add your desired toppings, and freeze them for up to 1 month. On busy days, all I have to do is put a frozen pizza in the oven and dinner is ready in 15 minutes!*

# mini egg salad sandwiches

**KETO** | **NUT FREE**

**PREP TIME:** 15 minutes

**COOK TIME:** 20 minutes

**YIELD:** 24 mini sandwiches (4 per serving)

## FOR THE PUFFS

3 large eggs, separated

½ teaspoon cream of tartar

2 tablespoons unflavored egg white protein or ¼ cup unflavored whey protein

⅓ cup sour cream or cream cheese (about 3 ounces), or 3 reserved egg yolks if dairy-sensitive

## FOR THE EGG SALAD

8 large eggs

½ cup mayonnaise

2 tablespoons Dijon mustard (page 49)

1 tablespoon chopped fresh dill or 1 teaspoon dried dill weed

½ teaspoon fine sea salt

¼ teaspoon fresh ground black pepper

1. Preheat the oven to 375°F. Grease a cookie sheet.

2. Make the puffs: In a large bowl, whip the egg whites and cream of tartar until very stiff. Then add the protein powder. Using a spatula, gradually fold the sour cream into the egg white mixture, being careful not to collapse the whites.

3. Place twenty-four 2-inch balls of dough on the greased cookie sheet. Bake for 10 minutes, then turn the oven off (but keep the oven door shut) and leave the puffs in the oven for another 5 minutes, or until cool.

4. Make the egg salad: Place the eggs in a saucepan and cover with cold water. Bring the water to a boil, cover, and remove from the heat. Let the eggs stand in the hot water for 10 to 12 minutes. Remove from the hot water, cool in ice water or under cold running water, then peel and chop.

5. In a large bowl, combine the chopped eggs, mayonnaise, mustard, dill, salt, and pepper. Mash well with a fork or wooden spoon.

6. Assemble the sandwiches: Split the mini puffs and place about a tablespoon of egg salad into each puff.

| NUTRITIONAL INFO (per serving) | | | | |
|---|---|---|---|---|
| calories | fat | protein | carbs | fiber |
| 433 | 36 g | 23.5 g | 4 g | 0 g |
| | 75% | 22% | 4% | |

# dutch baby pizza

## WITH "HONEY" DRESSING

KETO

**PREP TIME:** 10 minutes

**COOK TIME:** 23 minutes

**YIELD:** One 8-inch pizza (2 servings)

2 tablespoons unsalted butter or coconut oil

3 large eggs

¾ cup unsweetened almond milk

¼ cup unflavored egg white protein or egg whites (or unflavored whey protein if not dairy-sensitive)

¼ teaspoon fine sea salt

**TOPPINGS**

1 yellow tomato, quartered, or 1 cup yellow cherry tomatoes, halved

1 (2½-ounce) ball Burrata cheese, sliced

½ cup arugula

¼ cup "Honey" Dressing (page 53)

**SPECIAL EQUIPMENT**

Blender

1. Preheat the oven to 425°F.

2. In a medium cast-iron skillet, melt the butter over medium heat and set aside. In a blender, combine the eggs, almond milk, protein powder, and salt. Blend for about 1 minute, or until foamy. Pour the batter into the skillet and place the skillet in the oven. Bake for about 18 to 20 minutes, until the pancake is puffed and golden brown.

3. Meanwhile, cook the tomatoes: Preheat a broiler or grill to high heat.

4. If broiling, place the oven rack in the upper-middle position (about 6 inches from the heat). Place the tomato quarters on a rimmed baking sheet and broil for 2 to 3 minutes, until coloring or char appears.

If grilling, place the tomato quarters on the grill and cook for 2 to 3 minutes, until grill marks appear.

Remove the pancake from the oven. Top with the broiled or grilled tomatoes, sliced Burrata, arugula, and the dressing. Cut into wedges and enjoy!

**VARIATION: DUTCH BABY PIZZA WITH PROSCIUTTO.** *If you're not a vegetarian, try placing 3 slices of prosciutto on the pancake before topping with the tomatoes, Burrata, arugula, and dressing.*

| NUTRITIONAL INFO (per serving) | | | | |
|---|---|---|---|---|
| calories | fat | protein | carbs | fiber |
| 493 | 38 g | 29.7 g | 6.8 g | 1.2 g |
| | 69% | 24% | 6% | |

# slow cooker pesto pasta
## WITH CRISPY BASIL

**KETO**

**PREP TIME:** 6 minutes

**COOK TIME:** 8 hours

**YIELD:** 4 servings

1 (1-pound) package kelp noodles

**FOR THE PESTO (MAKES 3½ CUPS)**

2 packed cups fresh basil

¼ cup roasted, unsalted walnuts (omit if you don't tolerate nuts)

3 cloves garlic

½ teaspoon fine ground sea salt

¼ teaspoon fresh ground black pepper

½ cup MCT oil or equal parts MCT oil and melted coconut oil

1 tablespoon seeded and chopped fresh red chili pepper (or more or less depending on desired heat)

2 tablespoons lime juice (optional)

½ cup grated Parmesan cheese (about 4 ounces) (use nutritional yeast if dairy-sensitive)

**FOR THE FRIED BASIL**

1 cup coconut oil or ghee

Leaves from 1 large bunch fresh basil, well washed and dried

Several slices Garlic Keto Bread (page 276), for serving (optional)

**SPECIAL EQUIPMENT**

Food processor    Slow cooker

1. Rinse and drain the kelp noodles very well and place into a 4-quart slow cooker.

2. Make the pesto: Place the basil, walnuts, if using, garlic, salt, pepper, oil, chili pepper, lime juice, and Parmesan in a food processor and blend until smooth.

3. Pour the pesto over the kelp noodles.

4. Cook on low for 6 to 8 hours, until the kelp noodles are very soft.

5. Make the fried basil: Heat the oil to 350°F on a candy thermometer in a large saucepan over high heat. Standing as far back from the pot as possible and wearing an oven mitt, drop the basil leaves into the hot oil. The oil may bubble and splatter. Fry for about 1 minute, or until the leaves are crisp. Using a slotted spoon, transfer the leaves to a double layer of paper towels to drain. Serve over the kelp noodles along with garlic keto bread, if desired.

| NUTRITIONAL INFO (per serving) | | | | |
|---|---|---|---|---|
| calories | fat | protein | carbs | fiber |
| 359 | 34.1 g | 9.4 g | 2.6 g | 0.6 g |
| | 85% | 10% | 3% | |

sides

# keto bread

**KETO** ■■□
**NUT FREE**
**DAIRY FREE**

**PREP TIME:** 10 minutes

**COOK TIME:** 40 minutes

**YIELD:** One 9-by-5-inch loaf (14 slices, 2 slices per serving)

6 large eggs, separated

¼ cup unflavored egg white protein powder (or ½ cup unflavored whey protein if not dairy-sensitive)

**OPTIONAL SEASONINGS**

½ teaspoon onion powder or other seasonings and spices to your liking

*This light and airy bread is superior; in fact, it's so light that it's been called "Wonder Bread" by many of my clients. It has basically zero carbs and is 100 percent nut-free. The trick to making this bread is to not underwhip the whites: when you think the whites are stiff enough, continue whipping. I like to fry slices of this bread in a generous amount bacon fat to enhance the flavor and fat ratio, but this extra step is completely optional. (A helpful video on making my keto bread can be found on my blog, mariamindbodyhealth.com.)*

1. Preheat the oven to 325°F. Grease a 9-by-5-inch loaf pan.

2. Whip the egg whites for a few minutes until *very* stiff. Slowly fold in the protein powder and any seasonings, if using. Then slowly fold the reserved yolks into the whites (making sure the whites don't fall).

3. Fill the prepared pan with the "dough." Bake for 40 to 45 minutes, until golden brown. Let completely cool before cutting or the bread will fall. Cut into 14 slices.

**VARIATION: GARLIC KETO BREAD.** *To make garlic bread, brush slices of keto bread with butter or MCT oil and rub on roasted garlic. Toast in a 400°F oven for 3 to 6 minutes, until golden brown.*

**VARIATION: KETO BUNS.** *To make buns instead of a loaf of bread, first grease 2 cookie sheets.*

*To form hamburger buns, use a spatula to gently scoop up about ⅓ cup of the dough and form into a round bun about 3½ inches in diameter. Repeat with the rest of the dough.*

*To form hot dog or hoagie buns, use a spatula to gently scoop up about ⅓ cup of the dough and form into an oblong shape about 6 inches long and 2 inches wide. Repeat with the rest of the dough.*

*Bake for 15 to 20 minutes, until golden brown. Let cool completely before cutting. Makes about 14 buns.*

| NUTRITIONAL INFO (per serving) | | | | |
|---|---|---|---|---|
| calories | fat | protein | carbs | fiber |
| 70 | 4.3 g | 7.5 g | 0.4 g | 0 g |
| | 55% | 43% | 2% | |

# keto naan

**PREP TIME:** 7 minutes

**COOK TIME:** 10 minutes per piece

**YIELD:** 6 servings

3 eggs, separated

½ teaspoon cream of tartar

¼ cup unflavored egg white protein (or whey protein if not dairy-sensitive)

1 teaspoon curry powder (optional)

1 tablespoon coconut oil, for greasing the pan

*Naan is an oven-baked flatbread from South Asia and is particularly popular in India. My keto version is fried instead, but it still works great for picking up food instead of using utensils. It makes for a fun dinner...unless you are in charge of cleanup!*

1. Whip the egg whites in a clean, dry, nonreactive metal bowl for a few minutes, until *very* stiff. Blend in the yolks, cream of tartar, protein powder, and curry powder, if using.

2. Heat the coconut oil in a skillet over medium-high heat until a drop of water sizzles in the pan. Once it is hot, place a 3-inch circle of dough in the pan. Fry for about 3 to 5 minutes, until golden brown, then flip and fry for another 3 to 5 minutes. Remove from heat. Repeat with the remaining dough.

| NUTRITIONAL INFO (per serving) | | | | |
|---|---|---|---|---|
| calories | fat | protein | carbs | fiber |
| 64 | 4.5 g | 5.2 g | 0.6 g | 0.5 g |
| | 63% | 33% | 4% | |

# braised swiss chard

■■□ KETO  NUT FREE  DAIRY FREE

**PREP TIME:** 5 minutes

**COOK TIME:** 50 minutes

**YIELD:** 4 servings

2 tablespoons plus 1 teaspoon fine sea salt, divided

1½ pounds Swiss chard, roughly chopped

4 ounces bacon, chopped into ½-inch pieces

¼ cup diced yellow onion

1½ cups chicken or beef bone broth (page 42)

1 tablespoon finely chopped fresh herbs, such as basil, thyme, or tarragon (optional)

| NUTRITIONAL INFO (per serving) | | | | |
|---|---|---|---|---|
| calories | fat | protein | carbs | fiber |
| 199 | 14.5 g | 11 g | 7 g | 3 g |
| | 66% | 22% | 14% | |

1. Fill a large pot with water and add the 2 tablespoons of salt. Bring to a boil, then add the Swiss chard and cook until tender, about 5 minutes. Remove from the heat and drop the Swiss chard into a large bowl of ice water. Drain in a colander and set aside.

2. Place the bacon pieces in a large sauté pan and cook over medium-high heat for about 3 minutes, until the bacon is browned and the fat is rendered, stirring occasionally. Remove the bacon and set aside, leaving the drippings in the pan.

3. Turn the heat to low, add the diced onion, and cook until softened and golden brown, 15 to 30 minutes. (The longer the onion cooks, the more the sugars in the onion will caramelize, which provides an amazing flavor.) Add the Swiss chard and turn to coat well.

4. Add the broth and deglaze the pan, scraping the bottom of the pan. Cook the greens for another 15 minutes, until the broth reduces and the chard gets very tender.

5. Add the cooked bacon pieces, the remaining 1 teaspoon of salt, and any herbs you desire, and serve.

# braised cabbage

**KETO** NUT **DAIRY**
FREE FREE

**PREP TIME:** 5 minutes

**COOK TIME:** 2 hours 15 minutes

**YIELD:** 4 servings

1 medium head purple or green cabbage

¼ cup diced yellow onion

½ teaspoon stevia glycerite (optional)

¼ cup beef or chicken bone broth (page 42)

¼ cup bacon fat, melted, plus more for greasing the pan

2 teaspoons fine sea salt

1 teaspoon fresh ground black pepper

1. Preheat the oven to 325°F. Liberally grease a 9-by-13-inch baking dish with bacon fat.

2. Cut the cabbage into 6 wedges, keeping the core attached so the leaves stay intact after cooking. Lay the wedges in the greased dish in a single layer. Add the diced onion.

3. If using the stevia, add it to the broth and mix well. Pour the broth and melted bacon fat over the cabbage. Season with the salt and pepper. Seal tightly with a cover or aluminum foil and place in the oven. Cook for 1 hour.

4. After 1 hour, uncover and gently flip the wedges. Place the cover back on and return to the oven. Cook for another hour.

5. Just before serving, remove the cover, increase the heat to 425°F, and bake for 15 minutes, or until browned.

**BUSY FAMILY TIP:** *Make extra wedges of cabbage for the week. Make sure you let the braised cabbage cool before storing in the fridge. It will keep for up to 3 or 4 days.*

| NUTRITIONAL INFO (per serving) | | | | |
|---|---|---|---|---|
| calories | fat | protein | carbs | fiber |
| 191 | 14.2 g | 3.1 g | 13 g | 5.8 g |
| | 67% | 6% | 27% | |

# slow cooker cabbage "pasta"

**■□□ KETO**  **NUT FREE**

**PREP TIME:** 15 minutes

**COOK TIME:** 4 to 6 hours

**YIELD:** 4 servings

1 small head cabbage, cored and sliced into thin "noodles"

¼ cup beef or chicken bone broth (page 42)

¼ cup unsalted butter (or coconut oil or duck fat if dairy-sensitive)

2 teaspoons fine sea salt

**SPECIAL EQUIPMENT**

Slow cooker

*Cabbage "pasta" may sound weird at first, but using vegetables as noodles adds much more flavor and texture to dishes. It's also economical: cabbage costs only a dollar or two a head and stores in the fridge for a very long time—up to 2 months! In ideal root cellar conditions, it can even last longer.*

Place all of the ingredients in a 4-quart slow cooker. Stir well to combine. Cook on low for 4 to 6 hours, until the cabbage is very soft. Drain and serve in place of pasta with your favorite dishes.

**BUSY FAMILY TIP:** *Save time by making a large batch of cabbage "pasta" and storing extras in an airtight container for easy additions to dinner. It keeps in the fridge for up to 5 days or in the freezer for up to 1 month. To reheat, place in a saucepan and warm, covered, on medium heat.*

**HELPFUL CABBAGE TIPS**

- *If you are gathering cabbage from your own garden, keep all the leaves on the head. The outer leaves of the cabbage protect the softer inner leaves and help them retain moisture.*

- *Do not wash cabbage before storing. Wait until you are ready to use it.*

- *To store, wrap cabbage in a plastic bag and place it in the crisper drawer of your refrigerator.*

- *Though cabbage is hardy, it still should be handled with care. Try to minimize bruising, which can cause cell damage and quickly degrades the amount of vitamin C in the cabbage.*

| NUTRITIONAL INFO (per serving) | | | | |
|---|---|---|---|---|
| calories | fat | protein | carbs | fiber |
| 147 | 11.7 g | 2.5 g | 8.4 g | 4.5 g |
| | 72% | 7% | 23% | |

# zucchini "pasta"

**KETO** ■□□  **NUT FREE**  **DAIRY FREE**

**PREP TIME:** 10 minutes

**YIELD:** 2 servings

1 medium zucchini

**SPECIAL EQUIPMENT**

Spiral slicer
(see Note)

*I love growing zucchini in my garden, but it does take over! I planted an heirloom variety my first year of gardening and it continued to grow up to three years later—even though I didn't plant any seeds those years. But if you have the space, garden-fresh zucchini is absolutely worth it.*

*The trick to making zucchini noodles is to use zucchini that's not too large. The seeds in large zucchini can make a mess out of your spiral slicer. I prefer to use zucchini no larger than 12 inches long and 2 inches wide.*

1. Cut the ends off the zucchini to have nice even edges. If you desire a white "noodle," peel the zucchini.

2. Using a vegetable spiral slicer, swirl the zucchini into long, thin, noodlelike shapes by gently pressing down on the handle while turning it clockwise.

3. Just before serving, toss the raw pasta with your desired sauce to coat. Do not sauce more noodles than you plan to eat at that moment—once covered in sauce, leftover noodles get a little soggy, so store leftover zucchini noodles and sauce separately in airtight containers. Store the noodles in the fridge for up to 5 days. Not recommended for freezing since it tends to get soggy.

**NOTE:** *I use the Joyce Chen 51-0662, Saladacco spiral slicer.*

| NUTRITIONAL INFO (per serving) | | | | |
| --- | --- | --- | --- | --- |
| calories | fat | protein | carbs | fiber |
| 20 | 0 g | 1 g | 4 g | 1 g |
| | 0% | 20% | 80% | |

# brown butter mushrooms

■■■ KETO    NUT FREE

**PREP TIME:** 5 minutes

**COOK TIME:** 15 minutes

**YIELD:** 4 servings

1 pound morels or other mushrooms, such as button or cremini, cleaned

¼ cup (½ stick) unsalted butter

2 teaspoons chopped fresh herbs, such as parsley, sage, thyme, or rosemary (optional)

½ teaspoon fine sea salt

| NUTRITIONAL INFO (per serving) | | | | |
|---|---|---|---|---|
| calories | fat | protein | carbs | fiber |
| 131 | 11.4 g | 3 g | 4.8 g | 1.7 g |
| | 78% | 9% | 15% | |

*When they're in season, my favorite mushrooms to use for this dish are morels. They require a few additional cleaning steps than button or portobello mushrooms, but they are well worth the extra effort. And unlike button and portobello mushrooms, morels can never be eaten raw. (See the facing page for instructions on cleaning and storing morel mushrooms.)*

1. Place the morels in a large sauté pan over medium heat. Cook until the mushrooms give up much of their liquid, about 10 minutes.

2. Meanwhile, heat the butter in a saucepan over medium-high heat until it sizzles and brown flecks appear (watch closely; you don't want black butter). Turn the heat down to medium and continue cooking, whisking the butter constantly, for about 5 minutes, until the butter is a dark golden brown. Remove from the heat. Add herbs if you want to infuse the butter with more flavor.

3. Pour off the liquid from the morel pan and reserve for broth. (It tastes amazing!) Pour the browned butter onto the morels and cook for 4 to 5 minutes, until they are golden brown. Season with the salt and serve immediately.

## ABOUT MOREL MUSHROOMS

- *How to clean:* One glance at morels will show you just how difficult they are to clean. The many crevices hold and hide pieces of soil or bugs. Cut fresh mushrooms into 4 wide slices and soak them in a bowl of salt water for a couple hours in the refrigerator to remove and kill all those little pesty critters.

- *How to store:* If you're not preparing the morels right away, store them on a rimmed baking sheet covered with a damp paper towel in the fridge, which helps them from getting too soggy and mushy. Use morel mushrooms within 7 days.

- *How to eat:* Morels should never be eaten raw. They contain poisonous toxins that are removed during cooking. Plus, the mycochitin in their cell walls can be difficult for people to digest, but the cooking process breaks down fungal cell walls, making the mushroom flesh readily digestible.

# creamy coleslaw

**■□□ KETO**    **NUT FREE**    **DAIRY FREE**

**PREP TIME:** 8 minutes, plus 1 hour to chill

**YIELD:** 6 servings

4 cups shredded cabbage (about 1 medium head)

¼ cup thinly sliced yellow onion

**FOR THE DRESSING**

½ cup mayonnaise or Copycat Baconnaise (page 65)

⅓ cup powdered erythritol or ¼ teaspoon stevia glycerite (optional)

¼ cup dill pickle juice

2½ tablespoons lemon juice

½ teaspoon celery seeds

½ teaspoon fine sea salt

⅛ teaspoon fresh ground black pepper

*This recipe is a favorite of many of my clients; they tell me that it reminds them of KFC coleslaw, which is creamy and sweet. If you prefer your coleslaw less sweet, just omit the erythritol. Add a few quartered yellow cherry tomatoes for a colorful garnish, if desired.*

1. In a large bowl, combine the cabbage and onion. Set aside.

2. In a separate bowl, combine the ingredients for the dressing and mix until well combined.

3. Pour the dressing over the cabbage and onion and gently stir to coat in the dressing.

4. Refrigerate for 1 hour before serving.

| NUTRITIONAL INFO (per serving) | | | | |
|---|---|---|---|---|
| calories | fat | protein | carbs | fiber |
| 162 | 13.6 g | 2.1 g | 9.4 g | 3.9 g |
| | 76% | 5% | 23% | |

# blt coleslaw

**KETO** **NUT FREE** **DAIRY FREE**

**PREP TIME:** 6 minutes, plus 20 minutes to chill

**COOK TIME:** 5 minutes

**YIELD:** 6 servings

5 slices bacon, cut into ½-inch pieces

¼ cup chopped yellow onion or green onions

1 to 3 jalapeño peppers (depending on desired heat), seeded and sliced (optional)

1 cup Copycat Baconnaise (page 65) or mayonnaise

¼ cup coconut vinegar

2 tablespoons powdered erythritol or 1 drop of stevia glycerite

5 cups chopped or shredded cabbage (about 1 large head)

1 large yellow tomato, chopped, or 6 yellow cherry tomatoes, halved or quartered

1. In a large skillet, fry the bacon, onion, and jalapeños, if using, for about 5 minutes, until the bacon is crisp and the onion is browned. Remove the bacon mixture from the pan with a slotted spoon and reserve the bacon fat.

2. In a medium-sized bowl, combine the baconnaise, vinegar, erythritol, and ¼ cup of the reserved bacon fat. Stir until well combined.

3. Place the cabbage, chopped tomato, and bacon and onion mixture in a large bowl. Pour the baconnaise mixture over it and stir until well coated. Cover and chill for at least 20 minutes.

| NUTRITIONAL INFO (per serving) | | | | |
|---|---|---|---|---|
| calories | fat | protein | carbs | fiber |
| 258 | 20.7 g | 5.5 g | 14.4 g | 1.7 g |
| | 72% | 9% | 22% | |

# paleo onion rings

**KETO** ■■□ | **NUT FREE** | **DAIRY FREE**

**PREP TIME:** 10 minutes

**COOK TIME:** 30 minutes

**YIELD:** 6 servings

3 large sweet onions

24 slices thin-cut bacon (about 1 pound)

1 cup homemade ranch dressing, regular or dairy-free (pages 54 to 55); hollandaise, dairy-free or traditional (page 47); or other keto condiment of choice, for serving (optional)

1. Preheat the oven to 375°F. Line a rimmed baking sheet with parchment paper.

2. Slice the onions into ⅔-inch-thick rings. Reserve the small inside rings for other recipes; you want large rings that are easy to wrap in bacon.

3. Wrap each onion ring tightly in bacon and use a toothpick to hold it in place.

4. Place the wrapped onion rings on the rimmed baking sheet and bake for 25 to 30 minutes, until the bacon is crispy.

5. Serve with a dipping sauce, if desired.

| NUTRITIONAL INFO (per serving) | | | | |
|---|---|---|---|---|
| calories | fat | protein | carbs | fiber |
| 242 | 16.1 g | 15.5 g | 7.9 g | 1.6 g |
| | 60% | 26% | 13% | |

# avocado fries

**KETO** ■■■  **NUT FREE**  **DAIRY FREE**

**PREP TIME:** 10 minutes

**COOK TIME:** 14 minutes

**YIELD:** 6 servings

3 firm, barely ripe avocados

1 (1-pound) package thin-cut bacon (20 slices)

1 tablespoon Taco Seasoning (page 74)

½ cup salsa, for serving

*Avocados may seem like an odd replacement for potatoes, but after they bake, these avocado fries truly take on a french fry–like texture. I was amazed at how fast they disappeared! When purchasing avocados for this recipe, choose firm ones so they are easy to slice and wrap.*

1. Preheat the oven to 425°F. Line a rimmed baking sheet with parchment paper.

2. Peel and pit the avocados, then slice them into thick-cut french fry shapes. Wrap each slice with bacon and secure with a toothpick. Season with the taco seasoning.

3. Bake for 12 to 14 minutes, until the bacon is crisp. Serve with salsa.

| NUTRITIONAL INFO (per serving) | | | | |
|---|---|---|---|---|
| calories | fat | protein | carbs | fiber |
| 635 | 51.6 g | 30.6 g | 12 g | 7.8 g |
| | 73% | 19% | 8% | |

# fried pickles

KETO  NUT FREE

**PREP TIME:** 5 minutes, plus 10 minutes to freeze

**COOK TIME:** 5 minutes

**YIELD:** 6 servings

1 cup grated Parmesan cheese (about 4 ounces)

1½ cups sliced dill pickles

¼ cup coconut oil, for frying

½ cup homemade ranch dressing, regular or dairy-free (pages 54 to 55), for serving

1. Place the Parmesan cheese in a large shallow dish. Dip the sliced pickles into the Parmesan. Freeze the coated pickles for 10 minutes, or until the day you want to consume them.

2. When ready to fry the pickles, heat the oil in a large sauté pan over medium-high heat.

3. Working in batches so you don't overcrowd the pan, place the frozen, Parmesan-coated pickles in the hot oil and fry for 1 minute, or until golden brown. Flip and fry for another minute, or until golden brown on both sides. Remove from the pan and place on paper towels to drain. Serve with the ranch dressing.

| NUTRITIONAL INFO (per serving) | | | | |
|---|---|---|---|---|
| calories | fat | protein | carbs | fiber |
| 191 | 17.5 g | 7 g | 2 g | 0 g |
| | 82% | 15% | 4% | |

# buffalo chicken deviled eggs

KETO   NUT FREE

**PREP TIME:** 8 minutes

**COOK TIME:** 12 minutes

**YIELD:** 6 servings

6 large eggs

2 tablespoons mayonnaise or Copycat Baconnaise (page 65)

2 tablespoons Buffalo-style hot sauce, plus more for garnish

¼ cup finely diced cooked chicken (about 1 ounce)

2 tablespoons finely diced celery

1 tablespoon finely chopped green onions

2 tablespoons finely crumbled blue cheese (about ½ ounce), plus more for garnish (omit if dairy-sensitive)

½ teaspoon fine sea salt

Chopped fresh cilantro, for garnish

Finely diced red onion, for garnish

1. Place the eggs in a saucepan and cover with cold water. Bring the water to a boil, cover, and remove from the heat. Let the eggs stand in the hot water for 10 to 12 minutes. Remove from the hot water, cool in ice water or under cold running water, then peel and cut in half lengthwise.

2. Scoop the yolks out of the whites. Place them in a medium-sized bowl and mash them until no chunks of yolk are left. Add the mayonnaise, hot sauce, chicken, celery, green onions, blue cheese, and salt and mix well.

3. Stuff each egg white half with 1½ tablespoons of the yolk mixture. Serve topped with extra hot sauce and extra blue cheese, garnished with cilantro and red onion.

| NUTRITIONAL INFO (per serving) | | | | |
|---|---|---|---|---|
| calories | fat | protein | carbs | fiber |
| 149 | 11.7 g | 10.2 g | 1.1 g | 0 g |
| | 71% | 27% | 3% | |

# cheddar deviled eggs

**KETO**

**NUT FREE**

**PREP TIME:** 6 minutes

**COOK TIME:** 17 minutes

**YIELD:** 24 eggs (2 per serving)

12 large eggs

4 slices bacon (optional)

½ cup guacamole, Copycat Baconnaise (page 65), or mayonnaise

2 tablespoons shredded cheddar cheese (about ½ ounce)

1 tablespoon preferred homemade mustard (pages 48 to 50)

Fine sea salt

Smoked paprika (optional)

*My first go at this recipe did not include bacon (reflected in the photo). Then, when preparing these deviled eggs for a potluck gathering, I decided to add everyone's favorite ingredient: bacon. They were a huge hit! If you are a vegetarian, you can certainly omit the bacon; if not, I highly suggest including it.*

1. Place the eggs in a saucepan and cover with cold water. Bring the water to a boil, cover, and remove from the heat. Let the eggs stand in the hot water for 10 to 12 minutes.

2. While the eggs are cooking, cook the bacon, if using, in a sauté pan over medium-high heat until evenly brown, about 5 minutes. Remove from the pan and lay on paper towels to drain. When cool enough to handle, crumble into very small pieces and set aside.

3. When the eggs are done, remove them from the hot water and cool in ice water or under cold running water. Peel and cut in half lengthwise.

4. Remove the yolks and place them in a bowl. Mash until no chunks of yolk are left, then mash the yolks with the crumbled bacon, if using, guacamole, and cheese. Stir in the mustard. Season with salt to taste.

5. Fill the egg white halves with the yolk mixture and sprinkle with smoked paprika, if using. Refrigerate until serving.

| NUTRITIONAL INFO (per serving) | | | | |
|---|---|---|---|---|
| calories | fat | protein | carbs | fiber |
| 175 | 15.2 g | 9.1 g | 0.8 g | 0 g |
| | 78% | 21% | 2% | |

# spinach dip

**KETO** **NUT FREE**

**PREP TIME:** 7 minutes

**COOK TIME:** 5 minutes

**YIELD:** 8 servings (¼ cup per serving)

## FOR THE DIP

1 head roasted garlic (see page 46)

1 (10-ounce) package frozen chopped spinach, thawed and drained well

½ cup chopped green onions (white portions only)

1 cup sour cream or cream cheese

1 cup mayonnaise

1 teaspoon chopped fresh thyme

1 teaspoon fish sauce

½ teaspoon fine sea salt

¼ teaspoon smoked paprika

Dash of cayenne pepper

## FOR SERVING

1 loaf Keto Bread (page 276)

3 tablespoons unsalted butter (or coconut oil if dairy-sensitive)

Celery pieces

Sliced cucumber

## SPECIAL EQUIPMENT

Food processor

1. Squeeze the roasted garlic from the head into a blender or food processor. Add the spinach, green onions, sour cream, mayonnaise, thyme, fish sauce, salt, paprika, and cayenne and blend until smooth. Taste and adjust the seasonings as needed.

2. Just before serving, make crostini: Cut the loaf of bread into ½-inch-thick slices, then cut the slices into triangles. Heat the butter in a sauté pan and fry the triangles until golden brown on each side, about 5 minutes.

3. Serve the spinach dip with fried keto bread, celery pieces, and cucumber slices.

**BUSY FAMILY TIP:** *The spinach dip can be made ahead and stored in the fridge for up to 2 days.*

| NUTRITIONAL INFO (per serving) | | | | |
|---|---|---|---|---|
| calories | fat | protein | carbs | fiber |
| 342 | 31.2 g | 11.8 g | 4.6 g | 1 g |
| | 82% | 14% | 5% | |

# zucchini tots

KETO ▪▪▪ NUT FREE

**PREP TIME:** 8 minutes, plus 15 minutes to drain zucchini

**COOK TIME:** 15 minutes

**YIELD:** 6 servings

2 cups shredded zucchini (about 1 medium zucchini)

1 teaspoon fine sea salt

1 tablespoon coconut flour

2 large eggs

1 cup shredded sharp cheddar cheese (about 4 ounces) (or nutritional yeast if dairy-sensitive)

½ cup finely chopped yellow onion

1 teaspoon smoked paprika

*These tots can be served on their own or can be used to make Zucchini Tot Hot Dish (page 186).*

1. Preheat the oven to 400°F. Spray a 24-cup mini-muffin pan with cooking spray.

2. Place the shredded zucchini in a medium-sized bowl and toss with the salt. Let sit for 10 to 15 minutes. Squeeze out any moisture and discard the liquid.

3. Sprinkle the coconut flour onto the zucchini and toss well to coat. Add the eggs, cheddar cheese, onion, and paprika and mix well to combine.

4. Fill each muffin cup with 1½ tablespoons of the zucchini mixture. Bake for 15 minutes, or until golden brown. Run a knife around the tots to loosen as soon as you get them out of the oven. Let cool for a minute to allow them to set up, then remove them from the muffin pan.

**BUSY FAMILY TIP:** *Make a double batch of these and freeze for up to 1 month for an easy dinner side dish.*

| NUTRITIONAL INFO (per serving) | | | | |
|---|---|---|---|---|
| calories | fat | protein | carbs | fiber |
| 116 | 8.2 g | 7.6 g | 3.3 g | 1.2 g |
| | 64% | 26% | 11% | |

treats

# tips for making keto desserts

## HOW TO USE SWEETENERS IN SWEETS AND TREATS

To create the best possible flavor in keto desserts, I use a mixture of sweeteners. I usually use powdered erythritol and a teaspoon or two of stevia glycerite (which doesn't have a bitter aftertaste like most stevia). Then I adjust to the desired sweetness. Be aware that when you bake a dish with erythritol or stevia glycerite, some of the sweetness diminishes after it is baked.

The secret to success when baking with erythritol (either pure erythritol or erythritol-based brands of sweeteners, such as Swerve or Organic Zero) is to cream the fat first, then add the sweetener. When making traditional baked goods, normally sugar and butter are beaten together; a chemical reaction between the two creates a lot of air. Since erythritol has a different chemical structure than sugar, the butter (or other fat) should be beaten on its own until light and fluffy. Only after that point is the erythritol added.

## HOW TO USE SALT IN SWEETS AND TREATS

When you think of sweets, salt is probably the last ingredient that comes to mind—unless you once accidentally used salt in place of sugar! But as contradictory as it may sound, salt can make your treats taste sweeter, and it truly changes a dessert from tasty to jaw-dropping. It adds complexity to the entire dish. Salt balances and elevates flavors, and it conveys tones that you wouldn't otherwise know were in the dish. For example, salt makes spices more fragrant and citrus more vibrant. The takeaway here is that salt is a flavor enhancer, not a flavor replacer.

Many pastry chefs suggest doubling the salt in any classic dessert recipe and cutting back on the sugar. Even fast food restaurants are familiar with the power of salt; a small fast food milkshake contains more sodium than an order of french fries!

Just don't use iodized table salt in your desserts. First, a form of sugar is often added to table salt as an anti-caking agent, and it's always best to avoid hidden sugars. Second, you want the salt to complement the components in the dessert, not make it taste of chemicals, which table salt can do. I love using crystalline sea salt in desserts because it adds a slightly crunchy profile. If you are making a creamy dessert and do not want any crunch, try using a salt that dissolves well, such as flaked sea salt, which is the fastest-dissolving of the salt grains.

# chocolate gingerbread cookies

**KETO**

**PREP TIME:** 6 minutes

**COOK TIME:** 10 minutes

**YIELD:** 24 cookies (1 per serving)

½ cup (1 stick) unsalted butter or coconut oil, softened

1½ cups powdered erythritol or ½ cup yacón syrup

1 teaspoon stevia glycerite

2 large eggs, beaten

¾ cup unsweetened cocoa powder

1 tablespoon ground cinnamon

2 teaspoons ginger powder

¼ teaspoon fine sea salt

2 teaspoons vanilla extract

½ teaspoon almond extract

**SPECIAL EQUIPMENT**

Handheld mixer or stand mixer

1. Preheat the oven to 350°F.

2. In a medium-sized bowl, using a handheld mixer, or in the bowl of a stand mixer, cream the butter, erythritol or yacón syrup, and stevia together. (If using erythritol or an erythritol-based sweetener like Swerve, cream the butter first, then add the erythritol.)

3. Add the eggs and stir until well combined. Mix in the cocoa powder, cinnamon, ginger powder, salt, vanilla extract, and almond extract.

4. Form the dough into 2-inch balls. Place the balls on 2 ungreased cookie sheets about 1 inch apart. Bake for 10 minutes, until cooked through. Allow to cool on the cookie sheets before removing.

5. Store in an airtight container in the fridge for up to 1 week or in the freezer for up to 1 month.

| NUTRITIONAL INFO (per serving) | | | | |
|---|---|---|---|---|
| calories | fat | protein | carbs | fiber |
| 51 | 4.7 g | 1.1 g | 1.2 g | 0.7 g |
| | 83% | 9% | 9% | |

# gingerbread house

■□□
KETO

NUT
FREE

DAIRY
FREE

**PREP TIME:** 10 minutes

**COOK TIME:** 2 hours

**YIELD:** 1 gingerbread house

## FOR THE DOUGH

1¼ cups ground cinnamon, plus more for rolling out the dough

1 cup applesauce

## FOR THE ROYAL ICING

1 pound powdered erythritol

3 large egg whites, room temperature

½ teaspoon cream of tartar

## SPECIAL EQUIPMENT

Gingerbread house
cookie cutters

Stand mixer

**NOTE:** *Although you can eat the royal icing, the dough has too much cinnamon to be appetizing, so limit your snacking to the icing.*

1. Preheat the oven to 200°F. Line a cookie sheet with parchment paper.

2. Make the gingerbread: In large bowl, combine the cinnamon and applesauce. Stir well. (I use a paddle attachment on my stand mixer.)

3. If the dough is too sticky, add more cinnamon; if it's too dry and you are unable to mold it, add more applesauce.

4. Sprinkle a clean surface with cinnamon, just as you'd dust a surface with flour if you were rolling out traditional cookies.

5. Place the dough on the cinnamon-dusted surface and dust with additional cinnamon. Sprinkle a rolling pin with cinnamon and roll the dough to ¼ inch thick, sprinkling with more cinnamon to keep the dough from sticking. Cut the dough into shapes with gingerbread house cookie cutters.

6. Place the house pieces on the lined cookie sheet. They can be very close together since they do not rise or spread.

7. Bake for 1½ to 2 hours, until rock hard, or allow to dry at room temperature for several days.

8. Make the royal icing: Combine the ingredients for the icing in the bowl of a stand mixer. Beat on high speed for 7 to 10 minutes.

**VARIATION: NONEDIBLE ROYAL ICING.** *If you don't plan to eat the icing, you can replace the powdered erythritol with confectioners' sugar.*

**TIPS:** *Royal icing is a hard-drying icing, so keep it covered with a damp cloth. Humidity will greatly affect its texture and prevent it from fully hardening, as will grease, so be sure to use clean, dry utensils. In addition to making an excellent "glue" for gingerbread houses, royal icing works beautifully with Easter eggs and cookies you want to dry hard.*

| NUTRITIONAL INFO (icing only) | | | | |
|---|---|---|---|---|
| calories | fat | protein | carbs | fiber |
| 813 | 16.7 g | 24.8 g | 140.8 g | 76.2 g |
| | 18% | 12% | 69% | |

# DAIRY-FREE KETO
## *vanilla bean ice cream*

**KETO**  DAIRY FREE

**PREP TIME:** 10 minutes, plus time to churn the ice cream

**YIELD:** About 3 cups (¼ cup per serving)

¾ cup plus 2 tablespoons coconut oil (or unsalted butter if not dairy-sensitive)

¼ cup MCT oil

½ cup unsweetened almond milk or water

4 large whole eggs

4 large egg yolks

1 vanilla bean (about 6 inches long), split lengthwise and seeds scraped, or 1 teaspoon vanilla extract

¼ cup powdered erythritol or 1 teaspoon stevia glycerite

¼ teaspoon fine sea salt

**SPECIAL EQUIPMENT**

Ice cream maker        Blender

*This recipe, and the Dairy-Free Keto Chocolate Ice Cream recipe on page 312, contains raw eggs. Salmonella is rare—only about 1 in 20,000 eggs are infected—but young children, pregnant women, the elderly, and people with compromised immune systems should probably avoid raw eggs just in case. For the rest of us, be aware of the risk and decide for yourself whether it's worth it. I love these ice cream dishes, and for me, the risk is low enough that it doesn't affect my enjoyment of them.*

*Adding salt to desserts naturally brings out flavor, including sweetness, which means that you often need less sweetener. Salt is even more important when making ice cream because it helps keep the ice cream soft and scoopable.*

*Please don't forget to add the MCT oil; if you do, the ice cream liquid will curdle.*

1. In a blender, place the coconut oil, MCT oil, almond milk, whole eggs, yolks, vanilla bean seeds, erythritol, and salt. Blend until very smooth. Taste and add more erythritol if desired.

2. Pour into an ice cream maker and churn according to the manufacturer's directions, and watch the magic happen!

3. Store in an airtight container in the freezer for up to a month.

**BUSY FAMILY TIP:** *Ice cream is the perfect make-ahead dessert for entertaining.*

| NUTRITIONAL INFO (per serving) | | | | |
| --- | --- | --- | --- | --- |
| calories | fat | protein | carbs | fiber |
| 210 | 21.4 g | 3.2 g | 1.6 g | 0 g |
| | 92% | 6% | 3% | |

DAIRY-FREE KETO

# chocolate ice cream with cherry glaze

KETO · DAIRY FREE

**PREP TIME:** 15 minutes, plus time to churn the ice cream

**YIELD:** About 3 cups (¼ cup per serving)

---

## FOR THE ICE CREAM

¾ cup plus 2 tablespoons coconut oil (or unsalted butter if not dairy-sensitive)

½ cup unsweetened almond milk or water

¼ cup MCT oil

4 whole large eggs

4 large egg yolks

1 vanilla bean (about 6 inches long), split lengthwise and seeds scraped, or 1 teaspoon vanilla extract

¼ cup powdered erythritol

1 teaspoon stevia glycerite

¼ cup unsweetened cocoa powder

¼ teaspoon fine sea salt

## FOR THE GLAZE

1 bag cherry tea or other fruit-flavored tea, such as raspberry

½ cup boiling water

¼ cup powdered erythritol

¼ teaspoon stevia glycerite

¼ cup Brown Butter (page 68), cooled to room temperature (or melted coconut oil if dairy-sensitive)

1 teaspoon cherry flavor or other fruit flavor, such as raspberry

⅛ teaspoon guar gum or xanthan gum

*If, like one of my recipe testers, you can't tolerate the additives and chemicals in store-bought ice cream, this homemade version is for you. She said, "This was so easy to make, and all three of my kids just devoured it. The ice cream was buttery and velvety and the glaze made us feel like we were eating sundaes."*

*Please don't skip the MCT oil; if you do, the ice cream liquid will curdle. Also, note that raw eggs are used in this recipe. For a brief discussion of salmonella and raw eggs, see page 310.*

1. Make the ice cream: In a blender, place the coconut oil, almond milk, MCT oil, whole eggs, yolks, vanilla bean seeds, erythritol, stevia, cocoa powder, and salt. Taste and add more erythritol and/or stevia if desired. Blend until very smooth.

2. Pour into an ice cream maker and churn according to the manufacturer's directions, and watch the magic happen!

3. Make the glaze: Steep the tea bag in the ½ cup of boiling water for at least 2 minutes (the longer it steeps, the stronger the flavor), and then pour the tea into a food processor or blender. Add the erythritol, stevia, brown butter, and cherry flavor. Puree until smooth. Sift in the guar gum and puree again until smooth. After 3 minutes, the mixture will be a little thick. Pour over the chocolate ice cream and enjoy!

4. The chocolate ice cream can be stored in the freezer for up to a month, and the cherry glaze can be stored in the fridge for up to 4 days. Rewarm the glaze in a saucepan on low heat for 2 to 3 minutes before pouring over the ice cream.

**SPECIAL EQUIPMENT**

Ice cream maker     Blender

| NUTRITIONAL INFO (per serving) | | | | |
|---|---|---|---|---|
| calories | fat | protein | carbs | fiber |
| 249 | 25.3 g | 3.5 g | 2.1 g | 0.6 g |
| | 91% | 6% | 3% | |

# *easy mocha fudge truffles*

**KETO** | **NUT FREE**

**PREP TIME:** 15 minutes, plus 8 hours to chill

**COOK TIME:** 10 minutes

**YIELD:** About 24 truffles (1 per serving)

1 cup (2 sticks) unsalted butter

¼ cup powdered erythritol

1 teaspoon stevia glycerite

8 ounces mascarpone cheese or cream cheese (about 1 cup)

1 teaspoon espresso powder

1 teaspoon Kahlúa extract or rum extract

Unsweetened cocoa powder, for dusting (optional)

**FOR THE CHOCOLATE COATING**

2 ounces unsweetened baking chocolate, chopped fine

2 tablespoons unsalted butter or coconut oil

½ cup powdered erythritol

1 teaspoon stevia glycerite

¼ cup heavy cream

¼ teaspoon fine sea salt

1 vanilla bean (about 6 inches long), split lengthwise and seeds scraped, or 1 teaspoon vanilla extract

½ teaspoon Kahlúa extract

**SPECIAL EQUIPMENT**

Handheld mixer

| NUTRITIONAL INFO (per serving) | | | | |
|---|---|---|---|---|
| calories | fat | protein | carbs | fiber |
| 116 | 11.5 g | 1.5 g | 1.6 g | 0.5 g |
| | 89% | 5% | 6% | |

1. In a large saucepan, melt the 1 cup of butter over medium-high heat and heat until it turns brown (not black), about 5 minutes. Add the erythritol and stevia and cook for about 5 minutes, until well combined, then remove the pan from the heat.

2. Using a handheld mixer on low speed, mix in the mascarpone cheese, espresso powder, and Kahlúa extract until combined. The mixture will not emulsify until it cools a little; until then, it will keep separating. So allow the mixture to cool to room temperature, then whip once more and then place in the refrigerator to chill and thicken overnight (or for 6 to 8 hours).

3. Remove from the fridge and roll into 1-inch balls. For an easy coating, just dust the balls in cocoa powder to finish. If you prefer to coat them with chocolate, place the balls in the freezer while you make the chocolate coating.

4. Make the chocolate coating: In a medium-sized saucepan or double boiler, melt the chocolate and butter over low heat. When the mixture is melted and smooth, stir in the erythritol, stevia, heavy cream, and salt. Remove from the heat and add the vanilla bean seeds and Kahlúa extract.

5. Remove the truffles from the freezer and dip them in the chocolate coating. Place the coated truffles in the fridge for a few minutes, until the chocolate is set. Store in an airtight container in the fridge for up to 1 week.

# chocolate mocha cake pops

 **KETO** | **DAIRY FREE**

**PREP TIME:** 30 minutes, plus 25 minutes to chill

**COOK TIME:** 45 minutes

**YIELD:** 24 cake pops (2 per serving)

## FOR THE CAKE

¾ cup coconut oil or unsalted butter

7 ounces unsweetened baking chocolate, chopped fine

1¼ cups powdered erythritol

1 teaspoon vanilla extract

1 teaspoon almond extract

6 large eggs, separated

## FOR THE FILLING

¼ cup powdered erythritol

1 teaspoon stevia glycerite

2 tablespoons brewed decaf espresso or coffee

1 large egg

½ tablespoon unsweetened cocoa powder

2 tablespoons coconut oil or unsalted butter

½ teaspoon vanilla extract

¼ teaspoon almond extract

## FOR THE WHITE CHOCOLATE COATING

2 ounces cocoa butter

⅓ cup powdered erythritol

1 teaspoon vanilla extract or other extract, such as strawberry

⅛ teaspoon fine sea salt

## FOR DECORATING THE POPS (OPTIONAL)

¼ ounce unsweetened baking chocolate, melted

| NUTRITIONAL INFO (per serving) | | | | |
|---|---|---|---|---|
| calories | fat | protein | carbs | fiber |
| 325 | 30.5 g | 6.3 g | 5.3 g | 3.7 g |
| | 84% | 8% | 7% | |

1. Preheat the oven to 325°F. Grease a 10-inch round cake pan and line it with parchment paper.

2. Place the coconut oil in a saucepan on medium heat and slowly stir in the chocolate (don't burn the chocolate). Add the erythritol, vanilla extract, and almond extract. Stir to mix well, remove from the heat, cover, and let cool in the fridge for about 15 minutes.

3. While the chocolate mixture is cooling, place the egg whites in a stand mixer and whip until stiff peaks form. Once the whites are stiff, slowly add the yolks while the stand mixer is on low.

4. Once the chocolate mixture has cooled a bit but is still warm to the touch, add it to the egg mixture while the stand mixer is on low. Mix until well combined and pour the resulting mixture into the prepared cake pan.

5. Bake the cake for 25 to 30 minutes, until a toothpick inserted into the center comes out clean and the cake begins to pull away from the sides of the pan. Let the cake cool in the pan on a cooling rack for 30 minutes.

6. Cut around the sides of the pan to loosen the cake. Slide a spatula under the parchment to loosen from the pan and invert the cake onto a work surface. If the cake falls apart, no worries! You are going to roll it into cake pops!

7. While the cake is cooling, make the filling and the chocolate coating.

8. To make the filling: Combine the erythritol, stevia, espresso, egg, and cocoa powder in a heavy medium-sized saucepan. Whisk to blend, then add the coconut oil. Whisk constantly over medium heat for about 12 minutes, until the mixture thickens and coats the back of a spoon thickly. (Do not boil.)

9. Pour the mixture through a fine-mesh strainer into a medium-sized bowl. Stir in the vanilla and almond extracts. Place the bowl in larger bowl filled with ice water and chill, whisking occasionally, for about 15 minutes, until the filling is completely cool.

10. To make the white chocolate coating: Place the cocoa butter in a double boiler and heat on medium-high until fully melted, about 5 to 8 minutes. (Alternatively, heat in a microwave-safe bowl in the microwave on high for 1 minute, then check. Continue heating for 30-second intervals until melted.) Stir in the erythritol, vanilla extract, and salt. Set aside.

11. Assemble the cake pops: Crumble the cake into a large bowl. Add the filling and mix completely. (If you don't mind getting a little messy, push up your sleeves and use your hands to mix the cake and filling!) Be careful not to add too much filling. You want the consistency to be sticky, not soggy. Roll the mixture into 1-inch balls and place on a cookie sheet.

**SPECIAL EQUIPMENT**

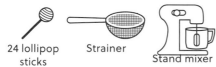

24 lollipop     Strainer     Stand mixer
sticks

12. Dip the ends of the lollipop sticks into the white chocolate coating and insert into the balls, then place the pops in the freezer for 5 to 10 minutes, until chilled. Dip the cake pops in the chocolate, then return them to the freezer for 15 minutes to chill.

13. If desired, use a toothpick to draw designs on the pops with melted unsweetened baking chocolate and set them in the fridge to set for 10 more minutes to let the designs harden.

# strawberry truffles

**KETO** | **NUT FREE** | **DAIRY FREE**

**PREP TIME:** 20 minutes, plus up to 1 hour to chill

**COOK TIME:** 20 minutes

**YIELD:** 24 truffles (1 per serving)

## FOR THE WHITE CHOCOLATE COATING

8 ounces cocoa butter

1⅓ cups powdered erythritol

2 teaspoons strawberry flavor

½ teaspoon fine sea salt

## FOR THE FILLING

1 cup powdered erythritol

1 teaspoon stevia glycerite

¾ cup very strong brewed strawberry tea

4 large eggs

2 teaspoons strawberry flavor

½ cup coconut oil

## SPECIAL EQUIPMENT

Truffle mold with 24 (1-inch) molds     Strainer

1. Make the white chocolate coating: Place the cocoa butter in a double boiler and heat on medium-high until fully melted, about 5 to 8 minutes. (Alternatively, heat in a microwave-safe bowl in the microwave on high for 1 minute, then check. Continue heating for 30-second intervals until melted.) Stir in the erythritol, strawberry flavor, and salt.

2. Pour the cocoa butter mixture into the truffle molds, filling them halfway. Let cool in the refrigerator or freezer until the white chocolate is solid, about 1 hour in the fridge or 5 minutes in the freezer.

3. While the coating chills, make the filling: Combine the erythritol, stevia, strong brewed tea, eggs, and strawberry flavor in a heavy medium-sized saucepan and whisk to blend. Add the coconut oil and heat, whisking constantly, over medium heat for about 12 minutes, until the mixture thickens and coats the back of a spoon thickly (do not boil.)

4. Pour the mixture through a fine-mesh strainer into a medium-sized bowl. Place the bowl in a larger bowl filled with ice water and chill, whisking occasionally, for about 15 minutes, until the mixture is cooled completely.

5. Make the truffles: Remove the mold from the fridge or freezer and cover the frozen cocoa butter mixture with the curd filling, leaving about ⅛ inch of space at the top. Top the filling with another layer of the cocoa butter mixture so that the curd is surrounded by the chocolate. Place back in the fridge or freezer to set: about 15 minutes in the freezer or 1 hour in the fridge.

6. Store the truffles an airtight container in the fridge for up to 1 week.

**VARIATION: DARK CHOCOLATE-COATED STRAWBERRY TRUFFLES.** *If you prefer your truffles to be coated in dark chocolate instead of white chocolate, chop ½ to 2 ounces unsweetened baking chocolate (depending on how dark you like your chocolate) and add it to the cocoa butter when you add the erythritol. Stir until it melts into the cocoa butter.*

*If you prefer half of your truffles coated in white chocolate and half in dark chocolate, set aside half of the cocoa butter mixture and stir the chopped unsweetened chocolate into the other half until melted.*

**BUSY FAMILY TIP:** *The filling can be made 1 day ahead and stored in the fridge until you're ready to assemble the truffles.*

| NUTRITIONAL INFO (per serving) | | | | |
|---|---|---|---|---|
| calories | fat | protein | carbs | fiber |
| 153 | 16.3 g | 1.1 g | 0 g | 0 g |
| | 96% | 3% | 0% | |

# chocolate mint cookies

 **KETO** | **NUT FREE** | **DAIRY FREE**

**PREP TIME:** 8 minutes, plus 10 minutes to cool

**COOK TIME:** 15 minutes

**YIELD:** 12 cookies (2 per serving)

½ cup coconut oil (or unsalted butter if not dairy-sensitive), softened

1¾ cups powdered erythritol

1 teaspoon stevia glycerite

2 large eggs

1 cup unsweetened cocoa powder

2 teaspoons mint flavor

¼ teaspoon fine sea salt

### FOR THE CHOCOLATE COATING

2 tablespoons coconut oil (or unsalted butter if not dairy-sensitive)

1 ounce unsweetened baking chocolate, chopped

6 tablespoons canned, full-fat coconut milk (or heavy cream if not dairy-sensitive)

¼ cup powdered erythritol

1 teaspoon mint flavor

### SPECIAL EQUIPMENT

Handheld mixer or stand mixer

*It can often seem impossible to enjoy treats when you've eliminated dairy, nuts, and grains from your diet. This tasty recipe is a great way to fill that sweet spot—especially if you have a weakness for Thin Mint Girl Scout cookies. When a client of mine brought a batch to work to share, no one could guess that they were healthy!*

1. Preheat the oven to 350°F.

2. In a medium-sized bowl, using a handheld mixer, or in the bowl of a stand mixer, cream the coconut oil, then add the erythritol and stevia. Add the eggs and stir until well combined. Finally, mix in the cocoa powder, mint flavor, and salt.

3. Form the dough into 2-inch balls and place on 2 cookie sheets about 1 inch apart. Bake for 10 minutes, until baked all the way through. Allow to cool on the cookie sheet for at least 10 minutes before removing. Place in the freezer for 10 minutes while you make the coating.

4. Make the chocolate coating: Place the coconut oil and chocolate in a double boiler over medium heat (or in a heat-safe dish over a pot of boiling water). Stir well until just melted (don't burn the chocolate!), then add the cream, erythritol, and mint flavor. Stir until smooth and thick. Remove from the heat.

5. Dip the frozen cookies in the chocolate coating and set on parchment paper to cool.

| NUTRITIONAL INFO (per serving) | | | | |
|---|---|---|---|---|
| calories | fat | protein | carbs | fiber |
| 304 | 28.6 g | 5.9 g | 7.3 g | 3.7 g |
| | 85% | 8% | 10% | |

# DARK CHOCOLATE
# *raspberry fat bombs*

**KETO** DAIRY FREE

**PREP TIME:** 10 minutes, plus 35 minutes to chill

**COOK TIME:** 5 minutes

**YIELD:** 12 fat bombs (1 per serving)

## FOR THE FILLING

1 cup coconut oil, softened

2 teaspoons raspberry flavor

⅔ cup powdered erythritol

1 teaspoon stevia glycerite

## FOR THE CHOCOLATE COATING

1 ounce unsweetened baking chocolate, chopped fine

½ cup powdered erythritol

¼ cup coconut oil (or unsalted butter if not dairy-sensitive)

¼ cup canned, full-fat coconut milk (or heavy cream if not dairy-sensitive)

1 teaspoon stevia glycerite

1 teaspoon raspberry flavor

½ teaspoon almond extract

⅛ teaspoon fine sea salt

1. Line a 12-well muffin pan with muffin liners.

2. Make the filling: In a medium-sized bowl, mix together the coconut oil, raspberry flavor, erythritol, and stevia until you have a paste.

3. Divide the mixture among the prepared muffin cups. Place in the freezer for about 30 minutes, or until frozen.

4. Meanwhile, make the chocolate coating: Place all of the ingredients in a double boiler over low heat (or in a heat-safe bowl over a pot of boiling water) to melt the chocolate, stirring often. When the chocolate is almost totally melted, remove from the heat (the chocolate will continue to melt). Continue stirring and, once the chocolate is totally melted and smooth, remove the raspberry bombs from the freezer.

5. Drizzle the melted chocolate over the raspberry bombs. Place back in the freezer to set for about 10 minutes before serving.

6. Store in the fridge for up to a week or in the freezer for up to 3 months.

| NUTRITIONAL INFO (per serving) | | | | |
|---|---|---|---|---|
| calories | fat | protein | carbs | fiber |
| 220 | 24 g | 0.3 g | 0.9 g | 0 g |
| | 98% | 1% | 2% | |

# chocolate berry pie

**KETO**  **NUT FREE**  **DAIRY FREE**

**PREP TIME:** 10 minutes, plus 10 minutes to chill

**COOK TIME:** 40 minutes

**YIELD:** One 8-inch pie (6 servings)

### FOR THE CRUST

3½ tablespoons coconut oil (or unsalted butter if not dairy-sensitive)

1½ ounces unsweetened baking chocolate

⅓ cup powdered erythritol

1 teaspoon stevia glycerite (or more or less for desired sweetness)

1 large egg

2 teaspoons raspberry flavor or other fruit flavor, such as strawberry or cherry

¼ teaspoon fine sea salt

### FOR THE FILLING

3 large eggs

½ cup powdered erythritol

¼ cup lime or lemon juice

2 teaspoons raspberry flavor or other fruit flavor, such as strawberry or cherry

1 teaspoon stevia glycerite

½ teaspoon baking powder

¼ teaspoon fine sea salt

¼ cup Dairy-Free Chocolate Syrup (page 330), for drizzling (optional)

*If you are looking for a special dessert that is not only pretty but also kid-friendly, this is a great one to try! One client of mine needed a dairy- and nut-free dessert for her son, who also doesn't eat fruit. She said he "loved feeling like he was getting a dessert baked with real fruit. It really satisfied that craving for him."*

1. Preheat the oven to 325°F. Grease an 8-inch pie pan and line it with parchment paper.

2. Make the crust: Heat the coconut oil in a saucepan over medium heat. (If using butter, take the additional step of browning the butter, if desired; it tastes way better! In a saucepan, heat the butter over high heat, stirring often. Once the butter foams and has brown flecks, not black, remove from the heat.) Slowly add the chopped chocolate (don't let it burn). Add the erythritol and stevia, then let cool in the fridge for about 10 minutes.

3. Once cool, add the egg, raspberry flavor, and salt, and stir to combine. Pour into the prepared pie pan.

4. Place the crust in the oven and prebake for 15 minutes. Remove from the oven and set aside to cool.

5. Make the filling: In a medium-sized bowl, mix the ingredients for the filling until well combined.

6. Pour the mixture evenly over the prebaked crust and bake again for 15 to 20 minutes, until set. Let cool and drizzle with chocolate syrup, if desired, before serving.

7. Store in an airtight container in the fridge or freezer for up to 1 week.

**MAKE-AHEAD WHIPPED CREAM:** *Have you ever made whipped cream ahead of time for a dinner party or holiday only to find that once the dessert is ready, the whipped cream has fallen? Well, I have a trick for you!*

*In a saucepan, sprinkle ½ teaspoon unflavored gelatin over 1½ tablespoons water. Let stand for 3 minutes, then gently heat over low heat until the gelatin is dissolved. (Alternatively, place the water and gelatin in a small, microwave-safe bowl and heat on high in 5-second increments until the gelatin is dissolved.)*

*Place 1½ cups cold heavy cream in a large bowl and add ¼ cup powdered erythritol or a few drops of stevia glycerite and the seeds from 1 vanilla bean or 1 teaspoon vanilla extract. Using a handheld mixer, whip the cream until the beaters leave a trail. Add the gelatin and continue to beat on high until peaks form. Cover and refrigerate until needed. Peaks will stay for up to a day!*

| NUTRITIONAL INFO (per serving) | | | | |
|---|---|---|---|---|
| calories | fat | protein | carbs | fiber |
| 177 | 15.6 g | 7 g | 2.8 g | 1.6 g |
| | 79% | 16% | 6% | |

# caramel apple fudge

■■■ KETO | NUT FREE

**PREP TIME:** 10 minutes, plus 8 hours to chill

**COOK TIME:** 5 minutes

**YIELD:** 24 pieces (2 per serving)

1 cup (2 sticks) unsalted butter

¼ cup powdered erythritol

1 teaspoon stevia glycerite

8 ounces mascarpone or cream cheese (about 1 cup)

1½ tablespoons unsweetened almond milk

1 teaspoon apple extract or a few drops apple oil

¼ teaspoon fine sea salt

**SPECIAL EQUIPMENT**

Handheld mixer

*I love to ask clients with young children to test new recipes, because kids can be so picky when it comes to trying new things. This recipe totally passed the kid test—one recipe tester reported that she had to hide some of the fudge so she could get a taste.*

1. Line an 8-inch square baking pan with parchment paper, allowing the paper to drape over the sides for easy removal.

2. In a small saucepan, melt the butter over medium-high heat (until it turns brown, but not black). Add the erythritol and stevia and continue to cook for about 5 minutes, until well combined.

3. Using a handheld mixer on low speed, mix in the mascarpone, almond milk, apple extract, and salt until combined and emulsified. Allow the mixture to cool for about 5 minutes, then continue blending until smooth. Alternatively, transfer the mixture to a blender and combine until smooth.

4. Pour the mixture into the prepared baking pan and refrigerate overnight. The mixture will thicken a lot. Remove from the pan, peel away the parchment, and cut into 1-inch cubes.

5. Store in an airtight container in the fridge for up to a week or in the freezer for up to a month.

| NUTRITIONAL INFO (per serving) | | | | |
|---|---|---|---|---|
| calories | fat | protein | carbs | fiber |
| 205 | 22 g | 1.6 g | 0.6 g | 0 g |
| | 96% | 3% | 1% | |

# dairy-free chocolate egg cream

**KETO** ■■■ · **DAIRY FREE**

**PREP TIME:** 2 minutes

**YIELD:** 1 serving

2 tablespoons Dairy-Free Chocolate Syrup (page 330)

3 ounces unsweetened almond milk

5 ounces seltzer water

*If you have ever had a chocolate egg cream at a restaurant or deli, most likely the chocolate syrup was drizzled down the spoon. But this isn't done because it makes it taste great; it is only for looks. And actually, drizzling the chocolate down the spoon kills carbonation because the more you stir, the more you dissipate the carbonation, resulting in a flat drink. To make a tasty and fizzy chocolate egg cream, combine the chocolate and milk in the bottom of the glass and stir that first. Add the carbonated water last and you will end up with the best chocolate egg cream ever!*

Pour the chocolate syrup into the bottom of a glass. Add the almond milk and stir to mix well. Add the seltzer last and enjoy!

| NUTRITIONAL INFO (per serving) | | | | |
|---|---|---|---|---|
| calories | fat | protein | carbs | fiber |
| 78 | 7.3 g | 1.1 g | 2.1 g | 0 g |
| | 84% | 6% | 11% | |

# cookie dough brownies

**KETO**

**PREP TIME:** 12 minutes, plus 40 minutes to chill

**COOK TIME:** 35 minutes

**YIELD:** 16 brownies (1 per serving)

### FOR THE BROWNIES

¾ cup coconut oil or unsalted butter

7 ounces unsweetened baking chocolate, chopped fine

1¼ cups powdered erythritol

1 vanilla bean (about 6 inches long), seeds scraped clean and pod discarded, or 1 teaspoon vanilla extract

1 teaspoon almond extract

¼ teaspoon fine sea salt

6 large eggs, separated

### FOR THE "HEALTHIFIED" CHOCOLATE CHUNKS OR CHIPS

2 ounces cocoa butter

4 ounces unsweetened baking chocolate, chopped fine

⅓ cup powdered erythritol

1 teaspoon vanilla extract or other extract, such as mint

⅛ teaspoon fine sea salt

### FOR THE FROSTING

1 cup (2 sticks) unsalted butter

¼ cup powdered erythritol

1 teaspoon stevia glycerite

8 ounces mascarpone or cream cheese (about 1 cup)

½ cup unsweetened almond milk

¼ teaspoon fine sea salt

"Healthified" chocolate chunks (from above)

¼ cup Dairy-Free Chocolate Syrup (page 330), for drizzling (optional)

*As one of my clients reported after she tried this recipe, the brownies and frosting balance each other in this dish: "The brownies are rich, dark chocolate gooey goodness, and the frosting adds a sweetness and creaminess that pairs exceptionally well."*

1. Preheat the oven to 325°F. Grease a 9-inch square brownie pan.

2. Make the brownies: Melt the coconut oil in a saucepan over medium heat, then slowly add the chocolate. Continue to heat, stirring often, until the chocolate is completely melted. Stir in the erythritol, vanilla bean seeds, almond extract, and salt. Let cool in the fridge for about 10 minutes.

3. While it is cooling, place the egg whites in a stand mixer and whip until stiff peaks form. Once the whites are stiff, slowly add the yolks while mixing on low speed.

4. Once the chocolate mixture is cooled a bit but still warm to the touch, add it to the egg mixture with the stand mixer on low. Pour the mixture into the prepared pan and smooth the top. Place in the oven and bake for about 18 minutes, until a toothpick inserted in the center comes out clean and the brownie begins to pull away from the sides of the pan. Cool the brownie in the pan on a cooling rack for 30 minutes.

5. While the brownie cools, make the chocolate chunks or chips: Place the cocoa butter and unsweetened baking chocolate in a double boiler and heat over medium-high heat until fully melted, about 5 to 8 minutes. (Alternatively, heat in a microwave-safe bowl in the microwave on high for 1 minute, then check. Continue heating for 30-second intervals until melted.) Stir in the erythritol, vanilla extract, and salt.

6. To make into chunks: Pour the melted chocolate into a truffle mold or 8-inch square baking dish lined with parchment paper and chill in the refrigerator or freezer until the chocolate is solid, about 1 hour in the fridge or 5 minutes in the freezer. Chop into chunks.

   To make into chips: Line a rimmed baking sheet with parchment paper. Place the melted chocolate in a small piping bag. Squeeze ¼ teaspoon of chocolate onto the parchment in a chocolate chip shape and repeat until you've used all the chocolate, keeping the chips about ⅛ inch apart. Chill in the fridge or freezer until the chocolate is solid, about 1 hour in the fridge or 5 minutes in the freezer.

7. Make the frosting: In a saucepan, heat the butter over medium-high heat until it turns brown, not black. Add the erythritol and stevia and continue to cook for about 5 minutes, until well combined. Remove from the

**SPECIAL EQUIPMENT**

Stand mixer

heat and, using a handheld mixer on low speed, mix in the mascarpone, almond milk, and salt until smooth. Allow the mixture to cool completely, about 15 minutes in the fridge (you don't want the chocolate chips to melt), then stir in the "healthified" chocolate chunks or chips.

8. When the brownie has cooled completely, cut it into pieces and spread the frosting over the number of brownies you plan to serve. The brownies are best served at room temperature or slightly warm. For an extra-fancy presentation, drizzle with the chocolate syrup, if desired.

9. Store leftover frosting and brownies separately in airtight containers in the fridge for up to a week or in the freezer for up to a month. When ready to serve, take the brownies out of the fridge and gently warm them in the microwave on medium heat for a few seconds or until the bottom is warm and gooey, then top with the frosting.

| NUTRITIONAL INFO (per serving) | | | | |
|---|---|---|---|---|
| calories | fat | protein | carbs | fiber |
| 427 | 41.6 g | 6.5 g | 6.4 g | 4.2 g |
|  | 88% | 6% | 6% |  |

# dairy-free chocolate syrup

**KETO** **NUT FREE** **DAIRY FREE**

**PREP TIME:** 5 minutes

**COOK TIME:** 10 minutes

**YIELD:** 1 pint (1 generous tablespoon per serving)

2 ounces unsweetened baking chocolate, chopped fine

2 tablespoons coconut oil

¾ cup canned, full-fat coconut milk

1 cup powdered erythritol

1 teaspoon stevia glycerite

¼ teaspoon fine sea salt

1 vanilla bean (about 6 inches long), split lengthwise and seeds scraped, or 1 teaspoon vanilla extract

½ teaspoon almond extract

1. In a medium-sized saucepan or double boiler, melt the chocolate and coconut oil over medium-low heat until melted and smooth. Stir in the coconut milk, erythritol, stevia, and salt.

2. Continue to cook, stirring constantly, until it begins to boil, then remove the pan from the heat and add the vanilla bean seeds and almond extract. The mixture will thicken as it cools.

3. Once cool, transfer to a jar. Seal and store in the fridge for up to 2 weeks.

| NUTRITIONAL INFO (per serving) | | | | |
|---|---|---|---|---|
| calories | fat | protein | carbs | fiber |
| 33 | 3.1 g | 0.4 g | 0.9 g | 0 g |
| | 84% | 5% | 11% | |

# chocolate crème de menthe pops

**KETO**

**PREP TIME:** 10 minutes, plus 3½ hours to freeze

**COOK TIME:** 5 minutes

**YIELD:** 12 pops (1 per serving)

2 cups unsweetened vanilla almond milk

4 ounces cream cheese (about ½ cup)

½ cup chopped avocado (about ½ avocado)

½ cup fresh mint leaves

2 tablespoons powdered erythritol

1 teaspoon stevia glycerite (or more to desired sweetness)

1 teaspoon mint flavor

**HEALTHY ADDITIONS (OPTIONAL)**

1 tablespoon aloe vera

1 tablespoon l-glutamine powder

1 tablespoon grass-fed powdered gelatin

**FOR THE CHOCOLATE DRIZZLE**

2 tablespoons unsalted butter or coconut oil

1 ounce unsweetened baking chocolate, chopped

10 tablespoons heavy cream or canned, full-fat coconut milk

¼ cup powdered erythritol

1 teaspoon stevia glycerite

**FOR GARNISH**

Fresh mint leaves

1. Place the almond milk, cream cheese, avocado, mint, erythritol, stevia, mint flavor, and any of the healthy additions, if desired, in a blender and blend until very smooth. Pour into 12 mini paper cups. Cut the Popsicle sticks in half crosswise and insert the rough end into the mixture so the rounded edge is showing. Place in the freezer for at least 3 hours, or until frozen.

2. When the pops are fully frozen, make the chocolate drizzle: Place the butter and chocolate in a double boiler over medium heat (or in a heat-safe bowl over a pot of boiling water) and heat, stirring constantly, until just melted (don't burn the chocolate!). Add the cream, erythritol, and stevia. Remove from the heat and stir until smooth and thick.

3. Line a rimmed baking sheet with parchment paper. Remove the pops from the freezer and rip off the paper cups. Dip the top end of each ice pop into the chocolate. Place a mint leaf on the top of the ice pop and place the pops on their sides on the lined baking sheet. Place back in the freezer and freeze for at least 30 minutes, until the chocolate is set.

**SPECIAL EQUIPMENT**

Blender

6 Popsicle sticks

12 mini paper cups

| NUTRITIONAL INFO (per serving) | | | | |
|---|---|---|---|---|
| calories | fat | protein | carbs | fiber |
| 96 | 8.3 g | 2.7 g | 2.9 g | 1.5 g |
| | 78% | 11% | 12% | |

# *pumpkin pie frozen custard*

KETO   NUT FREE   DAIRY FREE

**PREP TIME:** 20 minutes

**COOK TIME:** 10 minutes

**YIELD:** 5 cups (½ cup per serving)

2 cups canned, full-fat coconut milk (or heavy cream if not dairy-sensitive)

5 large egg yolks

⅔ cup powdered erythritol

1 vanilla bean (about 6 inches long), split lengthwise and seeds scraped, or 1 teaspoon vanilla extract

2 teaspoons pumpkin pie spice extract

1 teaspoon natural orange food coloring

1 teaspoon butter flavor or a few drops of butter oil (optional)

½ teaspoon fine sea salt

½ teaspoon ground cinnamon

¼ teaspoon ground nutmeg

**SPECIAL EQUIPMENT**

Ice cream maker        Strainer

1. In a large bowl, whisk together all of the ingredients until well combined. If you prefer not to use raw egg yolks, place the mixture in a medium-sized saucepan and cook for about 10 minutes, until the mixture thickens and coats the back of a spoon thickly, stirring often so the eggs don't curdle. Remove from the heat and strain the custard through a fine-mesh strainer to remove any cooked egg yolks. Let cool.

2. Churn the cooled mixture in an ice cream maker according to the manufacturer's directions, or until thick, about 20 minutes. Remove the frozen custard from the ice cream maker and serve.

3. Store leftovers covered tightly in the freezer.

| NUTRITIONAL INFO (per serving) | | | | |
| --- | --- | --- | --- | --- |
| calories | fat | protein | carbs | fiber |
| 112 | 11.2 g | 1.8 g | 1.2 g | 0 g |
| | 90% | 6% | 4% | |

# cinnamon swirl cheesecake

**KETO**

**PREP TIME:** 15 minutes

**COOK TIME:** 1 hour 10 minutes, plus 4 hours to chill

**YIELD:** One 8-inch cheesecake (12 servings)

## FOR THE CRUST

3½ tablespoons unsalted butter or coconut oil

1½ ounces unsweetened baking chocolate, chopped

⅓ cup powdered erythritol

1 teaspoon stevia glycerite

1 large egg, beaten

2 teaspoons ground cinnamon

1 vanilla bean (about 6 inches long), split lengthwise and seeds scraped, or 1 teaspoon vanilla extract

¼ teaspoon fine sea salt

## FOR THE FILLING

32 ounces cream cheese (about 4 cups), softened

¾ cup powdered erythritol

1 teaspoon stevia glycerite

½ cup unsweetened almond milk

1 vanilla bean (about 6 inches long), split lengthwise and seeds scraped, or 1 teaspoon vanilla extract

¼ teaspoon almond extract

¼ teaspoon fine sea salt

3 large eggs

## FOR THE CINNAMON SWIRL

6 tablespoons unsalted butter

½ cup powdered erythritol

½ teaspoon stevia glycerite

1 vanilla bean (about 6 inches long), split lengthwise and seeds scraped, or 1 teaspoon vanilla extract

1 tablespoon ground cinnamon

¼ teaspoon fine sea salt

1. Preheat the oven to 325°F. Grease an 8-inch springform pan and line it with parchment paper.

2. Make the crust: If using butter, take the additional step of browning the butter, if desired; it tastes way better! In a saucepan, heat the butter over high heat, stirring often. Once the butter foams and has brown flecks (not black), remove from the heat and allow to cool for 10 minutes. If using coconut oil, melt the oil in a saucepan over medium-low heat.

3. Slowly add the chocolate to the butter or oil (don't burn the chocolate), stirring constantly. When the chocolate is melted, add the erythritol and stevia. Let cool in the fridge.

4. Once cool, add the egg, cinnamon, vanilla bean seeds, and salt. Place the mixture in the prepared springform pan, spreading it with your hands to cover the bottom completely.

5. Make the filling: In a large bowl, using a handheld mixer, or in the bowl of a stand mixer, beat the cream cheese, erythritol, stevia, almond milk, vanilla bean seeds, almond extract, and salt until well blended.

6. Add the eggs one at a time, mixing on low speed after each addition just until blended. Pour half of the batter into the prepared springform pan. Reserve the rest.

7. Make the cinnamon swirl: In a saucepan, heat the butter over high heat, stirring often, until the butter froths and brown flecks appear. Whisk in the erythritol, stevia, vanilla bean seeds, cinnamon, and salt. Remove from the heat and let cool slightly.

8. Spoon half of the cinnamon swirl onto the top of the cheesecake batter in the springform pan. Using a knife, cut the cinnamon swirl through the batter several times for a marble effect. Top with the rest of the cheesecake batter and cinnamon swirl. Cut through the cheesecake batter again several times for a marble effect.

9. Set up a water bath: Wrap aluminum foil entirely around the bottom and halfway up the sides of the springform pan to prevent water from leaking into the removable bottom of the springform pan. Place the cheesecake in a roasting pan (or any baking pan with sides) and place the pans into the oven. Pour hot water into the roasting pan so that it comes halfway up the sides of the springform pan.

10. Bake for 55 minutes, or until the center is almost set. Remove from the oven and let cool completely in the pan before removing it.

11. Refrigerate for 4 hours or overnight before serving. Store leftover cheesecake in the refrigerator for up to 7 days.

## SPECIAL EQUIPMENT

Handheld mixer or stand mixer

| NUTRITIONAL INFO (per serving) | | | | |
|---|---|---|---|---|
| calories | fat | protein | carbs | fiber |
| 252 | 19.7 g | 12.2 g | 6.8 g | 1.3 g |
| | 70% | 19% | 11% | |

TIP: *A water bath helps the cheesecake cook evenly; however, it can be baked without this step. If you are not using a water bath, place the cheesecake on a lined rimmed baking sheet to catch any overflow or leaking. When done baking, turn the oven off and let the cake cool in the oven with the door closed for 5 to 6 hours; this prevents cracking.*

# chai panna cotta

**KETO**  **NUT FREE**  **DAIRY FREE**

**PREP TIME:** 7 minutes, plus 2 hours to chill

**YIELD:** 6 servings

1 cup strongly brewed chai tea

1 tablespoon grass-fed powdered gelatin

2 cups coconut cream or canned, full-fat coconut milk (or heavy cream if not dairy-sensitive)

1 vanilla bean (about 6 inches long), split lengthwise and seeds scraped, or 1 teaspoon vanilla extract

⅓ cup powdered erythritol

1 teaspoon stevia glycerite

1 tablespoon ground cinnamon

¼ teaspoon fine sea salt

1. Place the brewed chai tea in a large heat-safe bowl. Sift in the gelatin while whisking so no clumps form. Once the gelatin is dissolved, add the coconut cream and vanilla bean seeds and stir to mix.

2. Add the erythritol, stevia, cinnamon, and salt. Stir well.

3. Pour the mixture into cute cups for serving. Refrigerate until set, about 2 hours.

| NUTRITIONAL INFO (per serving) | | | | |
|---|---|---|---|---|
| calories | fat | protein | carbs | fiber |
| 176 | 16.3 g | 3 g | 4.1 g | 0 g |
|  | 83% | 7% | 9% |  |

# lemon curd ice cream

KETO   NUT FREE   DAIRY FREE

**PREP TIME:** 30 minutes, plus 15 minutes to chill

**COOK TIME:** 12 minutes

**YIELD:** 6 cups (½ cup per serving)

**FOR THE LEMON CURD**

1 cup powdered erythritol

1 teaspoon stevia glycerite

½ cup lemon juice

1 tablespoon finely grated lemon zest

4 large eggs

½ cup coconut oil or unsalted butter

¼ teaspoon fine sea salt

1½ cups canned, full-fat coconut milk or heavy cream

1 teaspoon strawberry flavor or other flavor (optional)

**SPECIAL EQUIPMENT**

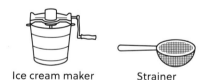

Ice cream maker    Strainer

1. Make the lemon curd: Combine the erythritol, stevia, lemon juice, lemon zest, and eggs in a heavy medium-sized saucepan and whisk to blend. Add the butter and salt. Place over medium heat and cook, whisking constantly, for about 12 minutes, or until the mixture thickens and coats the back of a spoon thickly (do not boil).

2. Strain the mixture through a fine-mesh strainer into a medium-sized bowl. Place the bowl in a larger bowl filled with ice water and chill, whisking occasionally, for about 15 minutes, until the lemon curd is cooled completely.

3. Add the cream and strawberry flavor to the curd and stir to combine.

4. Pour the mixture into an ice cream machine and churn according to the manufacturer's instructions. Store leftovers in a tightly sealed container in the freezer.

**BUSY FAMILY TIP:** *The lemon curd can be made 1 day ahead and stored in the refrigerator until you're ready to make the ice cream.*

| NUTRITIONAL INFO (per serving) | | | | |
|---|---|---|---|---|
| calories | fat | protein | carbs | fiber |
| 101 | 10 g | 2.3 g | 0.5 g | 0 g |
| | 89% | 9% | 2% | |

# almond roca mocha cake

KETO

**PREP TIME:** 40 minutes

**COOK TIME:** 50 minutes

**YIELD:** One 4-layer (6-inch) round cake (16 servings)

### FOR THE CAKE

¾ cup coconut oil or unsalted butter

7 ounces unsweetened baking chocolate, chopped fine

1¼ cups powdered erythritol

1 teaspoon vanilla extract

1 teaspoon almond extract

¼ teaspoon fine sea salt

6 large eggs, separated

### FOR THE SOAKING SYRUP

⅔ cup decaf espresso or coffee

¾ cup unsweetened vanilla almond milk

⅓ cup powdered erythritol

½ teaspoon stevia glycerite

1 teaspoon Kahlúa extract

¼ teaspoon fine sea salt

### FOR THE ESPRESSO MOUSSE

½ cup powdered erythritol

1 teaspoon stevia glycerite

¼ cup decaf espresso or coffee

2 large eggs

1 tablespoon unsweetened cocoa powder

¼ cup coconut oil (or unsalted butter if not dairy-sensitive)

½ teaspoon fine sea salt

1 teaspoon vanilla extract

½ teaspoon almond extract

1. Preheat the oven to 325°F. Grease two 6-inch round cake pans or line with parchment paper.

2. Melt the coconut oil in a saucepan over medium heat and slowly add the chocolate (don't burn the chocolate). Add the erythritol, vanilla and almond extracts, and salt. Let cool in the fridge for a while.

3. While it is cooling, place the egg whites in a stand mixer and whip until stiff peaks form. Once the whites are stiff, lower the speed to very low and slowly add the yolks one at a time and mix until just combined.

4. Once the chocolate mixture has cooled a bit but is still warm to the touch, fold it into the egg mixture using a spatula. Pour the batter into the prepared baking sheet and smooth the top.

5. Bake the cake for about 18 minutes, until a toothpick inserted into the center comes out clean and the cake begins to pull away from the sides of the pan. Let the cake cool in the pans on a cooling rack for 30 minutes.

6. Cut around the pan sides and invert the cake onto a work surface, peeling off the parchment paper if used. Cut each cake in half crosswise, so that you have 4 thin round cakes.

7. While the cake cools, make the syrup, mousse, and frosting.

8. To make the soaking syrup: Bring the espresso, almond milk, erythritol, stevia, Kahlúa extract, and salt to a boil in small saucepan. Remove from the heat and set aside.

9. To make the mousse: Combine the erythritol, stevia, espresso, eggs, and cocoa powder in heavy medium-sized saucepan and whisk to blend. Add the coconut oil and salt. Place over medium heat and cook, whisking constantly, for about 12 minutes, until the mixture thickens and coats back of spoon thickly (do not boil).

10. Strain the mixture through a fine-mesh strainer into a medium-sized bowl. Stir in the vanilla and almond extracts. Place the bowl in a larger bowl filled with ice water and chill, whisking occasionally, for about 15 minutes, until the filling is cooled completely.

11. To make the frosting: In a saucepan, melt the butter over medium-high heat until it turns brown, not black. Add the erythritol and stevia and continue to cook for 5 to 8 minutes, until well combined. Remove from the heat and, using a handheld mixer on low speed, mix in the mascarpone, almond milk, and salt until smooth. Allow to cool before using.

## FOR THE FROSTING

1 cup (2 sticks) unsalted butter

¼ cup powdered erythritol

1 teaspoon stevia glycerite

8 ounces mascarpone or cream cheese (about 1 cup)

½ cup unsweetened almond milk

¼ teaspoon fine sea salt

Sliced almonds, for garnish (optional)

## SPECIAL EQUIPMENT

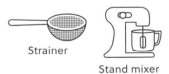

Strainer

Stand mixer

12. Assemble the cake. Place 1 cake circle on a platter. Brush the cake layer with 2 tablespoons of the soaking syrup. Spread one-third of the espresso mousse (about ¾ cup) on the cake layer, leaving a ½-inch border. Repeat twice more with cake, syrup, and mousse. Top with the fourth cake layer and press lightly to adhere.

13. Spread the frosting over the top and sides of the cake to seal, then adhere sliced almonds to the sides, if desired.

BUSY FAMILY TIP: *This cake will be more cakelike after resting a night. You can make the cake part the night before if desired. You can also make the mousse 1 day ahead and refrigerate until you're ready to assemble the cake.*

| NUTRITIONAL INFO (per serving) | | | | |
|---|---|---|---|---|
| calories | fat | protein | carbs | fiber |
| 375 | 36.9 g | 6.4 g | 4.4 g | 2 g |
| | 89% | 7% | 5% | |

# iced mocha pops

**KETO** ■■□  **NUT FREE**

**PREP TIME:** 5 minutes, plus 2 hours to chill

**COOK TIME:** 5 minutes

**YIELD:** 4 pops (1 per serving)

1 ounce brewed decaf espresso

4 ounces mascarpone cheese (about ½ cup), softened (or ½ cup coconut cream if dairy-sensitive)

¾ cup unsweetened vanilla almond milk or canned, full-fat coconut milk

¼ cup powdered erythritol

¼ teaspoon stevia glycerite

1 teaspoon rum extract

¼ teaspoon fine sea salt

**FOR THE CHOCOLATE COATING**

¼ cup coconut oil (or unsalted butter if not dairy-sensitive)

¼ cup unsweetened cocoa powder

2 tablespoons powdered erythritol

¼ teaspoon stevia glycerite

⅛ teaspoon rum extract

Pinch of fine sea salt

**SPECIAL EQUIPMENT**

2 Popsicle sticks    4 mini paper cups

1. In a medium-sized bowl, combine the espresso, mascarpone, almond milk or coconut milk, erythritol, stevia, rum extract, and salt and mix until smooth. Pour into 12 mini paper cups. Cut the Popsicle sticks in half crosswise and insert the rough end into the mixture so the rounded edge is showing. Place in the freezer for at least 2 hours.

2. Meanwhile, make the chocolate coating: In a saucepan, melt the coconut oil over low heat. Stir in the cocoa powder, erythritol, stevia, rum extract, and salt until smooth. Allow to cool to room temperature.

3. Dip the frozen pops into the chocolate or use a spoon to drizzle the coating over the pops. Place on a piece of parchment and return to the freezer for a moment so the shell can harden.

| NUTRITIONAL INFO (per serving) | | | | |
|---|---|---|---|---|
| calories | fat | protein | carbs | fiber |
| 251 | 25.3 g | 3.2 g | 3.1 g | 1.2 g |
| | 91% | 5% | 5% | |

# easy toffee fudge pops

KETO

**PREP TIME:** 5 minutes, plus 2 hours to chill

**YIELD:** 4 pops (1 per serving)

1 cup unsweetened almond milk

2 ounces cream cheese (about ¼ cup), softened

3 tablespoons unsweetened cocoa powder

2 teaspoons powdered erythritol or 1 drop of stevia glycerite

1 teaspoon toffee extract

Pinch of fine sea salt

**SPECIAL EQUIPMENT**

Ice pop molds

1. Place all of the ingredients in a large bowl or blender and combine until very smooth. Taste and adjust to the desired sweetness.

2. Pour into ice pop molds. Place in the freezer for 2 hours, or until completely frozen.

| NUTRITIONAL INFO (per serving) | | | | |
|---|---|---|---|---|
| calories | fat | protein | carbs | fiber |
| 46 | 2.7 g | 2.8 g | 2.6 g | 0 g |
| | 53% | 24% | 23% | |

# chai "sugar"

**KETO** ■□□  **NUT FREE**  **DAIRY FREE**

**PREP TIME:** 2 minutes

**YIELD:** About 2 cups (2 tablespoons per serving)

2 cups granulated erythritol

2 teaspoons ground cardamom

2 teaspoons ground cinnamon

¼ teaspoon ginger powder

¼ teaspoon ground cloves

2 vanilla beans (about 6 inches long), split lengthwise and seeds scraped

¼ teaspoon fine sea salt

*This is a tasty natural sweetener that can be used in a cup of tea or in any recipe where you'd like to add a lovely chai flavor. I use it to make Chai Streusel Candy (page 349) for a crunchy fat bomb.*

1. In a medium-sized bowl, combine the erythritol, cardamom, cinnamon, ginger powder, cloves, vanilla bean seeds, and salt until well mixed. Divide the mixture into small jars.

2. Cover and place in a cool, dry place. Keeps for up to 6 months.

| NUTRITIONAL INFO (per serving) | | | | |
|---|---|---|---|---|
| calories | fat | protein | carbs | fiber |
| 3 | 0 g | 0 g | 0.5 g | 0 g |
|  | 0% | 0% | 100% |  |

# chai streusel candy

**KETO** | **NUT FREE** | **DAIRY FREE**

**PREP TIME:** 2 minutes

**COOK TIME:** 15 minutes

**YIELD:** 4 servings

1 cup Chai "Sugar" (page 348)

3 tablespoons coconut oil

### FOR SERVING (OPTIONAL)

Dairy-Free Keto Vanilla Bean Ice Cream (page 310)

Dairy-Free Keto Chocolate Ice Cream with Cherry Glaze (page 312)

Lemon Curd Ice Cream (page 340)

| NUTRITIONAL INFO (per serving) | | | | |
|---|---|---|---|---|
| calories | fat | protein | carbs | fiber |
| 91 | 10.2 g | 0 g | 0.1 g | 0 g |
| | 100% | 0% | 0% | |

1. Preheat the oven to 350°F. Line a rimmed baking sheet with parchment paper.

2. Combine the Chai "Sugar" and coconut oil with a fork until small crumbs form. Place on the baking sheet and spread into a thin layer. Bake for 12 to 15 minutes, until the Chai "Sugar" melts.

3. Remove from the oven and allow to cool completely. The candy hardens as it cools. Store in an airtight container in the fridge for up to 1 month.

4. Serve with keto ice cream or eat plain!

# chocolate-covered toffee

**KETO**  **NUT FREE**

**PREP TIME:** 8 minutes, plus 15 minutes to chill

**COOK TIME:** 10 minutes

**YIELD:** 12 servings

¼ cup (½ stick) unsalted butter

1 cup powdered erythritol

1 teaspoon stevia glycerite

1 vanilla bean (about 6 inches long), split lengthwise and seeds scraped, or 1 teaspoon vanilla extract

**FOR THE CHOCOLATE DRIZZLE**

¼ cup heavy cream

¼ cup powdered erythritol

½ teaspoon stevia glycerite

1 vanilla bean (about 6 inches long), split lengthwise and seeds scraped, or 1 teaspoon vanilla extract

1½ ounces unsweetened baking chocolate, chopped fine

1. Line an 8-inch square baking dish with parchment paper.

2. In a medium-sized saucepan, simmer the butter until it froths and brown flecks appear. Whisk in the erythritol, stevia, and vanilla bean seeds and continue to heat for about 5 minutes, until well combined. Remove from the heat and allow to cool for 5 minutes. Pour into the prepared pan and place in the fridge to set, about 15 minutes.

3. Meanwhile, make the chocolate drizzle: In a small saucepan over medium heat, stir together the heavy cream, erythritol, stevia, and vanilla bean seeds. Bring to a light simmer, then remove from the heat and add the chocolate. Stir until the mixture is smooth and the chocolate is totally melted.

4. Remove the cooled toffee from the fridge. Drizzle the chocolate over the hardened toffee. Break into pieces for serving.

5. Store in an airtight container in the fridge for up to 2 weeks.

| NUTRITIONAL INFO (per serving) | | | | |
|---|---|---|---|---|
| calories | fat | protein | carbs | fiber |
| 60 | 6 g | 0.5 g | 1.1 g | 0.8 g |
| | 90% | 3% | 7% | |

# easy peppermint fudge

**KETO** **NUT FREE**

**PREP TIME:** 3 minutes, plus 2 hours to chill

**COOK TIME:** 5 minutes

**YIELD:** 18 pieces (1 piece per serving)

2 cups heavy cream (or canned, full-fat coconut milk if dairy-sensitive)

¾ cup powdered erythritol

1 teaspoon stevia glycerite

1 teaspoon peppermint flavor

6 ounces unsweetened baking chocolate, chopped fine

¼ teaspoon fine sea salt

1. Line an 8-inch square baking dish with parchment paper. Grease the parchment lightly for easy removal.

2. In a small saucepan over medium heat, stir together the heavy cream, erythritol, stevia, and peppermint flavor. Bring to a light simmer, then remove from the heat and add the chocolate and salt. Stir until the mixture is smooth and the chocolate is totally melted.

3. Pour the chocolate mixture into the prepared pan and spread evenly to the edges. Cover and refrigerate until set, about 2 hours or overnight. Cut into 18 squares for serving.

4. Store in an airtight container in the fridge for up to 1 week.

| NUTRITIONAL INFO (per serving) | | | | |
|---|---|---|---|---|
| calories | fat | protein | carbs | fiber |
| 99 | 8.2 g | 2 g | 4 g | 3 g |
| | 75% | 8% | 16% | |

# tiramisu fudge

**KETO** · **NUT FREE**

**PREP TIME:** 10 minutes, plus 2½ hours to chill

**COOK TIME:** 5 minutes

**YIELD:** 24 pieces (1 piece per serving)

1 cup heavy cream

8 ounces mascarpone or cream cheese (about 1 cup), softened

¼ cup brewed decaf espresso

½ cup powdered erythritol

1 teaspoon stevia glycerite

½ teaspoon rum extract or Kahlúa extract

¼ teaspoon fine sea salt

4 ounces unsweetened baking chocolate, chopped fine

### FOR THE CREAM LAYER

8 ounces mascarpone or cream cheese (about 1 cup), softened

¼ cup powdered erythritol

1 teaspoon espresso powder

½ teaspoon rum extract or Kahlúa extract

Unsweetened cocoa powder, for dusting

### SPECIAL EQUIPMENT

Strainer

1. Line an 8-inch square baking pan with parchment paper. Grease the parchment lightly for easy removal.

2. In a small saucepan over medium heat, stir together the heavy cream, mascarpone, espresso, erythritol, stevia, rum or Kahlúa extract, and salt. Bring to a light simmer, then remove from the heat and add the finely chopped chocolate. Stir until the mixture is smooth and the chocolate is totally melted.

3. Pour the chocolate mixture into the prepared pan and spread evenly to the edges. Place the pan in the freezer for 30 minutes, or until the fudge is firm.

4. Meanwhile, make the cream layer: Place the mascarpone in a small mixing bowl. Stir in the erythritol, espresso powder, and rum or Kahlúa extract.

5. Remove the chocolate layer from the freezer and spread the mascarpone layer evenly over the top, all the way to the edges. Using a small fine-mesh strainer, dust the top with unsweetened cocoa powder.

6. Cover and refrigerate until set, about 2 hours or overnight. Cut into 24 squares for serving.

| NUTRITIONAL INFO (per serving) | | | | |
|---|---|---|---|---|
| calories | fat | protein | carbs | fiber |
| 113 | 10.8 g | 2.2 g | 2.0 g | 0 g |
| | 86% | 8% | 7% | |

# tiramisu panna cotta

**KETO** · **NUT FREE**

**PREP TIME:** 6 minutes, plus 4 hours to chill

**COOK TIME:** 3 minutes

**YIELD:** 6 servings

1 tablespoon grass-fed powdered gelatin

½ cup brewed decaf espresso, cooled completely

2 cups heavy cream

4 ounces mascarpone cheese (about ½ cup)

⅓ cup powdered erythritol

1 vanilla bean (about 6 inches long), split lengthwise and seeds scraped, or 1 teaspoon vanilla extract

1 teaspoon Kahlúa extract or rum extract

¼ teaspoon fine sea salt

Unsweetened cocoa powder or Dairy-Free Chocolate Syrup (page 330), for garnish (optional)

*I love making panna cotta for dinner parties because it looks fancy and the taste is divine, yet it is very easy to make and can be made up to two days ahead of time. This dessert also gives me a chance to bring out my martini glasses, which are usually tucked away.*

1. In a medium-sized saucepan, sprinkle the gelatin over the cooled espresso and let stand about 1 minute to soften. Heat the gelatin mixture over low heat until the gelatin is dissolved. Add the cream, mascarpone, erythritol, and vanilla bean seeds to the saucepan. Heat over medium heat for 1 minute. Remove from the heat and stir in the Kahlúa or rum extract and salt.

2. Divide the panna cotta among 6 martini glasses or ½-cup ramekins and cool to room temperature. Chill, covered, for at least 4 hours or overnight.

3. Served dusted with unsweetened cocoa powder or drizzled with chocolate syrup, if desired.

| NUTRITIONAL INFO (per serving) | | | | |
|---|---|---|---|---|
| calories | fat | protein | carbs | fiber |
| 105 | 10.2 g | 2.5 g | 0.7 g | 0 g |
| | 87% | 10% | 3% | |

# Resources

## INGREDIENT BRANDS AND SOURCES

*I've created an online store where you can find specialty ingredients used in the recipes in this book, at the best prices I have found. To access it, go to my site, mariamindbodyhealth.com, and click on "Maria's Amazon Store." Or go directly to the following URL:*

http://astore.amazon.com/marisnutran05-20.

### COCONUT PRODUCTS (coconut flour, coconut oil)
Tropical Traditions, www.tropicaltraditions.com

### EXTRACTS AND FLAVORS
Frontier, www.frontiercoop.com
Best Flavors, www.bestflavors.com

### HOT SAUCE
Dark Star Sriracha Hot Chili Sauce, www.20brix.com/DS
Xyla Xylitol Buffalo Wing Sauce, store.xylitolusa.com

### PROTEIN POWDERS
Jay Robb, www.jayrobb.com

### MCT OIL
SKINNYFat, www.caltonnutrition.com/skinnyfat (For $5 off, enter "$5KetoOil" at checkout.)

### NOODLES
Kelp noodles: Sea Tangle, www.kelpnoodles.com
Miracle Noodle, www.miraclenoodle.com

### LIQUID SMOKE
Wright's Liquid Smoke, www.wrightsliquidsmoke.com

### POWDERED ERYTHRITOL
Swerve, www.swervesweetener.com
Wholesome Sweeteners Zero,
www.wholesomesweeteners.com

### STEVIA GLYCERITE
NOW, www.nowfoods.com

### XANTHAN GUM AND GUAR GUM
NOW, www.nowfoods.com

### YACÓN SYRUP
Sunfood Superfoods, www.sunfood.com

## BOOKS

Atkins, Dr. Robert C. *Dr. Atkins' Diet Revolution.* New York: Bantam, 1972.

Atkins, Dr. Robert C. *Dr. Atkins' New Diet Revolution.* New York: Harper, 2002.

Briffa, Dr. John. *Waist Disposal: The Ultimate Fat-Loss Manual for Men.* New York: Hay House, 2011.

Cantin, Elaine. *The Cantin Ketogenic Diet: For Cancer, Type I Diabetes & Other Ailments.* Williston, VT: Elaine Cantin, 2012.

Carlson, Dr. James. *Genocide: How Your Doctor's Dietary Ignorance Will Kill You.* James Carlson, 2007.

Carpender, Dana. *200 Low-Carb, High-Fat Recipes: Easy Recipes to Jumpstart Your Low-Carb Weight Loss.* Minneapolis, MN: Fair Winds Press, 2014.

Carpender, Dana, Amy Dungan, and Rebecca Latham. *Fat Fast Cookbook: 50 Easy Recipes to Jump Start Your Low Carb Weight.* Las Vegas, NV: CarbSmart Press, 2013.

Davis, Ellen. *Fight Cancer with a Ketogenic Diet: A New Method for Fighting Cancer*, Second Edition. 2014. Ebook.

Emmerich, Maria. *Keto-Adapted: Your Guide to Accelerated Weight Loss and Healthy Healing.* Maria and Craig Emmerich, 2013. Kindle edition.

Groves, Dr. Barry. *Natural Health & Weight Loss.* London: Hammersmith Press, 2007.

Jacoby, Dr. Richard. *Sugar Crush: How to Reduce Inflammation, Reverse Nerve Damage, and Reclaim Good Health.* New York: Harper Collins, 2015.

Kiefer, John. *The Carb Nite Solution: The Physicist's Guide to Power Dieting.* Kiefer Productions, 2005.

Kossoff, Dr. Eric H., Dr. John M. Freeman, Zahava Turner, and Dr. James E. Rubenstein. *Ketogenic Diets: Treatments for Epilepsy and Other Disorders*, Fifth Edition. New York: Demos Health, 2011.

McCleary, Dr. Larry. *The Brain Trust Program: A Scientifically Based Three-Part Plan to Improve Memory, Elevate Mood, Enhance Attention, Alleviate Migraine and Menopausal Symptoms, and Boost Mental Energy.* New York: Penguin, 2007.

McDonald, Lyle. *The Ketogenic Diet: A Complete Guide for the Dieter and Practitioner.* Lyle McDonald, 1998.

Moore, Jimmy, and Dr. Eric Westman. *Cholesterol Clarity: What the HDL Is Wrong with My Numbers?* Las Vegas, NV: Victory Belt Publishing, 2013.

Moore, Jimmy, and Dr. Eric Westman. *Keto Clarity: Your Definitive Guide to the Benefits of a Low-Carb, High-Fat Diet.* Las Vegas, NV: Victory Belt Publishing, 2014.

Newport, Dr. Mary. *Alzheimer's Disease: What If There Was a Cure?: The Story of Ketones.* Laguna Beach, CA: Basic Health Publications, 2011.

Ottoboni, Dr. Fred, and Dr. Alice Ottoboni. *The Modern Nutritional Diseases and How to Prevent Them*, Second Edition. Femly, NV: Vincente Books, 2013.

Perlmutter, Dr. David. *Grain Brain: The Surprising Truth about Wheat, Carbs, and Sugar—Your Brain's Silent Killers.* New York: Little, Brown, 2013.

Phinney, Dr. Stephen, and Dr. Jeff Volek. *The Art and Science of Low Carbohydrate Living.* Beyond Obesity, 2011.

Phinney, Dr. Stephen, and Dr. Jeff Volek. *The Art and Science of Low Carbohydrate Performance.* Beyond Obesity, 2012.

Seyfried, Dr. Thomas. *Cancer as a Metabolic Disease: On the Origin, Management, and Prevention of Cancer.* Hoboken, NJ: John Wiley & Sons, 2012.

Skaldeman, Sten Sture. *The Low Carb High Fat Cookbook: 100 Recipes to Lose Weight and Feel Great.* New York: Skyhorse Publishing, 2013.

Snyder, Dr. Deborah. *Keto Kid: Helping Your Child Succeed on the Ketogenic Diet.* New York: Demos Medical Publishing, 2006.

Taubes, Gary. *Good Calories, Bad Calories: Challenging the Conventional Wisdom on Diet, Weight Control, and Disease.* New York: Anchor Books, 2007.

Taubes, Gary. *Why We Get Fat: And What to Do About It.* New York: Anchor Books, 2011.

Tiecholz, Nina. *The Big Fat Surprise: Why Butter, Meat, and Cheese Belong in a Healthy Diet.* New York: Simon & Schuster, 2014.

Volek, Dr. Jeff, and Adam Campbell. *Men's Health TNT Diet: The Explosive New Plan to Blast Fat, Build Muscle, and Get Healthy in 12 Weeks.* New York: Rodale, 2008.

Wahls, Dr. Terry, and Eve Adamson. *The Wahls Protocol: How I Beat Progressive MS Using Paleo Principles and Functional Medicine.* New York: Penguin, 2014.

Westman, Dr. Eric. *A Low Carbohydrate, Ketogenic Diet Manual: No Sugar, No Starch Diet.* Dr. Eric Westman, 2013.

Westman, Dr. Eric, Dr. Stephen D. Phinney, and Dr. Jeff S. Volek. *The New Atkins for a New You.* New York: Fireside, 2010.

## KETO BLOGS AND WEBSITES

Caveman Keto:
http://cavemanketo.com

The Charlie Foundation for Ketogenic Therapies:
www.charliefoundation.org

Defying Age with Food:
http://defyingagewithfood.com

Diet Doctor:
www.dietdoctor.com

Dietary Therapies, LLC: Ketogenic Diet for Cancer:
http://dietarytherapies.com

Dr. Dave Unleashed:
http://drdaveunleashed.wordpress.com

Eat Keto:
http://eatketo.com

Eat Low Carb High Fat:
www.eatlowcarbhighfat.com

The Eating Academy:
http://eatingacademy.com

Everything About Keto, Reddit:
www.reddit.com/r/keto

Fat for Fuel, My Ketogenic Diet Experiment While Endurance Training:
www.sftrails. com/2013/08/fat-for-fuel-my-ketogenic-diet.html

A Game of Keto:
http://jennynotketo.tumblr.com

Ketastic:
http://ketastic.com

Keto Cook:
http://ketocook.com

Keto Diet: Real Food & Healthy Living:
http://ketodietapp.com/Blog

The Ketogenic Diet:
www.theketogenicdiet.org

The Ketogenic Diet for Health:
www.ketotic.org

Ketogenic Diet Resource:
www.ketogenic-diet-resource.com

KetoNutrition:
http://ketonutrition.org

Ketopia:
http://ketopia.com

Kickin' into Keto:
www.ketoblog.net

Low Carb Genesis:
http://lowcarbgenesis.com

Matthew's Friends:
www.matthewsfriends.org

RunKeto:
www.runketo.com

Second Opinions:
www.second-opinions.co.uk

Wicked Stuffed: Whole Food Recipes in 10 Carbs or Less:
www.wickedstuffed.com

## FILMS AND DOCUMENTARIES ON KETOGENIC DIETS

*Carb-Loaded: A Culture Dying to Eat* (2014). Produced by Lathe Poland and Eric Carlsen.
http://carbloaded.com

*Cereal Killers.* Directed by Yolanda Barker. 2013.
www.cerealkillersmovie.com

*Cereal Killers II: Run on Fat.* Directed by Yolanda Barker. 2015.
www.cerealkillersmovie.com

*Fat Head.* Directed by Tom Naughton. 2009.
www.fathead-movie.com

*"...First Do No Harm."* Directed by Jim Abrahams. 1997. Walt Disney Home Video, 2002.
www.amazon.com/First-Do-No-Harm/dp/B000068MBW

*My Big Fat Diet.* Directed by Mary Bissell. 2008.
http://mybigfatdiet.net

## KETO CALCULATORS

The Low Carb Flexi Diet:
www.flexibleketogenic.com

Keto Calculator:
http://keto-calculator.ankerl.com

## FIND A KETO-FRIENDLY DOCTOR

List of Low-Carb Doctors:
http://lowcarbdoctors.blogspot.com

# Meal Plans

## 7-DAY DAIRY- AND NUT-FREE FAST WEIGHT LOSS AND HEALING MEAL PLAN

When starting a ketogenic diet, many people complain about low energy. It takes the body 2 to 4 weeks to adapt to keto, and during that time your liver releases a lot of salt and water it was holding on to with a higher carb diet. This can cause dehydration and depletion of electrolytes, which in turn can cause low energy, muscle aches, and headaches—what is called the "keto flu." So it is important to drink lots of water (at least half your body weight in ounces per day), and get plenty of electrolytes, such as salt, potassium, and magnesium. This meal plan is designed to replenish your electrolytes as you start keto, and it doesn't contain any dairy or nuts so that if you're sensitive to them, your body can begin to heal.

*"I started in mid-June and my family all joined me in July. My husband lost 67 lbs and went from size 38 to size 32 pants. He is off of blood pressure meds and his CPAP, and his cholesterol. I have lost 63 lbs. I have fibromyalgia and eating this way helps my pain so much! My daughter was told she was borderline insulin-resistant and had ADHD and a behavior disorder. She has lost 38 lbs and no longer has any symptoms of any of her conditions. My husband is at his goal. I have a long way to go yet, but I'm going to keep on trucking. Keto is the way to go." —Amanda*

## 7-DAY MAINTAIN OR GAIN WEIGHT AND HEALING MEAL PLAN

Keto isn't necessarily about weight loss; it's more about healing your body. This meal plan is designed to help you establish ketosis while maintaining or even gaining weight. If you find yourself losing weight you want to keep, feel free to add Dark Chocolate Raspberry Fat Bombs (page 322) or increase portion sizes to keep your macronutrient ratios the same.

*"About 8 months ago, I started following the 'Maria Way' for the sake of my 6-year-old daughter, who has struggled for years with stomach issues, irregularity, and loss of appetite because food made her miserable. I couldn't put her through any more doctor visits and uncomfortable attempts to 'fix' her problems. She weighed 35 lbs on her sixth birthday! Since following this lifestyle and recipes, she is so happy and is excited about dinner, cooking, dessert... She has learned so much about healthy choices and has taken ownership over her choices—I'm so proud of her. And most importantly, she is finally growing! Thank you from the bottom of my heart." —Melissa*

## 7-DAY EASY KETO MEAL PLAN

Busy lifestyles can make budgeting time for cooking a challenge. This meal plan is designed to be quick and easy to accommodate those busy times in our lives while providing what we need for weight loss as well as healing. If you find you're often short on time, make a larger batch of a recipe on the weekend, separate it into single servings, and store them in the fridge or freezer. All you have to do is reheat for easy meals during the week.

*"Words just cannot express how thankful and blessed I feel to have found you and your blog. I started grain-free back in March 2013 with moderate success in weight loss but hit a plateau after about 6–7 months, though I still had overall amazing success with eliminating stomach issues, fatigue, and joint pain. I am so happy to report that after 5 weeks with the advanced keto package, I have lost another 15–18 pounds BUT most amazingly I have gone from a size 8–10 in jeans to a 5–6! Lord, I've not worn a 5–6 in years and I feel amazing!" —Dawn*

## 7-DAY VEGETARIAN MEAL PLAN

Vegetarians can also reap the many benefits of a ketogenic diet. This plan has lots of healthy fats and helps you maintain moderate protein intakes. It's designed to heal your body and help you lose weight quickly.

*"Just wanted to give you a quick update after being on your vegetarian meal plan for 5 days. My itchy, rashy legs have always looked their worst when I'm in a bath or shower; something about the hot water would make them very red and more noticeable than they already were. I was so happy to take a bath tonight and realize the rash is almost all gone! I just wanted to thank you again for saving my skin!" —Malorie*

# 7-Day Dairy- and Nut-Free
# Fast Weight Loss and Healing Meal Plan

| | | Calories | Fat (g) | Protein (g) | Carbs (g) | % Fat | % Protein | % Carbs |
|---|---|---|---|---|---|---|---|---|
| **Day 1** | Breakfast: Ham-n-"Cheese" Omelet (page 112) | 552 | 48 | 25 | 4.9 | 78% | 18% | 4% |
| | Lunch: BLT Bites (page 142) | 274 | 25 | 10 | 3 | 82% | 15% | 4% |
| | Dinner: Asian Meatballs (page 158) | 403 | 28 | 33.2 | 3.1 | 63% | 33% | 3% |
| | Snack/Side: Pumpkin Pie Frozen Custard (page 334) | 112 | 11.2 | 1.8 | 1.2 | 90% | 6% | 4% |
| | Day Total | 1341 | 112.2 | 70 | 12.2 | 75% | 21% | 4% |
| **Day 2** | Breakfast: Dairy-Free Breakfast Pizza (page 84) | 571 | 53.5 | 19.5 | 5.8 | 84% | 14% | 4% |
| | Lunch: Pork Belly in Aromatic Spices (page 196) | 350 | 28.8 | 18.3 | 5.3 | 74% | 21% | 6% |
| | Dinner: Chimichurri Flank Steak (page 166) | 391 | 27.5 | 31.7 | 2.8 | 63% | 32% | 3% |
| | Snack/Side: Strawberry Truffles (page 318) | 153 | 16.3 | 1.1 | 0 | 96% | 3% | 0% |
| | Day Total | 1465 | 126.1 | 70.6 | 13.9 | 77% | 19% | 4% |
| **Day 3** | Breakfast: Mushroom and Onion Omelet (page 116) | 461 | 38.8 | 24 | 3.9 | 76% | 21% | 3% |
| | Lunch: Lamb Tikka Masala (page 182) | 489 | 37.8 | 29.7 | 6.8 | 70% | 24% | 6% |
| | Dinner: Broiled Sesame-Orange Salmon (page 250) | 531 | 42.8 | 25.6 | 11.5 | 73% | 19% | 9% |
| | Snack/Side: Lemon Curd Ice Cream (page 340) | 101 | 10 | 2.3 | 0.5 | 89% | 9% | 2% |
| | Day Total | 1582 | 129.4 | 81.6 | 22.7 | 74% | 21% | 6% |
| **Day 4** | Breakfast: Avocado Egg Cups (page 100) | 490 | 45.8 | 10.7 | 11.6 | 84% | 9% | 9% |
| | Lunch: Gumbo (page 222) | 330 | 25.3 | 20.1 | 5.7 | 69% | 24% | 7% |
| | Dinner: Smoked Pork Chops with Apple Glaze (page 190) | 418 | 36.6 | 19 | 3 | 79% | 18% | 3% |
| | Snack/Side: Dark Chocolate Raspberry Fat Bombs (page 322) | 220 | 24 | 0.3 | 0.9 | 98% | 1% | 2% |
| | Day Total | 1458 | 131.7 | 50.1 | 21.2 | 81% | 14% | 6% |
| **Day 5** | Breakfast: French Toast Custard (page 124) | 327 | 31 | 6.9 | 5.2 | 85% | 8% | 6% |
| | Lunch: Reuben (page 172) | 291 | 23.6 | 10.6 | 9.1 | 73% | 15% | 13% |
| | Dinner: Teriyaki Steak Roll-Ups with Sautéed Mushrooms (page 168) | 821 | 66 | 45.9 | 8 | 72% | 22% | 4% |
| | Snack/Side: Chai Panna Cotta (page 338) | 176 | 16.3 | 3 | 4.1 | 83% | 7% | 9% |
| | Day Total | 1615 | 136.9 | 66.4 | 26.4 | 76% | 16% | 7% |
| **Day 6** | Breakfast: Salmon and Chive Omelet (page 114) | 357 | 27.6 | 26.1 | 2 | 70% | 29% | 2% |
| | Lunch: Slow Cooker Beefy Asian Noodles (page 164) | 286 | 18.1 | 23.4 | 6.9 | 57% | 33% | 10% |
| | Dinner: Pork Belly in Aromatic Spices (page 196) (leftover) | 350 | 28.8 | 18.3 | 5.3 | 74% | 21% | 6% |
| | Snack/Side: Chocolate Mint Cookies (page 320) | 304 | 28.6 | 5.9 | 7.3 | 85% | 8% | 10% |
| | Day Total | 1297 | 103.1 | 73.7 | 21.5 | 72% | 23% | 7% |
| **Day 7** | Breakfast: Mock Apple Porridge (page 106) | 528 | 51.9 | 13.4 | 2.6 | 88% | 10% | 2% |
| | Lunch: Kielbasa and Braised Cabbage (page 192) | 351 | 26.1 | 17.1 | 12.2 | 67% | 19% | 14% |
| | Dinner: BBQ Meatloaf (page 156) | 569 | 36.8 | 48.9 | 8.4 | 58% | 34% | 6% |
| | Snack/Side: Strawberry Truffles (page 318) | 153 | 16.3 | 1.1 | 0 | 96% | 3% | 0% |
| | Day Total | 1601 | 131.1 | 80.5 | 23.2 | 74% | 20% | 6% |

Looking for more meal plans with intermittent fasting, weekly grocery lists, instructional and educational videos, exercise examples, and much more?  Go here for more of Maria's services: http://mariamindbodyhealth.com/my-services/.

## 7-Day Maintain or Gain Weight and Healing Meal Plan

| | | Calories | Fat (g) | Protein (g) | Carbs (g) | % Fat | % Protein | % Carbs |
|---|---|---|---|---|---|---|---|---|
| **Day 1** | Breakfast: Breakfast Sushi (page 92) | 717 | 63 | 28 | 10.3 | 79% | 16% | 6% |
| | Lunch: Armadillo Eggs (page 202) | 764 | 66.7 | 36.6 | 2.4 | 79% | 19% | 1% |
| | Dinner: Chimichurri Flank Steak (page 166) | 391 | 27.5 | 31.7 | 2.8 | 63% | 32% | 3% |
| | Snack/Side: Easy Toffee Fudge Pops (page 346) | 46 | 2.7 | 2.8 | 2.6 | 53% | 24% | 23% |
| | **Day Total** | **1918** | **159.9** | **99.1** | **18.1** | **75%** | **21%** | **4%** |
| **Day 2** | Breakfast: Dairy-Free Key Lime Shake (page 96) | 397 | 40.8 | 8.1 | 1.8 | 92% | 8% | 2% |
| | Lunch: Lasagna Roll-Ups (page 206) | 467 | 25.7 | 50 | 9.3 | 50% | 43% | 8% |
| | Dinner: Zesty Chicken Pizza (page 210) | 610 | 41.2 | 55.2 | 6 | 61% | 36% | 4% |
| | Snack/Side: BLT Coleslaw (page 289) | 258 | 20.7 | 5.5 | 14.4 | 72% | 9% | 22% |
| | Snack/Side: Almond Roca Mocha Cake (page 342) | 375 | 36.9 | 6.4 | 4.4 | 89% | 7% | 5% |
| | **Day Total** | **2107** | **165.3** | **125.2** | **35.9** | **71%** | **24%** | **7%** |
| **Day 3** | Breakfast: Ham-n-Cheese Mini Quiches (page 98) (2 servings) | 506 | 32.2 | 43.8 | 9.6 | 57% | 35% | 8% |
| | Lunch: Slow Cooker BBQ Short Ribs (page 174) | 749 | 68.6 | 28.4 | 1.8 | 82% | 15% | 1% |
| | Dinner: Grilled Trout with Lemon-Thyme Glaze (page 246) | 369 | 21 | 41.6 | 3.8 | 51% | 45% | 4% |
| | Snack/Side: Brown Butter Mushrooms (page 286) | 262 | 22.8 | 6 | 9.6 | 78% | 9% | 15% |
| | Snack/Side: Tiramisu Panna Cotta (page 356) | 210 | 20.4 | 5 | 1.4 | 87% | 10% | 3% |
| | **Day Total** | **2096** | **165** | **124.8** | **26.2** | **71%** | **24%** | **5%** |
| **Day 4** | Breakfast: Avocado Egg Cups (page 100) | 490 | 45.8 | 10.7 | 11.6 | 84% | 9% | 9% |
| | Lunch: Duck Confit (page 220) | 675 | 57.8 | 29 | 5.5 | 77% | 17% | 3% |
| | Dinner: Steak with Brown Butter Béarnaise (page 160) | 761 | 60 | 52 | 0 | 71% | 28% | 0% |
| | Snack/Side: Dairy-Free Keto Chocolate Ice Cream with Cherry Glaze (page 312) | 249 | 25.3 | 3.5 | 2.1 | 91% | 6% | 3% |
| | **Day Total** | **2175** | **188.9** | **95.2** | **19.2** | **78%** | **17%** | **4%** |
| **Day 5** | Breakfast: Caramel Apple Dutch Baby (page 104) | 698 | 67 | 23 | 3.5 | 86% | 13% | 2% |
| | Lunch: Buffalo Chicken Stuffed Avocados (page 208) | 475 | 40 | 23 | 8 | 76% | 19% | 7% |
| | Dinner: Philly "Cheese" Steak Stuffed Portobellos (page 176) | 651 | 57 | 31 | 5 | 79% | 19% | 3% |
| | Snack/Side: Tiramisu Fudge (page 354) | 113 | 10.8 | 2.2 | 2 | 86% | 8% | 7% |
| | **Day Total** | **1937** | **174.8** | **79.2** | **18.5** | **81%** | **16%** | **4%** |
| **Day 6** | Breakfast: Breakfast Lasagna (page 110) | 423 | 29.5 | 34.5 | 4.9 | 63% | 33% | 5% |
| | Lunch: Grilled Halibut with Smoky Avocado Cream (page 232) | 525 | 28.8 | 60 | 4.9 | 49% | 46% | 4% |
| | Dinner: Slow Cooker BBQ Short Ribs (page 174) (leftover) | 749 | 68.6 | 28.4 | 1.8 | 82% | 15% | 1% |
| | Snack/Side: Cookie Dough Brownies (page 328) | 427 | 41.6 | 6.5 | 6.4 | 88% | 6% | 6% |
| | **Day Total** | **2124** | **168.5** | **129.4** | **18** | **71%** | **24%** | **3%** |
| **Day 7** | Breakfast: Huevos Rancheros (page 122) | 524 | 39 | 35 | 9.5 | 67% | 27% | 7% |
| | Lunch: Chicken à la King (page 226) | 358 | 28.1 | 21.1 | 6.1 | 71% | 24% | 7% |
| | Dinner: Lamb Tikka Masala (page 182) | 489 | 37.8 | 29.7 | 6.8 | 70% | 24% | 6% |
| | Snack/Side: Dark Chocolate Raspberry Fat Bombs (page 322) | 220 | 24 | 0.3 | 0.9 | 98% | 1% | 2% |
| | **Day Total** | **1811** | **152.9** | **86.4** | **24.2** | **76%** | **19%** | **5%** |

# 7-Day Easy Keto Meal Plan

| | | Calories | Fat (g) | Protein (g) | Carbs (g) | % Fat | % Protein | % Carbs |
|---|---|---|---|---|---|---|---|---|
| **Day 1** | Breakfast: Keto Soft-Boiled Eggs (page 108) | 260 | 20.5 | 17.9 | 1.4 | 71% | 28% | 2% |
| | Lunch: Asian Meatballs (page 158) | 403 | 28 | 33.2 | 3.1 | 63% | 33% | 3% |
| | Dinner: Easy Mortadella Ravioli (page 188) | 677 | 55.6 | 34.7 | 9.1 | 74% | 21% | 5% |
| | Snack/Side: Lemon Curd Ice Cream (page 340) | 101 | 10 | 2.3 | 0.5 | 89% | 9% | 2% |
| | Day Total | 1441 | 114.1 | 88.1 | 14.1 | 71% | 24% | 4% |
| **Day 2** | Breakfast: French Toast Custard (page 124) | 332 | 31 | 6.9 | 5.2 | 84% | 8% | 6% |
| | Lunch: Slow Cooker Beefy Asian Noodles (page 164) | 286 | 18.1 | 23.4 | 6.9 | 57% | 33% | 10% |
| | Dinner: Steak with Brown Butter Béarnaise (page 160) | 761 | 60 | 52 | 0 | 71% | 28% | 0% |
| | Snack/Side: Lemon Curd Ice Cream (page 340) (leftover) | 101 | 10 | 2.3 | 0.5 | 89% | 9% | 2% |
| | Day Total | 1480 | 119.1 | 84.6 | 12.6 | 72% | 23% | 3% |
| **Day 3** | Breakfast: Dairy-Free Key Lime Shake (page 96) | 397 | 40.8 | 8.1 | 1.8 | 92% | 8% | 2% |
| | Lunch: Brown Butter Chicken and "Pasta" (page 218) | 459 | 37.6 | 24.7 | 5.9 | 74% | 22% | 5% |
| | Dinner: Grandpa Joe's Barramundi (page 242) | 580 | 44 | 43.9 | 1.5 | 68% | 30% | 1% |
| | Snack/Side: Braised Cabbage (page 280) | 191 | 14.2 | 3.1 | 13 | 67% | 6% | 27% |
| | Day Total | 1627 | 136.6 | 79.8 | 22.2 | 76% | 20% | 5% |
| **Day 4** | Breakfast: Creamy Breakfast Shake (page 94) | 213 | 18.6 | 6.4 | 5.3 | 79% | 12% | 10% |
| | Lunch: Slow Cooker BBQ Short Ribs (page 174) | 749 | 68.6 | 28.4 | 1.8 | 82% | 15% | 1% |
| | Dinner: Asian Meatballs (page 158) (leftover) | 403 | 28 | 33.2 | 3.1 | 63% | 33% | 3% |
| | Snack/Side: Cookie Dough Brownies (page 328) | 427 | 41.6 | 6.5 | 6.4 | 88% | 6% | 6% |
| | Day Total | 1792 | 156.8 | 74.5 | 16.6 | 79% | 17% | 4% |
| **Day 5** | Breakfast: Bagels and Lox (page 90) (2 servings) | 336 | 25.6 | 18.6 | 9.4 | 69% | 22% | 11% |
| | Lunch: Brown Butter Chicken and "Pasta" (page 218) (2 servings) (leftover) | 918 | 75.2 | 49.4 | 11.8 | 74% | 22% | 5% |
| | Dinner: Slow Cooker Beefy Asian Noodles (page 164) (leftover) | 286 | 18.1 | 23.4 | 6.9 | 57% | 33% | 10% |
| | Snack/Side: Easy Toffee Fudge Pops (page 346) (2 servings) | 92 | 5.4 | 5.6 | 5.2 | 53% | 24% | 23% |
| | Day Total | 1632 | 124.3 | 97 | 33.3 | 69% | 24% | 8% |
| **Day 6** | Breakfast: French Scrambled Eggs (page 83) | 476 | 37 | 32 | 4.4 | 70% | 27% | 4% |
| | Lunch: Easy Mortadella Ravioli (page 188) (leftover) | 677 | 55.6 | 34.7 | 9.1 | 74% | 21% | 5% |
| | Dinner: Slow Cooker Pesto Pasta with Crispy Basil (page 272) | 359 | 34.1 | 9.4 | 2.6 | 85% | 10% | 3% |
| | Snack/Side: Lemon Curd Ice Cream (page 340) (leftover) | 101 | 10 | 2.3 | 0.5 | 89% | 9% | 2% |
| | Day Total | 1613 | 136.7 | 78.4 | 16.6 | 76% | 19% | 4% |
| **Day 7** | Breakfast: Ham-n-Cheese Mini Quiches (page 98) | 253 | 16.1 | 21.9 | 4.8 | 57% | 35% | 8% |
| | Lunch: Slow Cooker Pesto Pasta with Crispy Basil (page 272) (leftover) | 359 | 34.1 | 9.4 | 2.6 | 85% | 10% | 3% |
| | Dinner: Slow Cooker BBQ Short Ribs (page 174) (leftover) | 749 | 68.6 | 28.4 | 1.8 | 82% | 15% | 1% |
| | Snack/Side: Braised Cabbage (page 280) (leftover) | 191 | 14.2 | 3.1 | 13 | 67% | 6% | 27% |
| | Day Total | 1552 | 133 | 62.8 | 22.2 | 77% | 16% | 6% |

# 7-Day Vegetarian Meal Plan

| | | Calories | Fat (g) | Protein (g) | Carbs (g) | % Fat | % Protein | % Carbs |
|---|---|---|---|---|---|---|---|---|
| **Day 1** | Breakfast: Floating Islands (page 86) (2 servings) | 361 | 28 | 21 | 3 | 71% | 23% | 4% |
| | Lunch: Creamy "Mac"-n-Cheese (page 258) | 241 | 23.3 | 7.5 | 1.8 | 87% | 12% | 3% |
| | Dinner: Mini Egg Salad Sandwiches (page 268) (2 servings) | 433 | 36 | 23.5 | 4 | 75% | 22% | 4% |
| | Snack/Side: Dairy-Free Keto Chocolate Ice Cream with Cherry Glaze (page 312) | 249 | 25.3 | 3.5 | 2.1 | 91% | 6% | 3% |
| | Day Total | 1284 | 113 | 55.5 | 11.3 | 79% | 17% | 4% |
| **Day 2** | Breakfast: Chai Muffins (page 120) | 218 | 21.6 | 3.7 | 3.2 | 88% | 7% | 6% |
| | Lunch: Yellow Tomato Soup and Grilled Cheese (page 262) | 463 | 37 | 26.3 | 8 | 72% | 23% | 7% |
| | Dinner: Dutch Baby Pizza with "Honey" Dressing (page 270) | 493 | 38 | 29.7 | 6.8 | 69% | 24% | 6% |
| | Snack/Side: Strawberry Truffles (page 318) | 153 | 16.3 | 1.1 | 0 | 96% | 3% | 0% |
| | Day Total | 1327 | 112.9 | 60.8 | 18 | 77% | 18% | 5% |
| **Day 3** | Breakfast: Keto Pancakes and Syrup (page 82) | 170 | 15 | 8.2 | 0.6 | 79% | 19% | 1% |
| | Lunch: Deep Dish Alfredo Pizza with Mushrooms (page 264) | 506 | 47 | 17.4 | 5 | 84% | 14% | 4% |
| | Dinner: Yellow Tomato and Burrata Salad with "Honey" Dressing (page 260) (2 servings) | 562 | 48.2 | 24 | 8 | 77% | 17% | 6% |
| | Snack/Side: Chocolate Berry Pie (page 324) | 177 | 15.6 | 7 | 2.8 | 79% | 16% | 6% |
| | Day Total | 1415 | 125.8 | 56.6 | 16.4 | 80% | 16% | 5% |
| **Day 4** | Breakfast: French Scrambled Eggs (page 83) | 476 | 37 | 32 | 4.4 | 70% | 27% | 4% |
| | Lunch: Toasted Open-Face Brie and Tomato Sandwich (page 261) | 310 | 27 | 13.5 | 2.7 | 78% | 17% | 3% |
| | Dinner: Dutch Baby Pizza with "Honey" Dressing (page 270) (leftover) | 493 | 38 | 29.7 | 6.8 | 69% | 24% | 6% |
| | Snack/Side: Dairy-Free Keto Vanilla Bean Ice Cream (page 310) | 176 | 16.3 | 3 | 4.1 | 83% | 7% | 9% |
| | Day Total | 1455 | 118.3 | 78.2 | 18 | 73% | 21% | 5% |
| **Day 5** | Breakfast: Creamy Zucchini Hash Browns (page 88) | 436 | 46 | 3 | 2.3 | 95% | 3% | 2% |
| | Lunch: Pizza Margherita (page 266) | 199 | 12.8 | 17 | 5 | 58% | 34% | 10% |
| | Dinner: Deep Dish Alfredo Pizza with Mushrooms (page 264) (leftover) | 506 | 47 | 17.4 | 5 | 84% | 14% | 4% |
| | Snack/Side: Celery Boats (page 136) | 192 | 17.2 | 7 | 3.2 | 81% | 15% | 7% |
| | Day Total | 1333 | 123 | 44.4 | 15.5 | 83% | 13% | 5% |
| **Day 6** | Breakfast: Mushroom and Onion Omelet (page 116) | 455 | 38.8 | 24 | 3.9 | 77% | 21% | 3% |
| | Lunch: Fried Parmesan Tomatoes (page 256) | 209 | 19 | 7 | 2.3 | 82% | 13% | 4% |
| | Dinner: Slow Cooker Pesto Pasta with Crispy Basil (page 272) | 359 | 34.1 | 9.4 | 2.6 | 85% | 10% | 3% |
| | Snack/Side: Chocolate Mocha Cake Pops (page 316) | 325 | 30.5 | 6.3 | 5.3 | 84% | 8% | 7% |
| | Day Total | 1348 | 122.4 | 46.7 | 14.1 | 82% | 14% | 4% |
| **Day 7** | Breakfast: Herb Goat Cheese Omelet (page 115) | 445 | 35.9 | 28.8 | 2.2 | 73% | 26% | 2% |
| | Lunch: Yellow Tomato and Burrata Salad with "Honey" Dressing (page 260) | 281 | 24.1 | 12 | 4 | 77% | 17% | 6% |
| | Dinner: Slow Cooker Pesto Pasta with Crispy Basil (page 272) (leftover) | 359 | 34.1 | 9.4 | 2.6 | 85% | 10% | 3% |
| | Snack/Side: Brown Butter Mushrooms (page 286) | 131 | 11.4 | 3 | 4.8 | 78% | 9% | 15% |
| | Day Total | 1216 | 105.5 | 53.2 | 13.6 | 78% | 18% | 4% |

Looking for more meal plans, videos and cookbooks? Go here: http://mariamindbodyhealth.com/my-services/.

# Acknowledgments

*Jimmy*

*After the huge success of my 2014 book,* Keto Clarity *(thanks to everyone who supported this book), which is all about how to follow a ketogenic diet to optimize your health, my publisher asked me to write a cookbook with ketogenic-friendly recipes as a follow-up. I asked them if I could collaborate with someone with experience writing cookbooks and making delicious and nutritious low-carb, high-fat meals. When they gave me the green light, I couldn't think of anyone better than the amazing Maria Emmerich, who had already self-published seven books. I'm so incredibly thrilled to have joined forces with her to make* The Ketogenic Cookbook *a reality. Maria is one of the most incredible people in the ketogenic community, and it's such an honor and a privilege to work with her on bringing this invaluable resource to you.*

**Thank you to my wife, Christine,** who has strongly supported me writing books for the past three years in a row (I promise to take a year off after this one, honey!). I'm so grateful for her constant encouragement of my work; she shares my passion for getting out quality information to the people who need it the most. Plus, she stepped up for this book by running all numbers in the nutritional information for each recipe. Thank you, baby!

I am extremely grateful to all those medical professionals who champion the ketogenic message both in the scientific community and with their patients, including my *Cholesterol Clarity* and *Keto Clarity* coauthor Dr. Eric Westman, Dr. Steve Phinney, Dr. Jeff Volek, Dr. Jeffry Gerber, Dr. Adam Nally, Dr. Ann Childers, Dr. Jay Wortman, Dr. Peter Attia, Gary Taubes, Nina Teicholz, Professor Tim Noakes, Dr. David Perlmutter, Dr. Terry Wahls, Dr. Dominic D'Agostino, Dr. Thomas Seyfried, Dr. William Davis, Dr. Andreas Eenfeldt, and many more. I'm also so thankful for the laypeople who are educating others online about the power of ketogenic diets, people like Ellen Davis, Emily Maguire, Stephanie Person, Luis Villasenor, Leanne Vogel, Katie Coleman, Amy Berger, and Miriam Kalamian, among others.

**To my publishing team, Erich, Michele, Erin, Holly, and everyone who worked behind the scenes at Victory Belt:** Thank you for giving me the great privilege of writing my third major book in three years. The lives of real people are being changed for the better as a result of these books, and I owe it all to you for taking a chance on this blogger and podcaster who works tirelessly to educate, encourage, and inspire others to be as healthy as possible.

# Maria

*I once heard someone say, "If you want to hear God laugh, tell him what you have planned!" That statement couldn't have been more true for the past few years of my life. I was a planner, and the more I tried to control how things happened, the more frustrated I got. My husband lost his job, my job as a rock-climbing guide didn't pay the bills, and we struggled to start our family. All of these trials helped inspire my nutrition business. Throughout this journey I have been able to befriend some amazing people that I need to thank.*

**Rebecca Oberle:** I remember meeting you for the first time in Body Pump! Your talent as an artist is amazing! Thank you for decorating the beautiful cake pops (page 316) and Almond Roca Mocha Cake (page 342) for this book. And thank you for all your support and encouragement.

**Micah and Kai Emmerich:** We were always meant to be together. I know it sounds crazy, but we are soulmates. Micah, you will do something and Craig will look at me and say, "Oh my, he takes after you!" And Kai, you're quiet like me, with a passion for being outdoors with nature. My life is so full with you in my life. My ideal day is cooking for you in the kitchen all day and hearing, "Mommy, try." You love trying my new food creations!

**Jamie Schultz:** I want to thank you for helping me start my blog; it helped me get up in the morning when I was going through the most difficult time in my life! Without you, who knows if my recipes would be published.

**Craig Emmerich:** To my love and best friend. Without your technical skills, patience, editing, encouragement, and APPETITE, none of this would have happened. SHMILY.

**Jimmy Moore:** I still remember when you first contacted me to do a podcast six years ago. I was in celebrity shock. I have always admired your work and dedication. When you contacted me to write a cookbook with you, I was in awe that I was the one chosen. You have truly been a blessing, not only to me and my family, but to all the dieters out there, who are lucky to have a trusted and respected pioneer like you.

**I also need to express my gratitude to the whole Victory Belt team.** I never thought I would have such amazing support and kindness from everyone at Victory Belt.

**Erich,** your fun attitude and encouragement made this adventure exciting and totally worth the hard work! Getting calls from you on a Friday evening just to check in on me and compliment my new photos made me so happy!

**Sean and Michele,** I truly appreciate the time you spent helping me and coaching me on how to take better photos. It was a pleasure getting to know both of you.

**Holly and Erin,** I can't express my gratitude for how hard you both worked on editing my recipes. Your attention to detail is remarkable! Thank you for all those early morning meetings while I was running.

**Bill and Haley,** I am honored to have your photo for the cover. I've always been a big fan of yours. My first Victory Belt cookbook was your book *Gather*. I've been in love with your artistry from the beginning. Thank you for taking the time to make my recipes and shoot the cover.

# Recipe Index

## condiments, dressings, broth, and other basics

42
slow cooker bone broth

44
herb-infused compound "butter"

46
roasted garlic

47
dairy-free hollandaise

48
homemade mustards

52
tartar sauce

53
"honey" dressing

54
dairy-free avocado ranch dressing

55
ranch dressing

56
dairy-free thousand island dressing

57
fat-burning salad dressing

58
greek salad dressing

59
tomato sauce

60
yellow marinara sauce

62
keto ketchup

63
keto bbq sauce

64
dairy-free nacho cheese sauce

65
copycat baconnaise

66
brown butter béarnaise

68
brown butter

70
fat-burning chimichurri sauce

72
enchilada sauce

74
taco seasoning

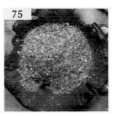
75
seafood seasoning

76
how to preserve herbs

78
brown butter syrup

# breakfast

82
keto pancakes and syrup

83
french scrambled eggs

84
dairy-free breakfast pizza

86
floating islands

88
creamy zucchini hash browns

90
keto bagels / bagels and lox

92
breakfast sushi

94
creamy breakfast shake

96
dairy-free key lime shake

98
ham-n-cheese mini quiches

100
avocado egg cups

102
strawberry popovers with strawberry "butter"

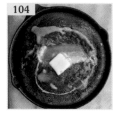
104
caramel apple dutch baby

106
mock apple porridge

108
keto soft-boiled eggs

110
breakfast lasagna

112
the perfect omelet

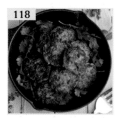
118
maple bacon breakfast patties

120
chai muffins

122
huevos rancheros

124
french toast custard

# appetizers

128
herb salmon dip

129
antipasti platter

130
beef carpaccio

132
curry chicken stuffed endive

134
grilled halloumi with prosciutto and pesto

135
pan-fried prosciutto-wrapped string cheese

136
celery boats

138
ham salad

140
mini frico cups

142
blt bites

144
nirvana meatballs

146
easy greek meze

148
spring rolls

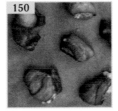
150
bacon-wrapped cheese curds

152
nacho cheese crisps

# beef and lamb

156
bbq meatloaf

158
asian meatballs

160
steak with brown butter béarnaise

162
meaty spaghetti

164
slow cooker beefy asian noodles

166
chimichurri flank steak

168
teriyaki steak roll-ups with sautéed mushrooms

170
swedish meatballs

172
reubens

174
slow cooker bbq short ribs

176
philly "cheese" steak stuffed portobellos

178
taco salad in a crispy cheese bowl

180
braised lamb shanks and mushrooms

182
lamb tikka masala

184
zucchini tot hot dish

## pork

188

easy mortadella ravioli

190

smoked pork chops with apple glaze

192

kielbasa and braised cabbage

194

asian lettuce wraps

196

pork belly in aromatic spices

198

stromboli

200

mini lettuce wraps

202

armadillo eggs

## poultry

206

lasagna roll-ups

208

buffalo chicken stuffed avocados

210

zesty chicken pizza

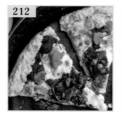

212

deep dish bbq chicken pizza

214

chicken enchiladas

216

herb and ricotta rotolo

218

brown butter chicken and "pasta"

220

duck confit

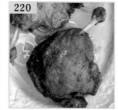

222

gumbo

224

bbq chicken and "faux"tatoes

226

chicken à la king

228

creamy chicken casserole

## fish and seafood

232
grilled halibut with smoky avocado cream

234
shrimp po' boys

236
gravlax

238
gravlax sushi

240
seafood salad

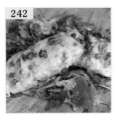
242
grandpa joe's barramundi

244
grilled whole mackerel with homemade tartar sauce

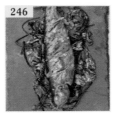
246
grilled trout with lemon-thyme glaze

248
canned salmon

250
broiled sesame-orange salmon

252
shrimp scampi with cabbage noodles

## vegetarian dishes

256
fried parmesan tomatoes

258
creamy "mac"-n-cheese

260
yellow tomato and burrata salad with "honey" dressing

261
toasted open-face brie and tomato sandwich

262
yellow tomato soup and grilled cheese

264
deep dish alfredo pizza with mushrooms

266
pizza margherita

268
mini egg salad sandwiches

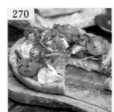
270
dutch baby pizza with "honey" dressing

272
slow cooker pesto pasta with crispy basil

# sides

276
keto bread

278
keto naan

279
braised swiss chard

280
braised cabbage

282
slow cooker cabbage "pasta"

284
zucchini "pasta"

286
brown butter mushrooms

288
creamy coleslaw

289
blt coleslaw

290
paleo onion rings

291
avocado fries

292
fried pickles

294
buffalo chicken deviled eggs

296
cheddar deviled eggs

298
spinach dip

300
zucchini tots

# treats

**304** tips for making keto desserts

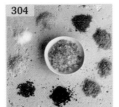

**306** chocolate gingerbread cookies

**308** gingerbread house

**310** dairy-free keto vanilla bean ice cream

**312** dairy-free keto chocolate ice cream with cherry glaze

**314** easy mocha fudge truffles

**316** chocolate mocha cake pops

**318** strawberry truffles

**320** chocolate mint cookies

**322** dark chocolate raspberry fat bombs

**324** chocolate berry pie

**326** caramel apple fudge

**327** dairy-free chocolate egg cream

**328** cookie dough brownies

**330** dairy-free chocolate syrup

**332** chocolate crème de menthe pops

**334** pumpkin pie frozen custard

**336** cinnamon swirl cheesecake

**338** chai panna cotta

**340** lemon curd ice cream

**342** almond roca mocha cake

**344** iced mocha pops

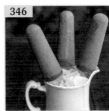

**346** easy toffee fudge pops

**348** chai "sugar"

**349** chai streusel candy

**350** chocolate-covered toffee

**352** easy peppermint fudge

**354** tiramisu fudge

**356** tiramisu panna cotta

# Index